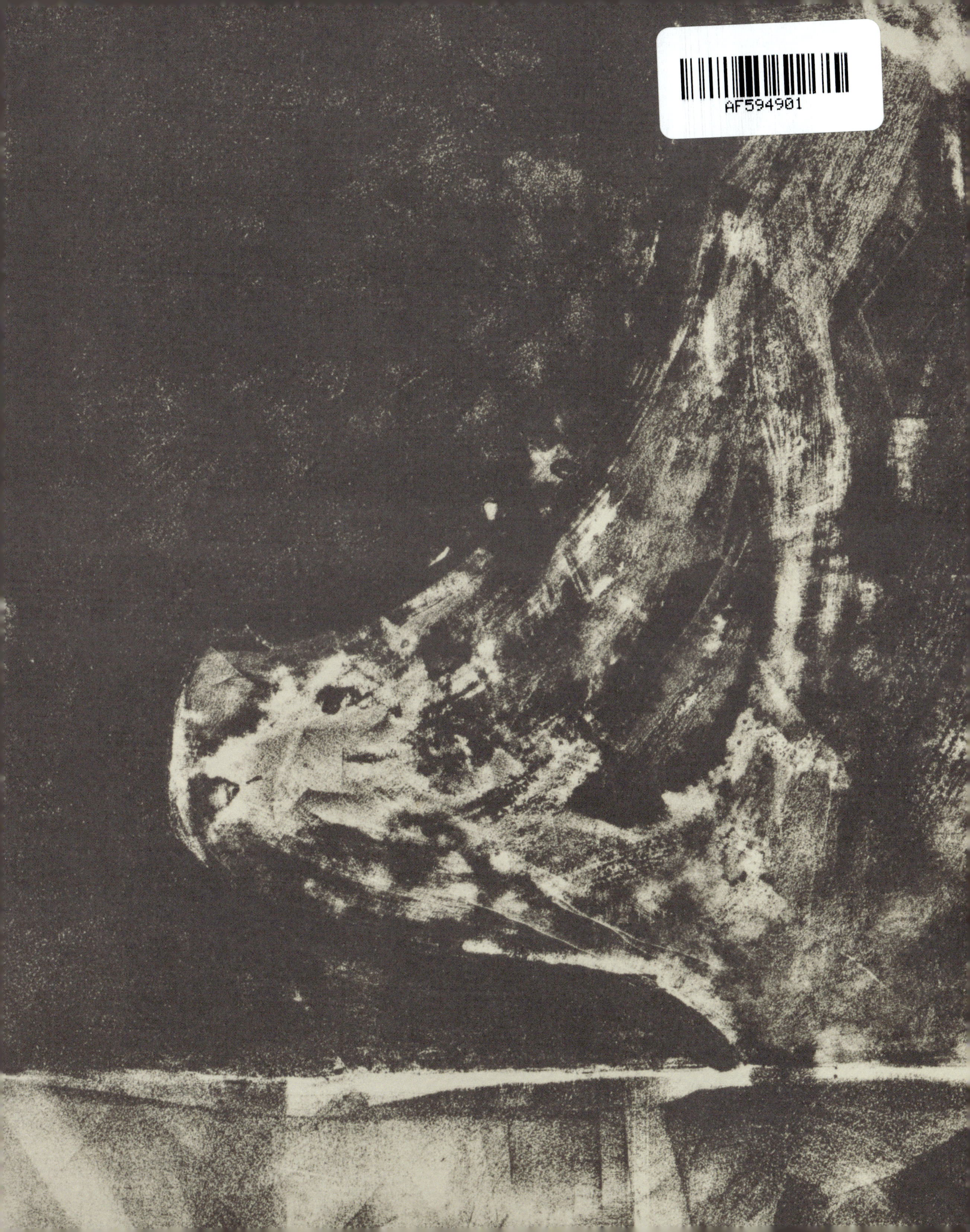

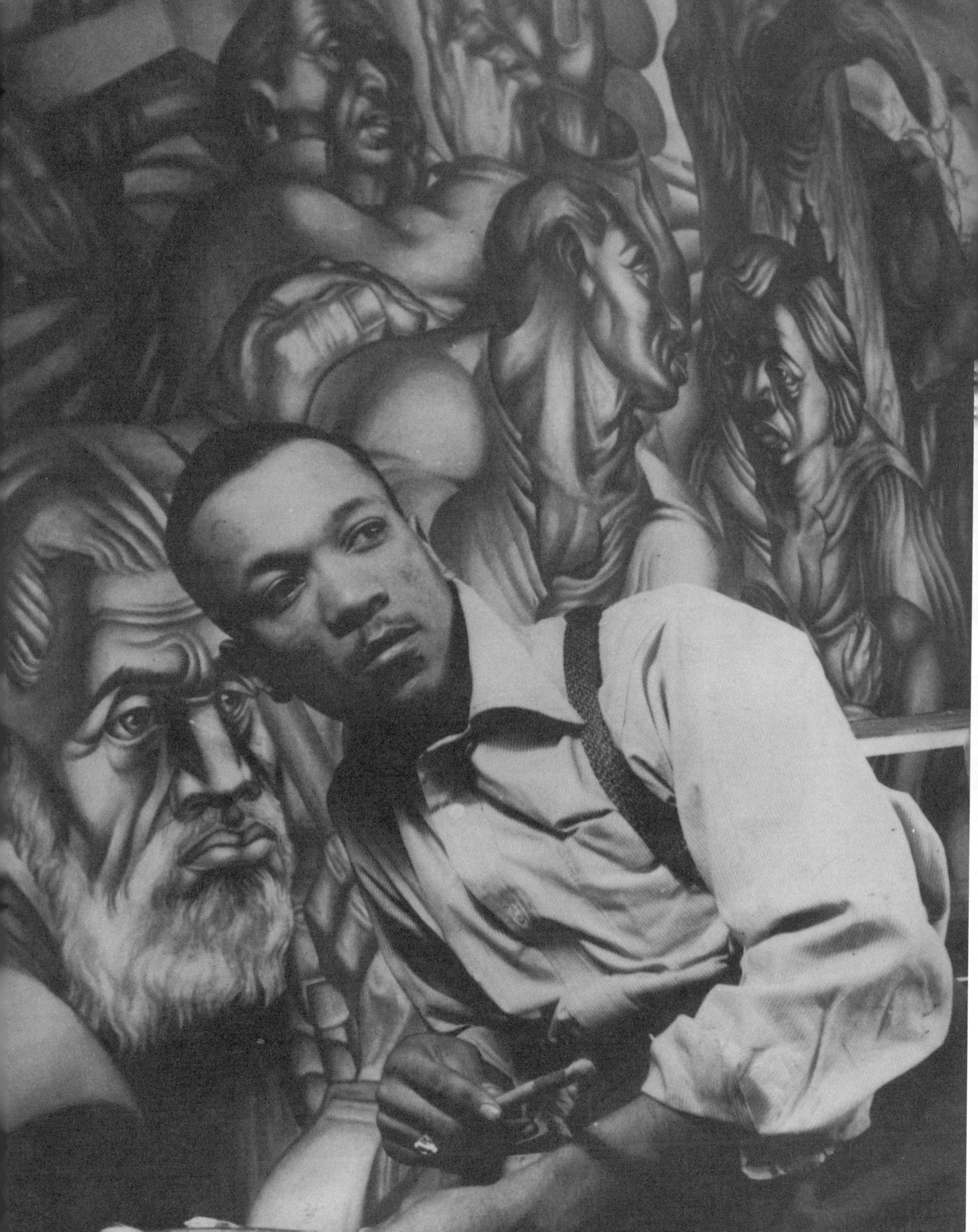

CHARLES WHITE

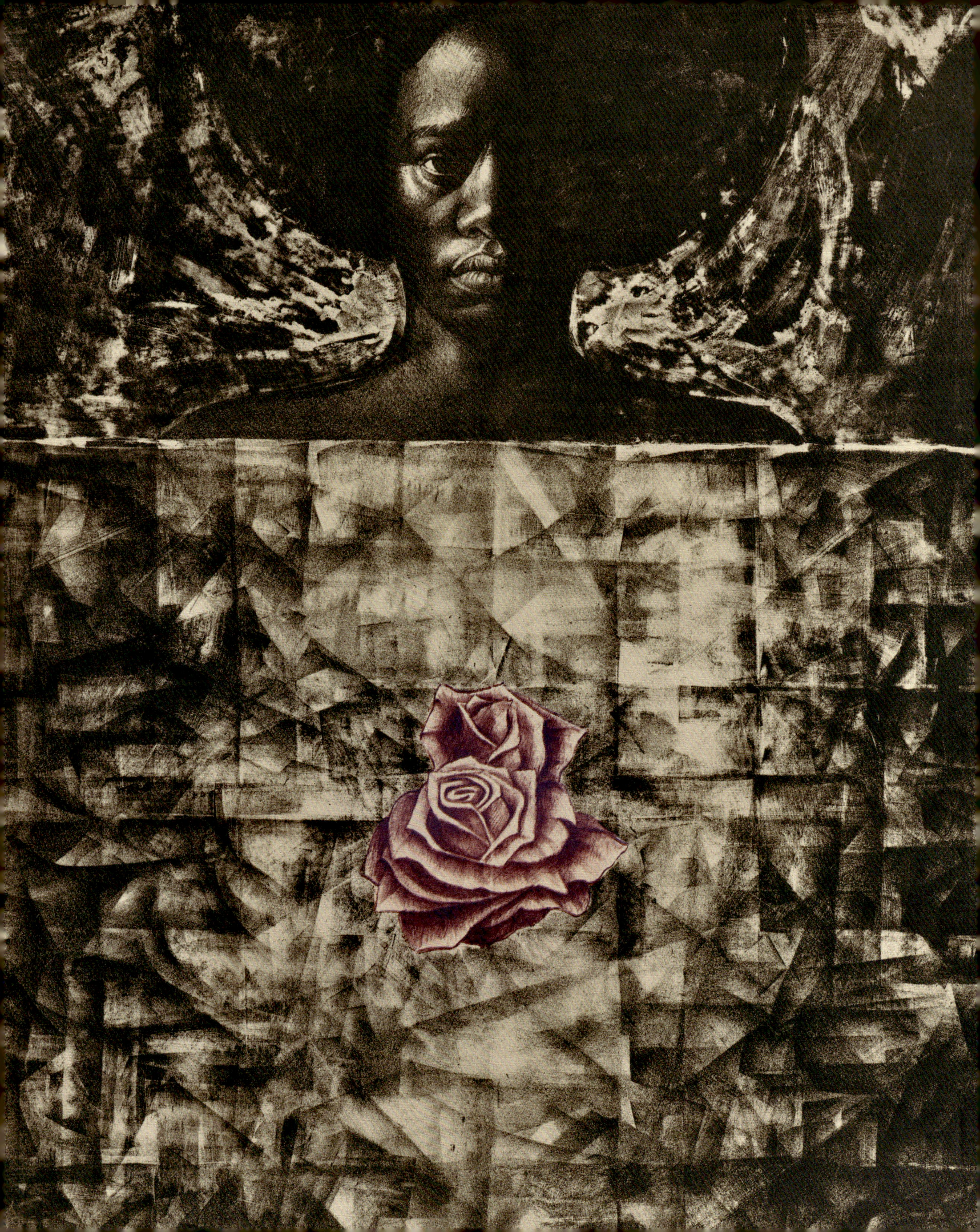

CHARLES WHITE

A Little Higher

Edited by Jill Deupi

Lowe Art Museum
Tra Publishing

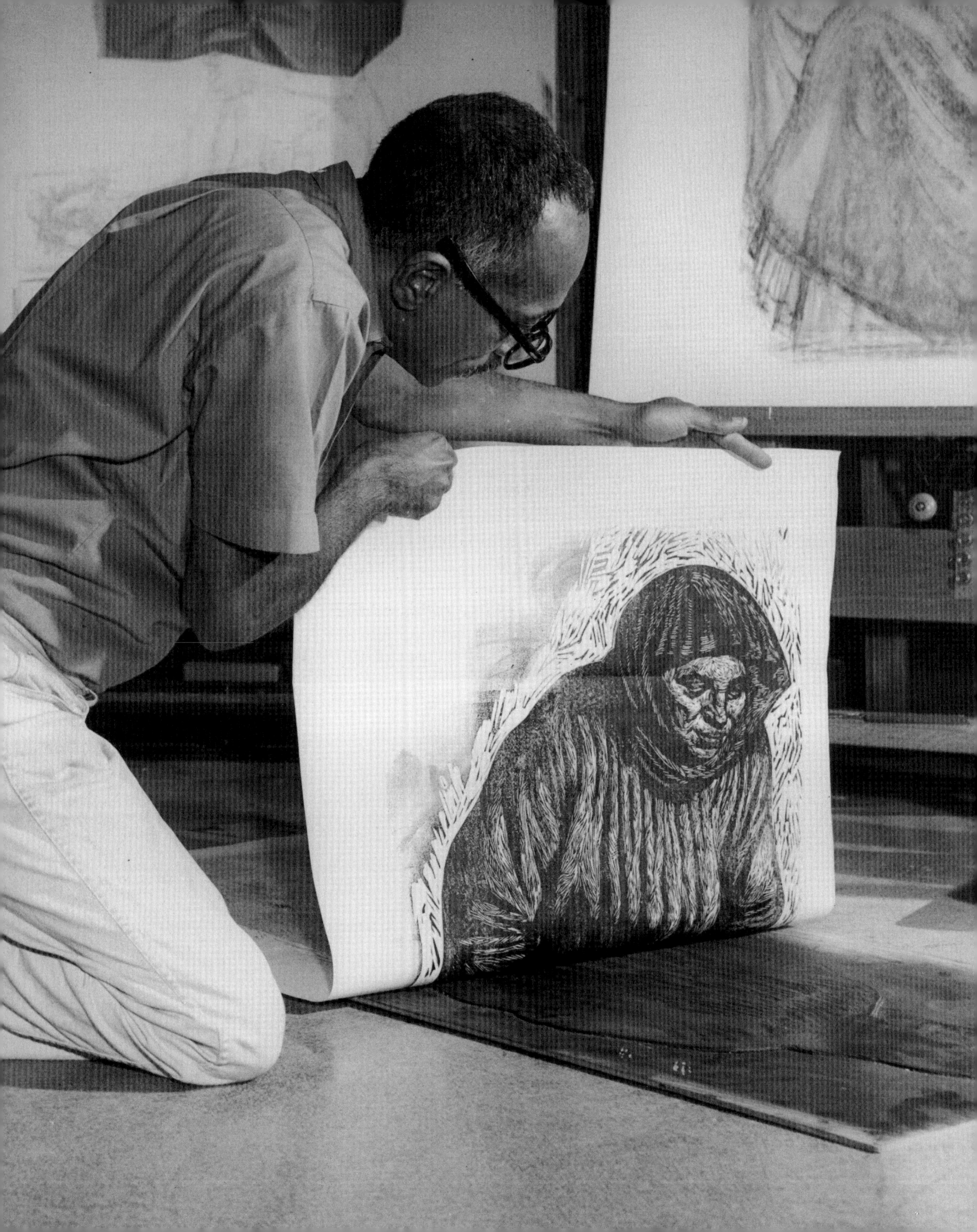

CONTENTS

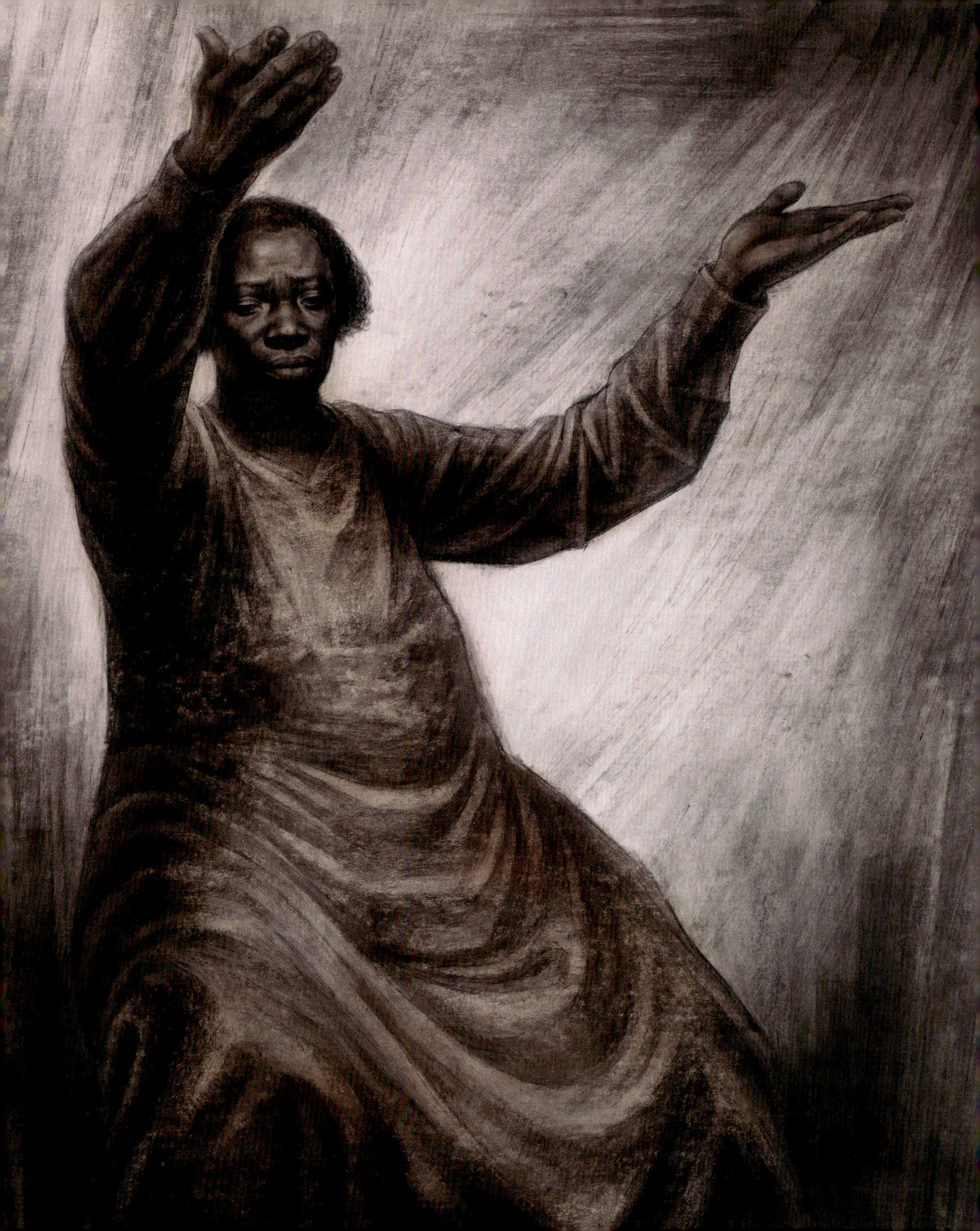

DIRECTOR'S FOREWORD

Jill Deupi

Gonna walk and never get tired
Gonna fly, Lord, and never falter
I'm gonna move up a little higher
—William Herbert Brewster[1]

Best remembered for his meticulously rendered drawings and paintings of people of color, Charles White (1918–1979) dedicated himself to creating "images of dignity," works that elevated and ennobled his subjects without shying away from the cruel realities of systemic racism. Beyond staying true to the norms of figurative art—even in the face of calls for non-representational forms, which many in mid-twentieth-century America considered better suited to the postwar zeitgeist—White bore witness to his lived experience as an African American man who fought the ill effects of racialized poverty, discrimination, denigration, and violence throughout his life. His art also reflects White's deep and abiding admiration for the Social Realists, American Regionalists, and Mexican Muralists as well as his steadfast commitment to battling toxic oppression while striving for a better tomorrow. A staunch activist with a generous spirit, White was a devoted teacher who touched the lives of an entire generation of students on both coasts, including Kerry James Marshall and David Hammons.

Two related anecdotes shed light not only on the rich tapestry of White's life but also on the shape and content of his life's work. A lover of the visual and the performing arts since youth, the artist kept a modest record collection in his apartment in New York City, where he lived between 1947 and 1956. While visiting White in his home one day, the multitalented athlete, performer, and activist Paul Robeson (1898–1976) put an LP featuring the great gospel singer Mahalia Jackson (1911–1972) on his host's turntable. As White's gallerist and biographer Benjamin Horowitz (1912–2004) later recounted, Robeson "became quite ecstatic. [He] had never heard of her before, and White had to play [her] records over and over again. From that point on, Robeson was a frequent visitor to [his friend's] apartment."[2] Ms. Jackson would emerge as the lynchpin in another important biographical event several years later. The setting was actor and singer Harry Belafonte's (B. 1927) Los Angeles home, which, according to novelist John Oliver Killens (1916–1987), was "a veritable Charles White museum."[3] White, who was close friends with Belafonte, and Jackson were among the invited guests. At a certain point in the evening, Belafonte called the singer over to a painting cloaked by a sheet, saying he wanted "to show [her] something." That "something" was White's portrait of Jackson, commissioned by Belafonte and now held in the Museum of Modern Art's permanent collection.[4] Reflecting on this 1955 charcoal and Conté crayon on board image decades later, the iconic performer and lifelong activist Belafonte noted: "Mahalia was…the greatest expression of the celebration

FIG. I
Charles White, *Move on Up a Little Higher*, 1961, detail. Charcoal black and carbon black pencil on illustration board, 102.2 x 121.9 x 0.5 cm (40 1/4 x 48 x 3/16 in.). Collection of the Smithsonian National Museum of African American History and Culture.Charles White Archives.

of Black Liberation…She welcomes you with her art. She seduces you into her space. Then she sings the songs of pain and sorrow."[5] These same words could aptly be used to describe Charles White, whose alluring images draw us in before delivering a walloping punch powered by centuries of race-based discrimination, inequity, and brutality in America, and unheeded calls for equity and true freedom.

White's fervent demands for racial justice parallel his steadfast commitment to celebrating Black achievement, autonomy, agency, and, of course, dignity. These beliefs inform this show's title, an allusion to a gospel hymn composed in 1946 by the Reverend William Herbert Brewster (1897–1987) and rendered famous by none other than by Mahalia Jackson the following year. Explaining his lyrics' meaning, Brewster noted: "We'll have to move in the field of education. Move into the professions and move into politics. Move in anything that any other race has to have to survive. That was a protest idea and inspiration. I was trying to inspire Black people to move up higher. Don't be satisfied with the mediocre."[6] White gave physical form to Brewster's inspiring, yet sobering, exhortation in his *Move on Up a Little Higher* (1961, FIG. 1). His protagonist—a woman of color with downcast eyes—raises her hands heavenward in a gesture of supplication, veneration, and praise. Though she has been victimized, she is not a victim. Though she has been held down, she rises up. And though she has been "[re]buked and scorned" (to borrow a title from an important work White created in 1956), she is "solid as a rock" (another phrase to which the artist would return several times in naming his work). A metaphor for Black Americans, White's protagonist is bathed by a providential light, which speaks to his persistent belief in society's capacity to effect positive change, if only we commit ourselves to doing so. In her we see not only Charles White's consummate skills of observation and powerful social critique but also a genuine love for his "folks" as well as humanity writ large.

This important exhibition would not have been possible were it not for Arthur Primas, Kathryn Primas, and the Primas Family Collection. I am deeply grateful to them for their extraordinary generosity. I am also indebted to Mr. Primas's associates Regina Glover and Nicole Coward as well as to photographer Chad Redmon for their important contributions to this project. The Charles White Archives' Pauline Alvarez provided invaluable support, as did countless individuals at the partner institutions named in this catalogue's image credits. Tra Publishing was peerless in its work, above all, Ilona Oppenheim, Jefferson Quintana, and Andrea Gollin, editor extraordinaire, who went above and beyond the call of duty, and image researcher Amanda Belli. I am equally grateful to contributors Mora J. Beauchamp-Byrd, Nijah Cunningham, Willis "Bing" Davis, Arthur Primas, and Will South for the insights they have provided into the life and work of Charles White and his circle of influence. Many thanks are due for the contributions of University of Miami's Assistant Professor, African, Black & Caribbean Art, Erica Moiah James. Benny Levin and his team at Miami Art Services ensured that this book's companion show was all that it could be, as did University of Miami's Assistant Vice President for Lifelong Learning and Engagement, Desiree Rodriguez, and above all, my colleagues at the Lowe: Juan Almeciga, Nathalia Bolivar, María Angeles Cardenas, Martin Casuso, Colbie Symone Cooke, Melinda DeDominicis, Amy Ferguson, Harry Hurns, Faviola Hurtado, Mary

Kramer, Marie Milhomme, Mark Osterman, Caitlin Swindell, and Natasha Zabala. Christopher Norwood, Imani Greene, and Darryl Neverson at Hampton Art Lovers, who share the Lowe's vision of "communities" flourishing as "community," were incredible collaborative partners who make me excited for the future. Much the same may be said for the University of Miami's Center for Global Black Studies; Miami MoCAAD; and the Historic Ward Rooming House, all of whom I thank. As ever, this project would not have been possible were it not for the University of Miami and its College of Arts and Sciences. Additional funding was provided by the State of Florida, Department of State, Division of Arts and Culture, the Florida Council on Arts and Culture, and the National Endowment for the Arts; the Miami-Dade County Department of Cultural Affairs and the Cultural Affairs Council, the Miami-Dade County Mayor and Board of County Commissioners; the City of Coral Gables; the Funding Arts Network; Beaux Arts Miami; and Lowe members.

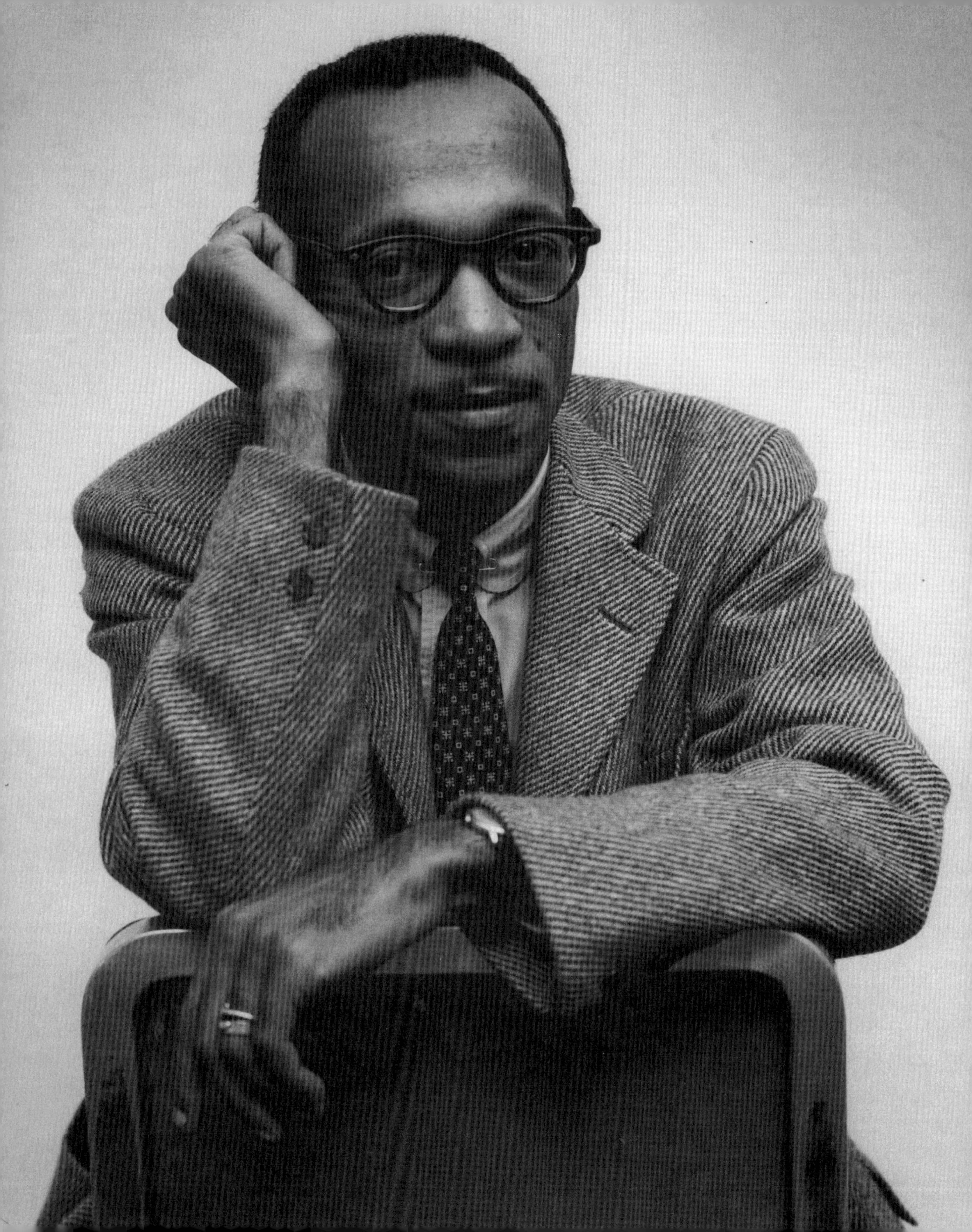

COLLECTOR'S NOTE

Arthur Primas

Please allow me to introduce you to Charles White (FIG. 1). If this is your first experience with Mr. White, welcome. If you are already familiar with Charles White's art, welcome back. I hope each of you enjoy his work as much as I do.

My decades-long journey with Charles White started with Adron Griffith, Jumaane N'Namdi, Charlotte Sherman, and *Images of Dignity: The Drawings of Charles White* (1967), the first book devoted to White's work, featuring more than ninety reproductions and valuable commentary. Charles White was a figurative artist dedicated to portraying people of color with strength and dignity. There is so much I want to say about Charles White, but he says it best with his art. I am humbled to have this opportunity to review his work again thanks to the Lowe Museum, its sponsors, and the partnering museums to which the show is traveling: the Hickory Museum of Art and the Cincinnati Art Museum.

In these pages, you will learn more about White's exceptional life and career, including his origins as an artist. You will become acquainted with the child who began to draw during the stretches he spent at the main branch of Chicago's public library, where his mother would drop him off while she went to work. You will learn that he won an award to attend drawing classes at the Art Institute of Chicago while in grammar school and later won a scholarship to enroll at the School of the Art Institute of Chicago full time—but only after two other art schools accepted him, then turned him down upon learning he was Black.

White's commitment to creating powerful images of African Americans—what his gallerist and, later, the artist himself, described as "images of dignity"—was unwavering over the course of his four-decade career. He believed that art had a role to play in changing the world.

I leave you with his powerful words: "Art must be an integral part of the struggle. It can't simply mirror what's taking place. It must adapt itself to human needs. It must ally itself with the forces of liberation. The fact is, artists have always been propagandists. I have no use for artists who try to divorce themselves from the struggle."[1]

FIG. 1
Charles White, n.d.
Charles White Archives.

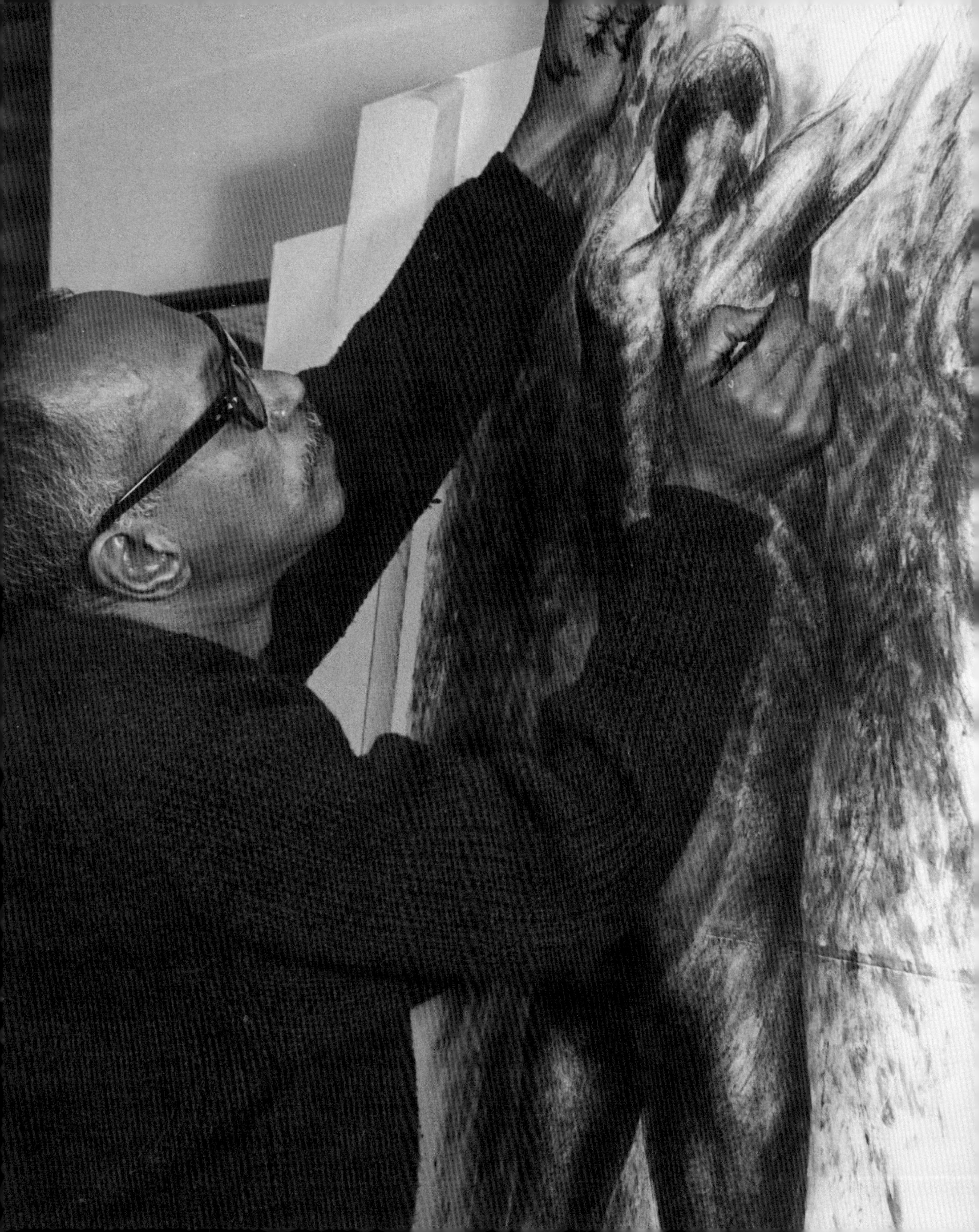

CHARLES WHITE: A LIFE, EXTRAORDINARY

Jill Deupi

My whole purpose in art is to make a positive statement about mankind, all mankind, an affirmation of humanity... This doesn't mean that I am a man without angers—I've had my work in museums where I wasn't allowed to see it—but what I pour into my work is the challenge of how beautiful life can be.

—Charles White[1]

One of the leading artists of his generation, Charles Wilbert White (1918–1979) is perhaps best remembered for his meticulously crafted works on paper (FIG. 1). His oeuvre, however, has a significance that resonates far beyond his virtuosic skills and beautifully finished drawings. Profoundly influenced in his youth and early adulthood by progressive thinkers, political activists, Social Realism as well as American Regionalism painters, and early-twentieth-century Mexican Muralists, White leveraged his art to expose and interrogate society's ills—above all, the nefarious legacies born of enslaving and chattelizing Black people in America. His powerful early murals, together with the easel paintings, drawings, and lithographs he created in the late 1930s and throughout the 1940s, were particularly compelling in this regard: They squarely critiqued the profound inequities, immense suffering, and unwarranted violence visited upon his fellow African Americans by a deeply racist nation. These same works spoke to the enduring dignity of people of color while elevating and amplifying their remarkable contributions to the very nation that degraded and brutalized them.[2] And though White's later works may appear initially less radical and more attenuated (both formally and ideologically), they, too, are powerful statements about the self-worth, agency, and pride of Black Americans in the face of ongoing discrimination, bigotry, racially motivated violence, and murder. From anonymous mothers and their children to towering historical figures like Frederick Douglass (1818–1895) and Harriet Tubman (1822–1913), White endowed the people he depicted—nearly all of whom were African American—with a solidity and a solemnity that transcended their two-dimensional forms and invoked the superlatives of human existence (FIG. 2).

Early Life

Born in Chicago on APRIL 2, 1918, White was a child of adversity (FIG. 3). Descended from enslaved people, his mother, Ethelene Gary (CA. 1898–1977), had been sent by her relatives from Richland, Mississippi, to Chicago in 1914 after her mother died.[3] She was just sixteen.[4] Like so many people of color who participated in the Great Migration—a demographic phenomenon fueled by economic as well as societal imperatives (above all, an urgent need to escape the repression and violence of the Jim Crow South)—Gary and her family surely hoped she would find greater opportunities and access to a better, more equitable life in Chicago.[5] As a single, young Black woman with a limited education and

FIG. 1
Charles White, n.d. Cleo Trumbo, photographer. Charles White Archives.

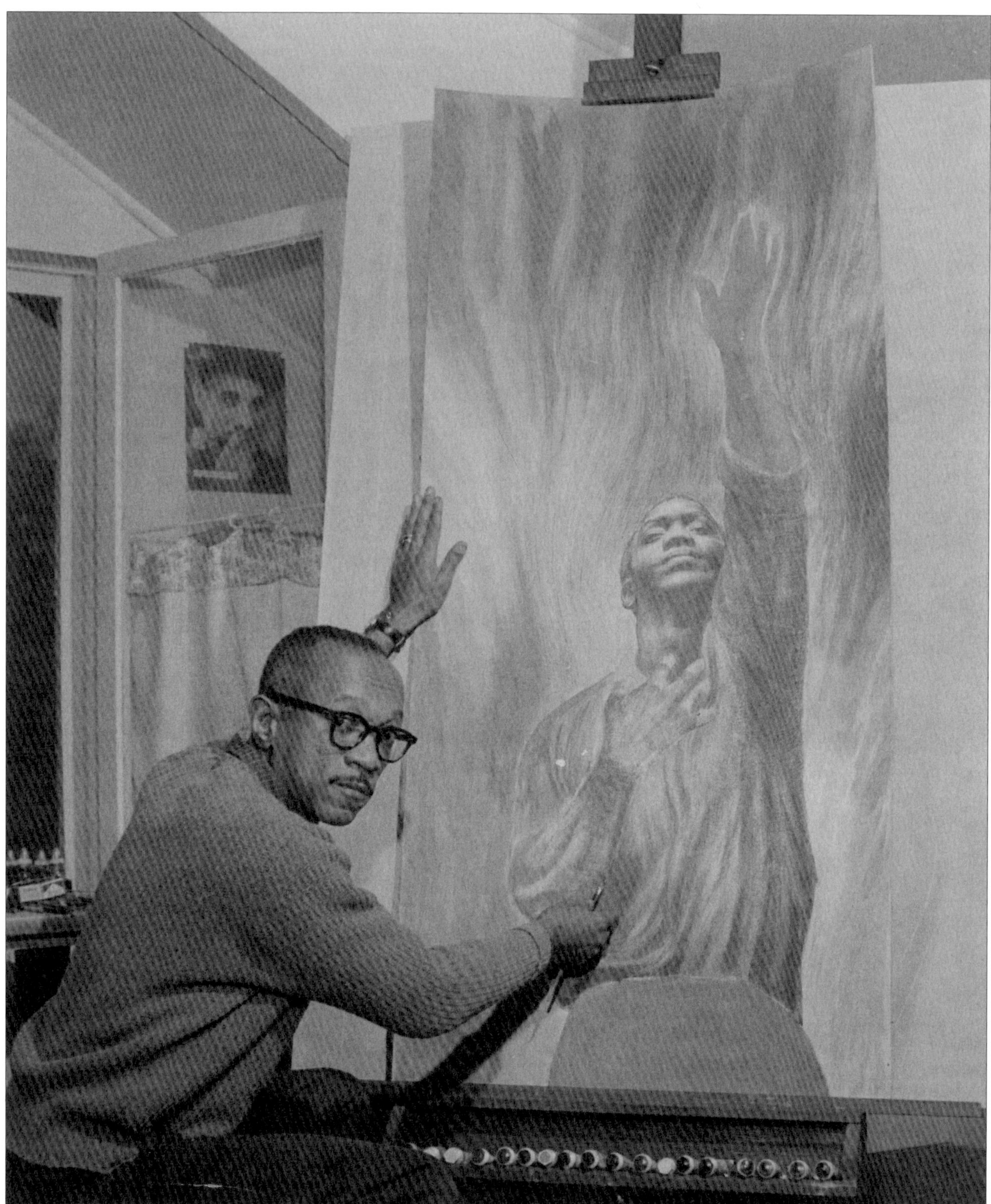

FIG. 2
Charles White in his attic studio
on Summit Ave. in Pasadena, California, n.d.
Howard Morehead, photographer.
Charles White Archives.

even fewer socioeconomic resources, however, her options were severely constrained. The challenges Gary faced were compounded by the fact that Chicago was not the colorblind city of dreams many Black Southerners may have imagined. Legislated discrimination in nineteenth-century Illinois had led to the creation of the so-called "Black Belt"—high density, high poverty, highly segregated neighborhoods on Chicago's South Side.[6] It was there that Gary settled, living her entire life in racialized poverty and working as a domestic servant for white families.[7] White's biological father, Charles (Charley) White Sr. (CA. 1884–1927), was a Creek Indian with ancestral roots in Georgia.[8] Gary and her son saw the elder White only on Sundays, as he was married with other children. This unorthodox arrangement came to an abrupt halt in March 1927 when White Sr. contracted pneumonia and died. He was forty-three years old and his son by Gary just eight.[9] Later that year, Charles's mother married Clifton Marsh, a broken, bitter man who sought solace in drink. Instead of comfort, however, he found there only temper and bile. Prone to violence, Marsh frequently lashed out at his stepson and fought bitterly with Gary.[10] The couple divorced when Charles was thirteen.[11]

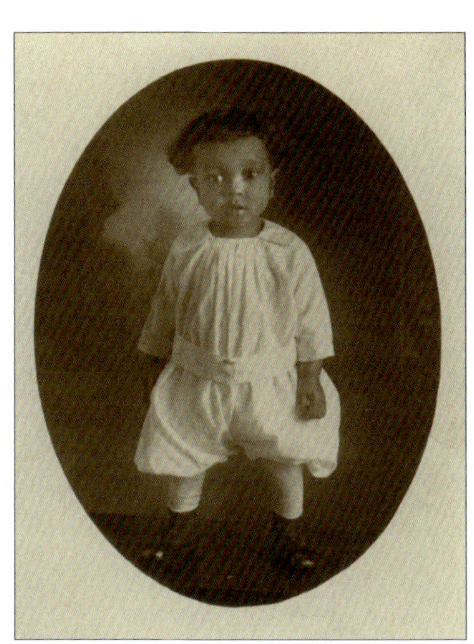

FIG.3
Charles White as a young boy, n.d.
Charles White Archives.

However high the hurdles and deep the disappointments Gary encountered, she remained focused on the future, funneling her love—together with her limited resources and boundless aspirations—into her only child, Charles. Having once dreamed of being a music instructor, Gary bought her son a violin when he was nine.[12] Though not a natural talent, he "scratched away on [it] for about seven years."[13] And while he grew to have an enduring appreciation of music—and, indeed, theater—painting and drawing were Charles's true passions.[14] Gary recognized the depth of her son's ardor, which she fueled with a coveted paint kit, presented to him on his seventh birthday. In contrast to the violin—a gift complemented by years' worth of lessons with a teacher—no formal instruction accompanied the paint set. Thus, White's early training was that of an autodidact. As a young boy of just six or seven, he regularly visited the Art Institute of Chicago (AIC) on his own, seeking inspiration in that venerable institution's great halls.[15] His artistic education continued at home, where White pored over cast-off magazines, sourcing images he wanted to incorporate into drawings of his own.[16] He also browsed the shelves at the main branch of Chicago's public library, where—from the time he could read—White devoured books while his mother worked. These early habits not only catalyzed a lifelong love of reading but also introduced him to the significant contributions Black individuals had made to American life.[17] Other informal learning opportunities included canvassing local art students working *en plein air* at a nearby park for technical pointers when he was still in elementary school, attending Saturday classes at the AIC (thanks to a scholarship from the James Nelson Raymond Lecture Fund), and, most impactfully, actively participating in the Art Crafts Guild, a group of Black artists that, under the informal leadership of George E. Neal (1906–1938), convened each Sunday to share their learning and ideas.[18]

Early Career

A pivotal moment in White's early career came on MAY 17, 1937, when he won a $240 scholarship from the AIC, enabling him to attend the prestigious School of the Art Institute of Chicago (SAIC) that fall.[19] He applied himself with diligence, making the most of this precious opportunity. It was one that White particularly cherished since two other awards, one from the Chicago Academy of Fine Arts and another from the Frederic Mizen Academy of Art, had been rescinded once the administrators realized he was Black ("a mistake," they mumbled, when White appeared in person to claim his prizes).[20] Beyond having to navigate restricted educational opportunities, the young artist also bore the economic brunt of systemic racism. Lacking cab fare, he frequently walked the sixty blocks between his South Side Chicago home and the SAIC.[21] He also worked as a valet and cook for the artist Antonio Beneduce (1900–1975) and was a part-time art teacher at Saint Elizabeth's, a local parochial high school, so that he could buy art supplies and cover basic living expenses.[22] Additionally, White taught life drawing at the South Side Community Arts Center (SSCAC), co-founded by him and other members of the Art Crafts Guild.[23] Despite the demands these very necessary extracurricular activities made on his time, he finished the SAIC's two-year program in a single year.

In September 1938, White joined the ranks of the federal Illinois Art Project (IAP), part of President Franklin D. Roosevelt's Works Progress Administration (WPA), established three years earlier to combat the Great Depression's devastating effects.[24] Under commission from the IAP, White—who initially had been assigned to the easel division but transferred to the mural unit in September 1939—produced commanding works that helped to establish his professional reputation. These include two powerful murals: *Progress of the American Negro: Five Great American Negroes* (1939–40, Howard University School of Law, Washington, D.C.) and *Techniques Used in the Service of Struggle* (1940–41, incomplete and now lost).[25] During this period, White was also extremely active at the SSCAC, where he spent time with other like-minded young artists, including Elizabeth Catlett (1915–2012). Catlett, who was at the time on the art faculty at Dillard University in New Orleans, spent the summer of 1941 in Chicago, studying lithography at the SSCAC as well as ceramics at the SAIC. She stayed with Margaret Burroughs (1915–2010), one of White's closest high school—and, ultimately, lifelong—friends. In December of that year, White and Catlett married (FIG. 4). It was a union the groom's mother, who felt that Catlett "looked down on her," frowned upon from the start.[26]

After honeymooning in New York, the newlyweds settled in New Orleans, where Catlett resumed her duties as chair of Dillard's art department while White taught drawing. They did not remain in New Orleans long, however. In April 1942, White received a $2,000 fellowship from the Julius Rosenwald Foundation, which enabled the couple to move to New York City.[27] There he immersed himself in the archives of the Schomburg Collection of Negro Literature, History and Prints (today, the New York Public Library's Schomburg Center for Research in Black Culture) and studied with Harry Sternberg (1904–2001) at the Art Students League (ASL).[28] That summer Catlett and White both worked as arts coordinators at the Workers Children's Camp (Wo-Chi-Ca), an interracial, coeducational camp in Washington Township, New Jersey, founded in 1934 to promote progressive socialist values (FIG. 5).[29] That fall, White and Catlett traveled extensively throughout Louisiana, Mississippi, Virginia, and Georgia, immersing themselves in Black history and culture.[30] The following spring (1943), White used his remaining Rosenwald funds to spend several months at Virginia's Hampton Institute (now University), where he

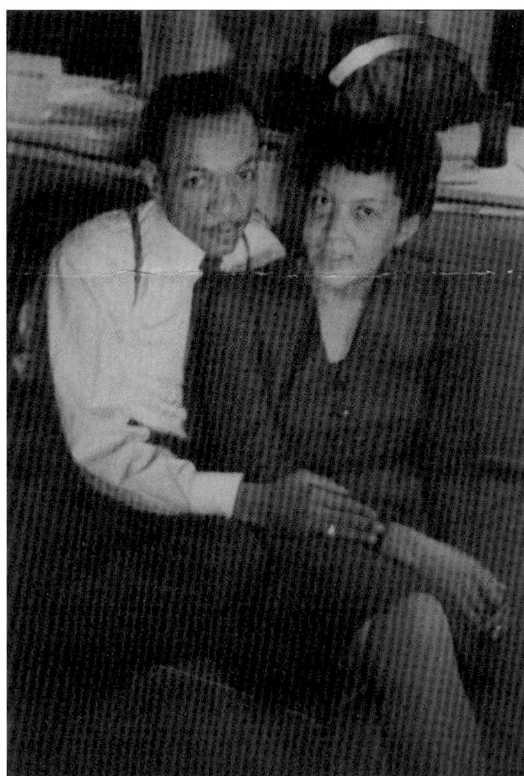

FIG. 4
Charles White and Elizabeth Catlett, n.d.
Charles White Archives.

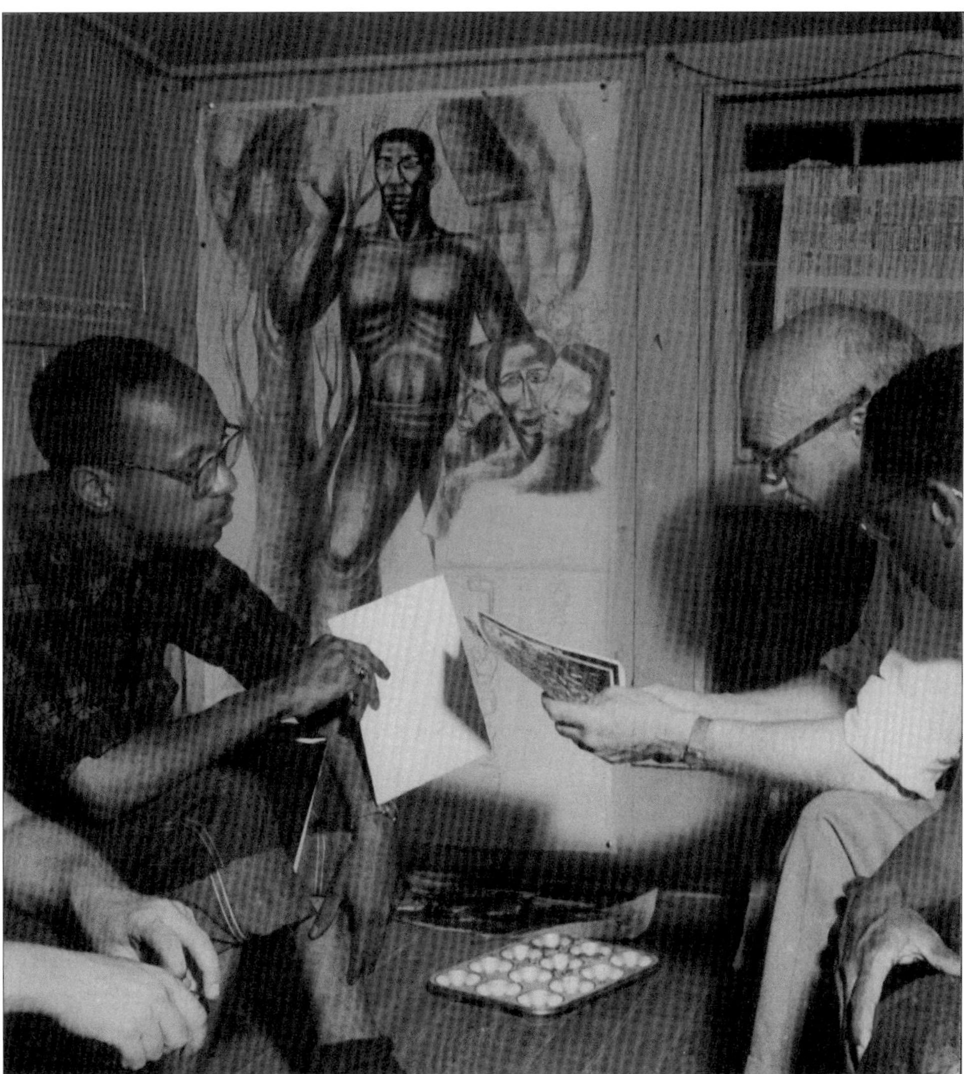

FIG. 5
Charles White with Ernest Crichlow, Rockwell Kent, and Richard Crosscup at Camp Wo-Chi-Ca, Washington Township, New Jersey. ca. 1945.
Charles White Archives.

painted *The Contribution of the Negro to Democracy in America* (1943, Hampton University, Hampton, Virginia). Following the unveiling of this powerful mural, the pair returned to New York, where they both went to work for the leftist George Washington Carver School in Harlem.[31] The renewal of White's Rosenwald Fund fellowship the following year enabled him to continue his studies at the ASL as well as his independent work as an artist, this time with a topical focus on the Black presence in the U.S. Armed Forces, including the loved ones whom enlisted men had left behind.[32]

Wartime, Illness, Mexico, and Divorce

As the Second World War continued to rage, storm clouds also gathered on White's personal horizon. In 1944, the artist was drafted. After completing basic training at the Army's Camp Ellis in Fulton County, Illinois, he was stationed at Jefferson Barracks outside of Saint Louis, Missouri.[33] Accorded the rank of corporal in the 1332ND Engineer General Service Regiment (an all-Black unit), White worked in the camouflage division, painting countless utilitarian objects in shades of green, until tasked with helping to sandbag the swollen Ohio and Mississippi Rivers. The reassignment required him to stand in raging floodwaters for hours, leaving White with tuberculosis (TB), a pulmonary disease that not only plagued him for the rest of his life but also greatly influenced his choice of media.[34] After a lengthy recuperation in a Castle Point, New York, veterans' hospital, White received a medical discharge from the Army in late 1944, less than a year after his conscription.

The following February he served as artist-in-residence at Howard University, remaining there until June. That same spring (1945), Catlett received a Rosenwald Fund fellowship of her own. When her award was renewed the following year, the couple was able to fulfill their long-standing dream of spending time in Mexico, intentions that the war—and the draft board—had stymied for White back in 1942.[35] Artistically, the period was a high point for White, who spent time with the great Mexican Muralists Diego Rivera (1886–1957), David Alfaro Siqueiros (1896–1974), Pablo O'Higgins (1904–1983), and José Clemente Orozco (1883–1949), in addition to studying at the Escuela Nacional de Pintura, Escultura y Grabado ("La Esmeralda") and working with artists from Mexico City's renowned Taller de Gráfica Popular, including Leopoldo Méndez (1902–1969).[36] He was profoundly influenced by "[t]he Taller's grounding in art as a fundamentally democratic practice and interest in making it available to all through multiples."[37] Indeed, the accessibility of his art—in every sense of the word—was a major concern of White's throughout his career.[38]

Though the couple's art-making may have flourished in Mexico (where Catlett worked on her important *The Negro Woman* series), they were not so fortunate in terms of their personal lives: In 1947, White and Catlett returned to New York, where they finalized their divorce.[39] This rupture coincided with further health setbacks for White, who underwent a series of pulmonary operations followed by a protracted period of in-patient recovery at Saint Anthony's Hospital in Queens, New York, between January 1948 and May 1949. While recovering, the now-established artist reconnected with Frances Barrett (1926–2000), a young social worker whom he had met several years earlier at Wo-Chi-Ca. They fell deeply in love and married on MAY 31, 1950, just months after their first date (FIG. 6).

Despite an almost boundless passion for and steadfast commitment to one another, the newlyweds found life in New York City challenging. Beyond the ordinary pressures of work and daily life, as a biracial couple (Barrett was Caucasian) the Whites faced countless acts of racism, including discriminatory housing practices that made finding a new home extraordinarily difficult. Fortunately, the Eastside Fair Housing Council intervened on their behalf, enabling them to secure a place to call their own on Twenty-Fourth Street and Second Avenue in 1950.[40] Unfortunately, this was not the only time they would need the supportive intervention of others to ensure they could rent or even purchase residential property.

Professional Growth and Recognition

Through it all, White continued to draw (the medium to which he increasingly devoted himself), often on a monumental scale. His talent was recognized by the American Contemporary Art (ACA) Gallery, which gave him his first solo show in 1947 (FIG. 7). He also became deeply involved with New York City's Committee for the Negro in the Arts (CNA), which was founded that same year as both an activist platform for the vocalization of Black grievances and a resource for technical training, advancement, and support.[41]

In 1951 the Whites traveled to Europe, visiting France, England, Italy, and East Germany, where White represented the CNA at the World Youth and Student Festival for Peace and participated in the Young People's Assembly for Peace "Friendship Tour."[42] They then visited Czechoslovakia, Poland, and—in an unplanned extension of their tour—the Soviet Union, where they remained for three weeks (FIG. 8). The trip was an eye-opening experience for White, who was lauded overseas as a world-class artist and a fully actualized man rather than a second-class citizen.[43] Reflecting on his time abroad, he noted: "I will never forget the hospitality and warmth showered upon me, and what I can call the affection bestowed upon me, as a representative of the oppressed Negro people and of the people striving for peace in the United States. If I had come back with nothing else, this would have been the most powerful experience and influence on my life from then on."[44] More directly, White's wife would write of their time in Paris: "Everything…was exciting and different…With the exception of his stay in Mexico City, Charlie had never before experienced an occasion when his color did not matter. He told me that he truly felt like a man. Except for the recognition he was met with as an artist, no one noticed what he looked like, who he was with, or where he went."[45]

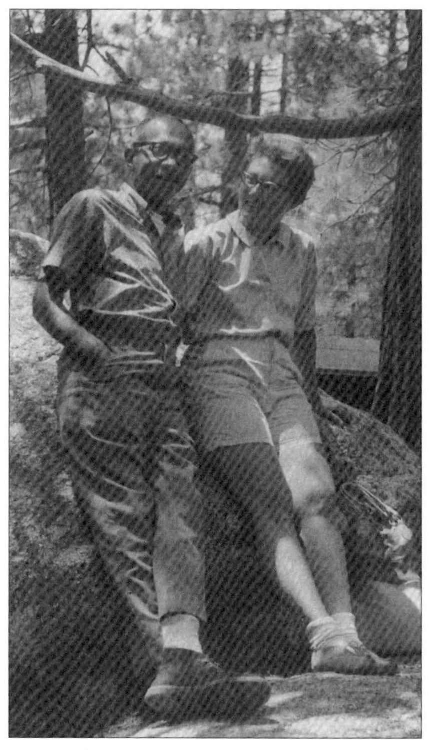

FIG. 6
Charles White and Frances Barrett White, n.d. Charles White Archives.

Despite the fact that racism continued to hamper White's professional trajectory back in the U.S., he enjoyed several important successes in the early 1950s, most notably, inclusion in group shows at both the Metropolitan Museum of Art and the Whitney Museum of American Art, as well as a $1,000 grant from the National Institute of Arts and Letters.[46] However, ongoing health setbacks as well as a February 1952 brush with the House Un-American Activities Committee (a product of Cold War America's "Red Scare") cast a pall over these successes.[47] While the Congressional subpoena came to naught, White was not so fortunate with his health. A serious tubercular infection led to testicular surgery that rendered a much-longed-for family with Frances highly improbable. White also suffered further infections in the fall of 1955 and spring of 1956, when his one functional lung (the other having been prophylactically collapsed in the late 1940s as he recovered from

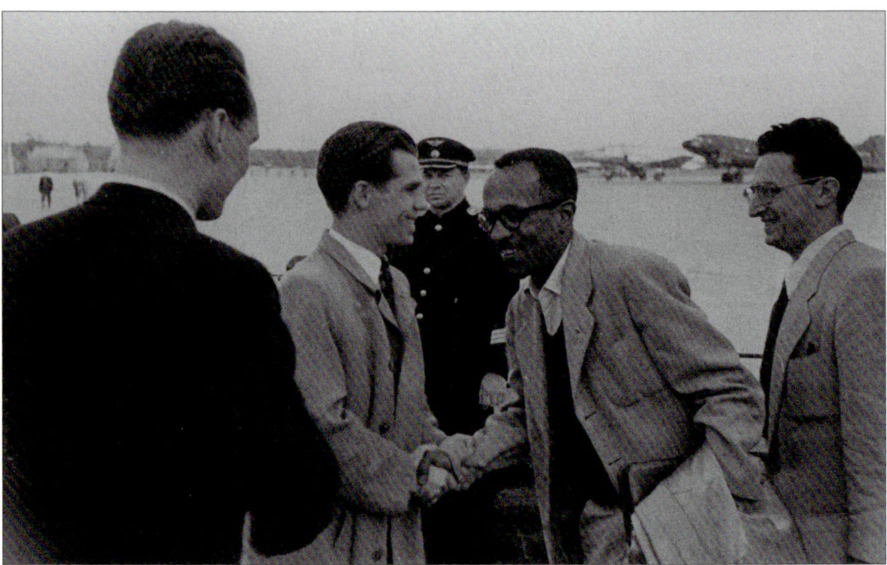

FIG. 8
Representatives of the Soviet Youth Antifascist Committee welcome Charles White in Moscow, 1951. Charles White Archives.

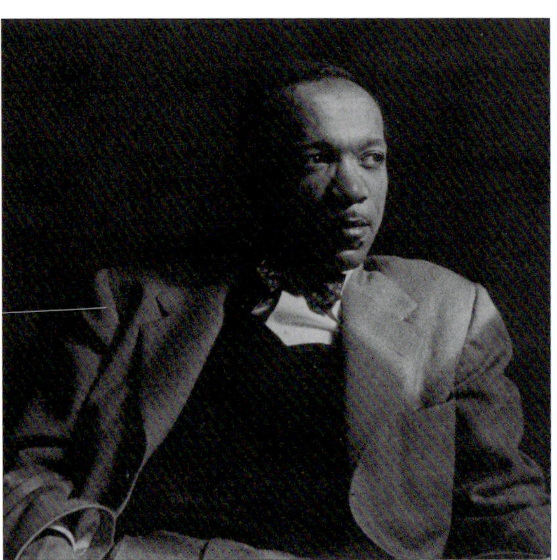

FIG. 7
Charles White at either ACA Gallery or the Workshop School of Advertising Art in New York City, ca. 1949–50. Charles White Archives.

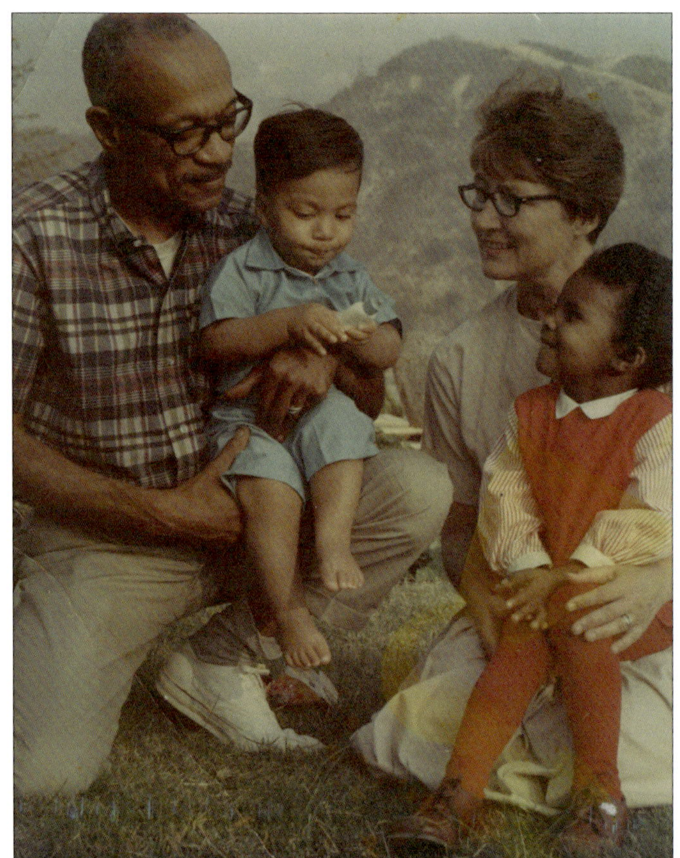

FIG. 9
Charles and Frances with their children, Jessica and Ian, n.d. Charles White Archives.

an earlier bout of TB) became infected. At the urging of his physicians, White severely curtailed the amount of time he devoted to work.[48] His healthcare providers also encouraged him to seriously consider exchanging New York for a more salubrious locale. After puzzling through the options, the Whites settled on California, to which they relocated in October 1956.[49]

Life in California: Starting a Family, Continuing a Career

Life on the West Coast was not without its challenges. White, who described Los Angeles as "a big sprawling country town," missed the creative energy and concentrated excitement of New York City.[50] And though racially motivated restrictive covenants had been overturned by the U.S. Supreme Court in *Shelley vs. Kraemer* (1948), a powerful coalition of realtors and fearful whites effectively continued this discriminatory practice in California for decades.[51] Further, marriage between individuals of different races had only been decriminalized in the Whites' new home state eight years before their arrival, meaning that the stigma, bigotry, and discrimination biracial couples faced was still very real when they settled there in the autumn of 1956. Just as they had in New York, the pair endured countless aggressions (both macro- and micro-) as racist neighbors as well as law enforcement officers and even strangers on the street went out of their way to make the Whites feel unwelcome, inferior, and somehow lesser. Adoption agencies similarly operated under the prejudiced assumption that "mixed raced" couples were incapable of creating loving, cohesive nuclear family units, a baseless conclusion Charles and Frances disproved with the adoption of their children, Jessica and Ian, in the mid-1960s (FIG. 9).[52] Undeterred, they drew strength from one another, their growing brood, their close-knit circle of supportive (and in many cases, hugely successful and highly influential) friends, and, of course, from White's art-making.

Settling first in Pasadena before moving to Altadena, then to Highland Park, and finally back to Altadena (all areas of greater Los Angeles), the Whites had access to more space, which stimulated Charles's creativity and encouraged him to be ever more introspective, allegorical, and lyrical in his work.[53] Supremely productive, the artist enjoyed successful solo and group presentations at museums and galleries in the U.S. and abroad during this period, in addition to expanded teaching responsibilities at Otis Art Institute (now Otis College of Art and Design). A devoted teacher throughout his career (FIG. 10), White's students included Alonzo Davis, Charles Dickson, Greg Dickson, Mark Steven Greenfield, David Hammond, Judith Hernandez, Suzanne Jackson, Ulysses Jenkins, John Lees, Collie Lowe, Gary Lloyd, Kerry James Marshall, Ronnie Nichols, Martin Payton, Luis Serrano, Joseph Sims, Kirk Silsbee, Stan Wilson, and Richard Wyatt Jr.[54]

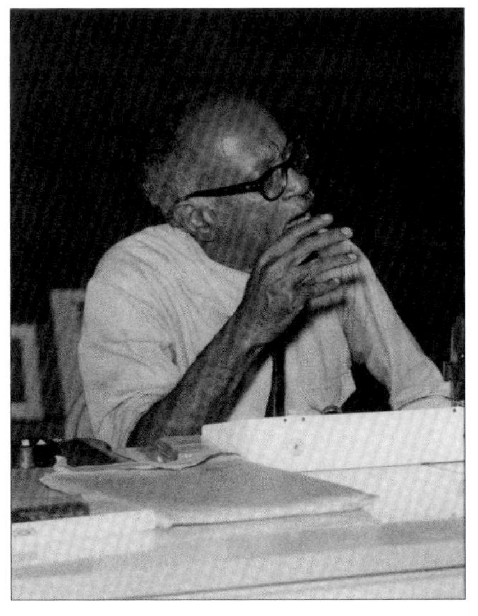

FIG. 10
Charles White at a teacher's symposium at UCLA, 1969. Charles White Archives.

In 1967, the Los Angeles–based Heritage Gallery published *Images of Dignity: The Drawings of Charles White*, which featured a powerful foreword by the artist's close friend and champion, Harry Belafonte (B.1927, FIG. 11).[55] Seven years later, the Johnson Publishing Company commissioned White to provide illustrations for the cover and chapter openers of Lerone Bennett Jr.'s *The Shaping of Black America*, a comprehensive overview of nearly four hundred years of Black enslavement and its treacherous legacy in the U.S. (PLATES 29–40). The book was published in 1975, a year after White had been elected a full member of the National Academy of Design.[56] His successes crested the

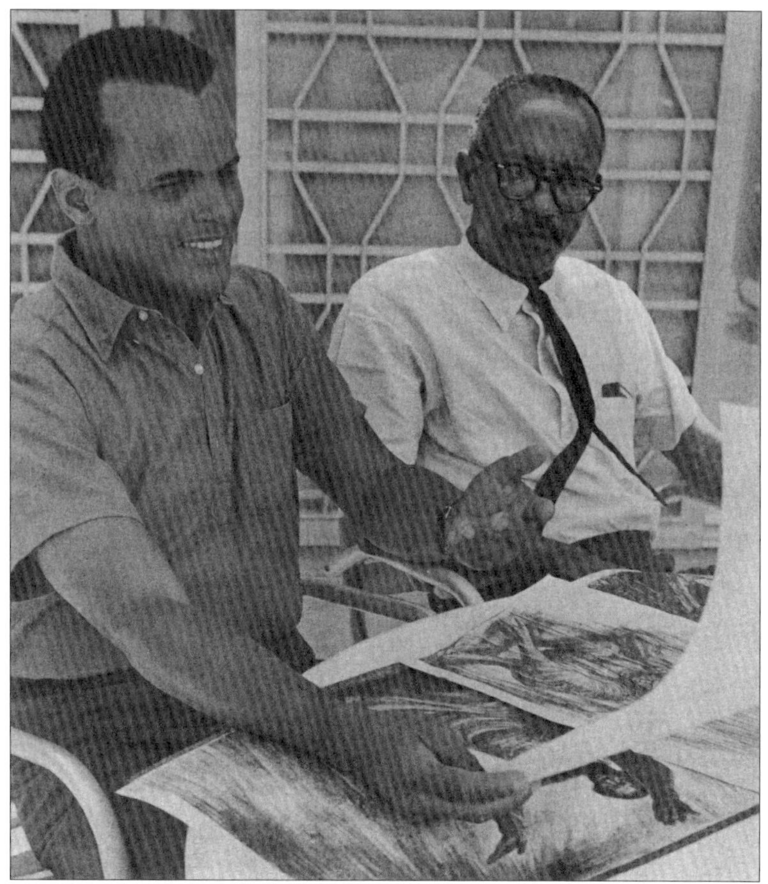

FIG.11

Charles White with Harry Belafonte, discussing what may be proofs for *Images of Dignity*, n.d. Charles White Archives.

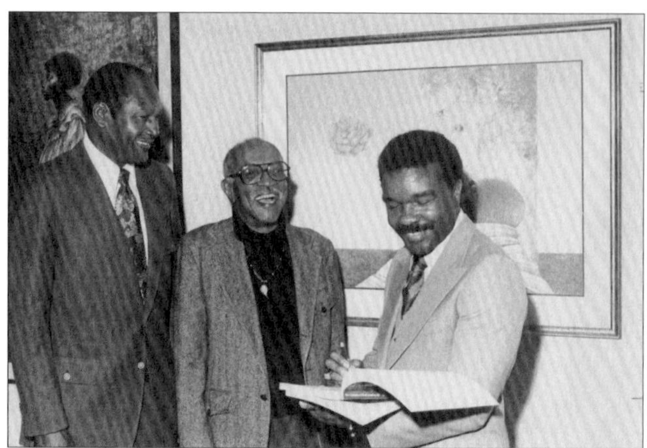

FIG.12

From left to right, Tom Bradley (mayor of L.A.), Charles White, and David C. Driskell at the *Two Centuries of Black American Art* exhibition at LACMA, 1976. Courtesy of the David C. Driskell Papers at the David C. Driskell Center at the University of Maryland, College Park. Gift of Prof. and Mrs. David C. Driskell. (MS01.11.01.P0305).

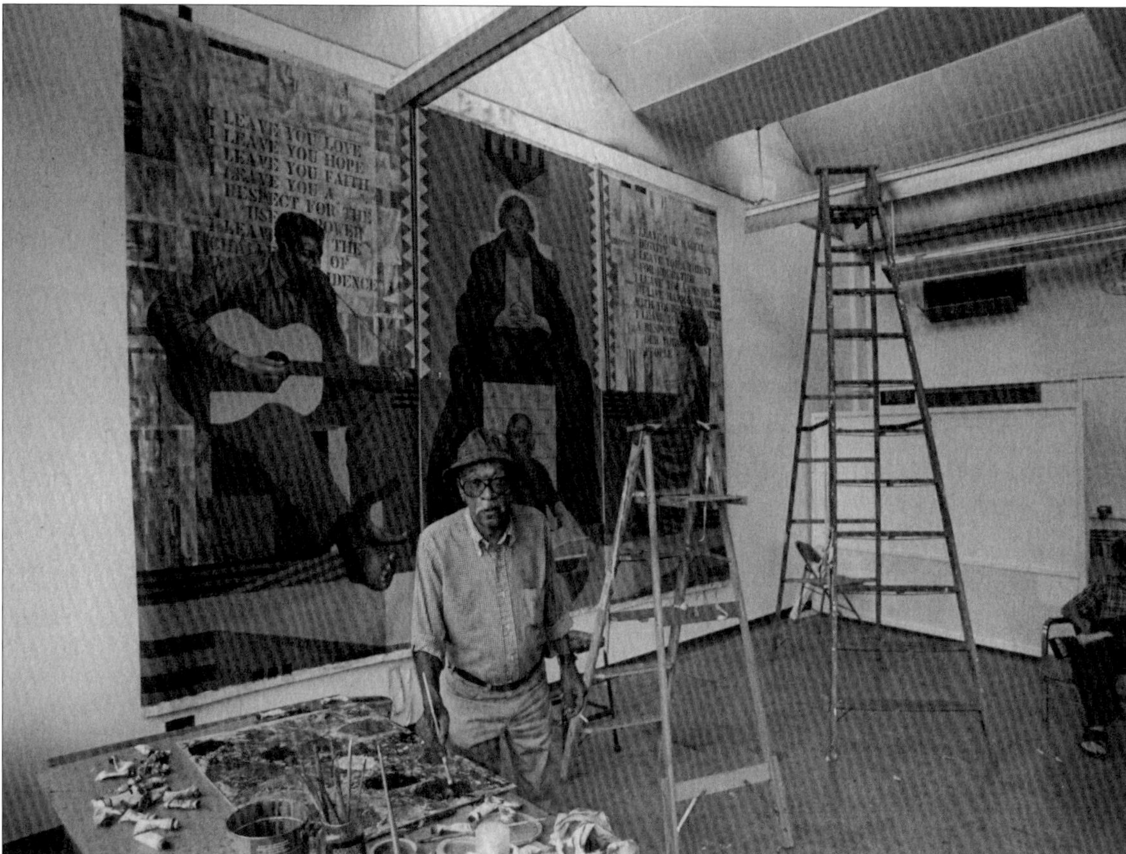

following year, the capstone of which was the September 1976 inauguration of *The Work of Charles White: An American Experience*, his first traveling solo exhibition, which premiered at Atlanta's High Museum before opening at the Montgomery Museum of Fine Arts, the Hunter Museum of American Art, the Arkansas Art Center, and in West Palm Beach. Then, on September 30, the Los Angeles County Museum of Art (LACMA) inaugurated its landmark exhibition *Two Centuries of Black Art*, guest curated by David C. Driskell, who was, at that time, chair of Fisk University's art department (FIG. 12).[57] Both events marked high points not only in White's career but also in the growing (though still paltry) recognition of Black artists' vital importance. As the promise of a new decade loomed ever closer, White joined the National Advisory Board for the National Council for Black Studies in addition to being named chair of Otis's drawing department. He accepted nominations to serve as both commissioner of California's new Afro-American Museum of History and Culture (today, the California African American Museum) and a member of the L.A. Advisory Committee on Cultural Affairs (gubernatorial and mayoral appointments, respectively).[58]

Final Days

In 1978 White executed his last great mural, dedicated to the legacy of Dr. Mary McLeod Bethune (1875–1955) at the eponymous public library branch in Los Angeles (FIG. 13), before traveling to Dresden in March as a corresponding member of Germany's Akademie der Künste. Upon his return to the States, he was invited by Howard University to serve as Distinguished Professor of Art in the Graduate School of Fine Arts, an invitation he felt compelled to accept, despite his mounting exhaustion and physical depletion.[59] Meanwhile, White continued to fulfill responsibilities on the New York boards of the Black Academy of Arts and Letters and the National Center for Afro-American Artists.[60] His schedule that fall was pummeling; so much so that White had to resign from his teaching duties at Howard before the autumn term had even concluded. Less than a year later, on OCTOBER 3, 1979, drained and suffering from chronic obstructive pulmonary disease, Charles White died of congestive heart failure. The *New York Times* neatly summarized his remarkable professional achievements in its obituary, noting: "His pictures are in 49 museums and have been seen in 123 institutional exhibitions, in 48 books illustrating and discussing his works, and in 53 one-man shows. They won him 39 American and European awards."[61]

Charles White masterfully balanced medium and message. He used his immense technical prowess to deliver critically important messages with laser accuracy and bore witness while inspiring people from all walks of life to do better, to be better. White was, in fact, an iron fist in a velvet glove. The artist once shared: "I had no other tools to fight with so the only way I had to fight was with my brushes."[62] And fight he did, harnessing his brilliance and virtuosity in the service of people of color as well as humanity writ large throughout his remarkably productive career.[63] Possessing a rare grace of character, tenacity of spirit, and nobility of mind, White brandished his unwavering commitment to justice, compassion, integrity, and education in his life and work. His personality, like his talents and his values, enabled him to overcome countless obstacles, such that, when White died, he left behind indelible legacies, both personal and professional.[64] His was truly a life, extraordinary.

FIG. 13
Charles White working on the Dr. Mary McLeod Bethune Mural in a studio at Otis Art Institute, with Kent Twitchell in the background, 1977. Charles White Archives.

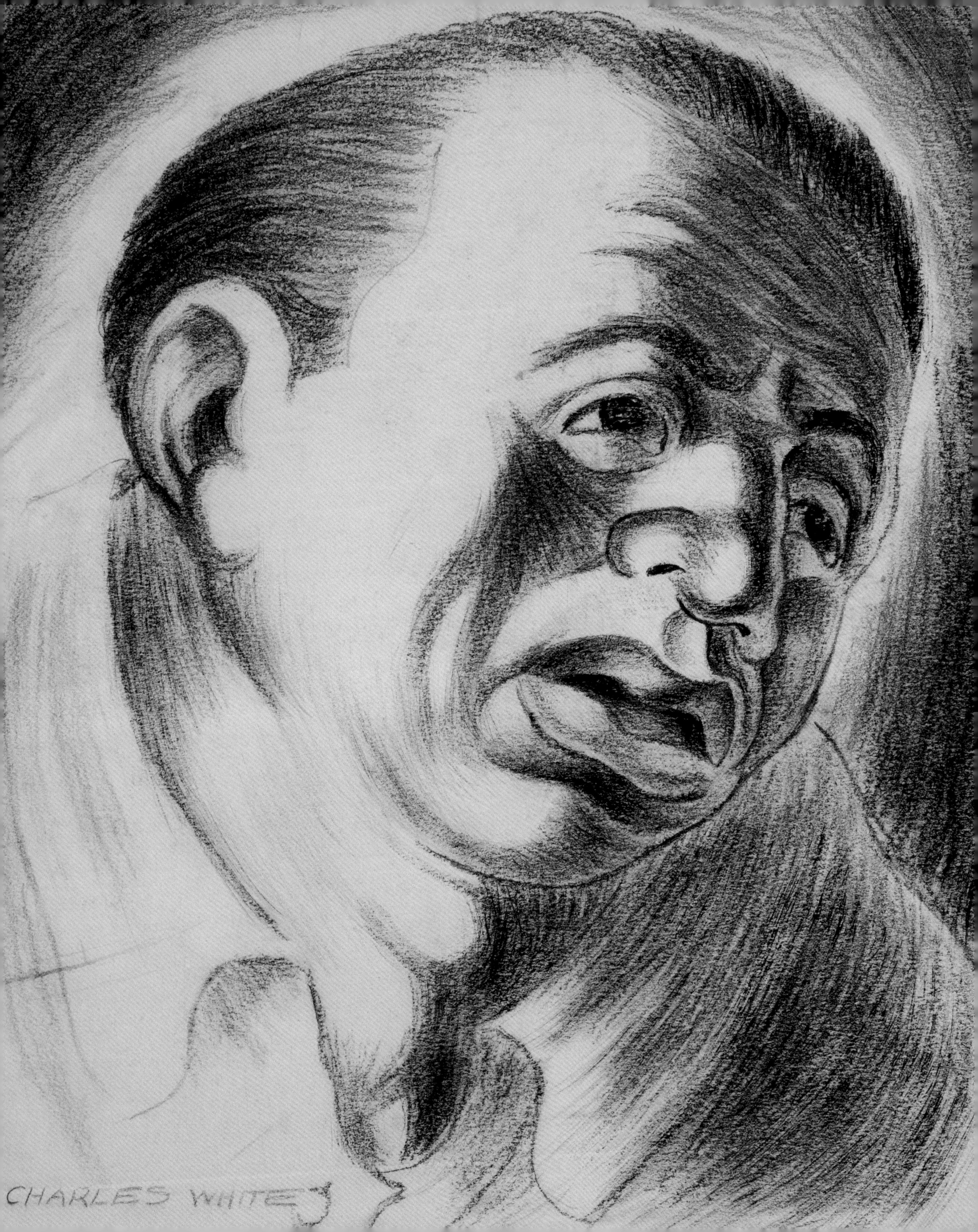
CHARLES WHITE

MEXICO WAS A MILESTONE—CHARLES WHITE'S *NEGRO: U.S.A.* PRINTS

Mora J. Beauchamp-Byrd

"Mexico was a milestone. I saw artists working to create an art about and for the people. This had the strongest influence on my whole approach."
—Charles White[1]

The Mexican Muralist painter Diego Rivera (1886–1957) completed a number of high-profile public art commissions in the United States between 1930 and 1934, including murals for the California School of Fine Arts in San Francisco (the now-closed San Francisco Art Institute), the Detroit Institute of Arts, and New York City's Rockefeller Center. Magazine and newspaper articles across the nation trumpeted his presence as well as that of his wife, the artist Frida Kahlo (1907–1954). Though it would be another decade before Charles White would meet Rivera and other Muralists in Mexico, White was likely exposed to Rivera's work through the extensive media coverage as well as his early, frequent visits to the Art Institute of Chicago. Later, he certainly engaged in dialogue regarding Rivera with his mentors, peers, and colleagues, many of whom revered the artist, and some of whom had worked with him directly.[2] It is not surprising, then, that in the mid- to late-1930s, White produced two portraits of Rivera, one in Conté crayon and pencil (1935–38, FIG. 1), and the other solely in Conté crayon (1936).[3] These two drawings are highly significant, evincing White's early awareness of Rivera, and of the Muralists as a whole; it is clear that their work had an enduring impact on White's oeuvre. In 1946–47, White and his first wife, the artist Elizabeth Catlett (1915–2012), spent time in Mexico with the Muralists and other artists associated with the Taller de Gráfica Popular, a printmaking collective founded in 1937 to promote Mexican culture and foster national pride.[4] White's interest was certainly further fueled by the time in Mexico with Catlett, who decided to study with the Taller after receiving a renewed Julius Rosenwald fellowship.[5]

This essay explores *Head of a Man* (FIG. 2) and *Our War* (FIG. 3), two offset lithographs White produced for *Negro: U.S.A. A Graphic History of the Negro People in America Workshop Prints No. 2*, a 1949 portfolio of twenty-six prints published by the New York City–based Workshop of Graphic Art, an interracial group of Social Realist artists. Produced relatively soon after White's time in Mexico, these prints have not yet been fully explored in scholarship on White. What was the stylistic and thematic impact of the Mexican Muralists and the Taller on White's subsequent work? And how might the trip to

FIG. 1
Charles White, *Diego Rivera (Portrait of a Man)*, ca. 1935–38. Conté crayon and pencil on illustration board. 25.4 x 20.3 cm (10 x 8 in.). Courtesy Petrucci Family Foundation Collection of African American Art. The Charles White Archives.

Mexico with Catlett, and her work, have influenced White? This essay provides historical and conceptual context for these images, proposing that his time in Mexico was highly impactful, and critical to a transformative shift in White's work.

Early Years: Chicago, Mural Traditions, and the Illinois Art Project

Often referred to as a Social Realist artist, White's paintings, drawings, and prints reflect the influence of American Regionalist, Cubist, German Expressionist, and Mexican Muralist aesthetic and thematic concerns. He began exploring the work of American Regionalist (or American Scene) painters like Grant Wood (1891–1942) and Thomas Hart Benton (1889–1975) in the mid-1930s.[6] During this period, he also engaged with leftist, Chicago-based artists, including African Americans in the arts, and became involved with the Art Crafts Guild, a group of Black artists that met on Sundays to offer skills training and support for its members and to sponsor exhibitions and other professional opportunities.[7] The group was organized in 1932 in Chicago by the artist William McGill, with George E. Neal (1906–1938) serving as a primary instructor by 1934. In addition to White, artists who attended regularly included Margaret Burroughs (1915–2010), Eldzier Cortor (1916–2015), Bernard Goss (1913–1966), Joseph Kersey (1909–1982), and Archibald Motley (1891–1981). Their efforts led to the founding of the South Side Community Arts Center in 1940.[8]

White's early career was also impacted by his time working for the Works Progress Administration (WPA), which was created in 1935 as one of numerous federal agencies established by President Franklin Roosevelt's New Deal legislation. In addition to providing employment for millions, the WPA sponsored projects that supported the visual arts, including the Federal Art Project (FAP), which established community and cultural centers and employed artists to produce public art such as murals and sculpture for buildings including schools, post offices, and hospitals. White joined the Illinois Art Project (IAP), a state affiliate of the FAP, in 1938, and began working on murals with artists such as Mitchell Siporin (1910–1976) and Edward Millman (1907–1964), both of whom were enthralled with the work of the Mexican Muralists. Indeed, Millman studied fresco painting with Rivera from 1934 to 1935, and in 1941, after Siporin and Millman won a major commission to produce murals for the Central Post Office in St. Louis, both artists traveled to Mexico to study the Muralists' work more closely. They and their colleagues also admired the Taller, a respect that assuredly fueled White's own desire to explore this Mexican collective more deeply. The impact of these influences is apparent in the murals that White completed for the IAP, and subsequently, including *Progress of the American Negro: Five Great American Negroes* (1939, FIG. 4); *A History of the Negro Press* (1940), a commission from the American Negro Press; and the well-known *The Contribution of the Negro to American Democracy* (1943) at Hampton University.[9]

Another New Deal program, the Farm Security Administration (FSA), also helped shape White's evolving style. Initially hired to document the devastation caused by widespread economic depression, FSA photographers' portfolios were later expanded, resulting in an extensive catalogue of American life—youngsters playing on city streets, mothers with children in parks, construction workers, and more.[10] From the late 1930s through the 1940s, White, too, explored these and other themes seen in the work of FSA photographers

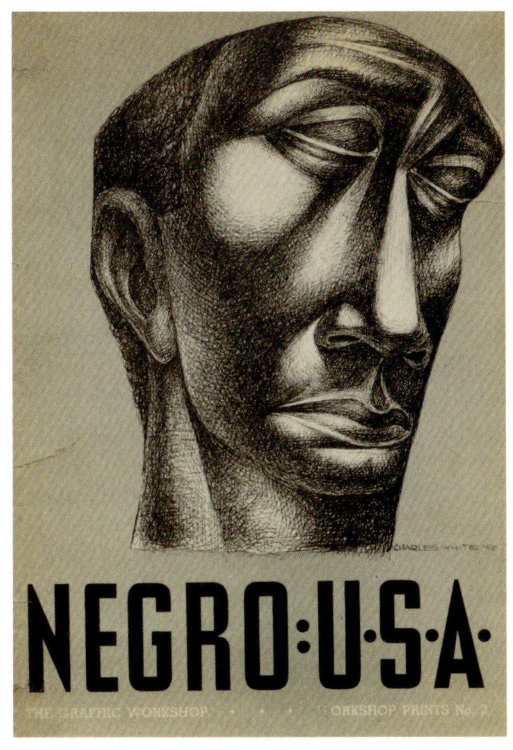

FIG. 2
Charles White, *Head of a Man*, 1948 (see plate 7).

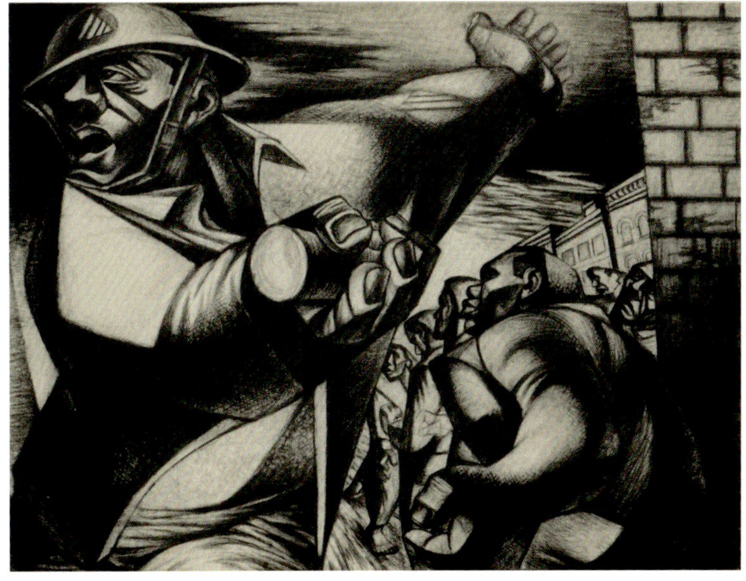

FIG. 3
Charles White, *Our War*, ca. 1948 (see plate 8).

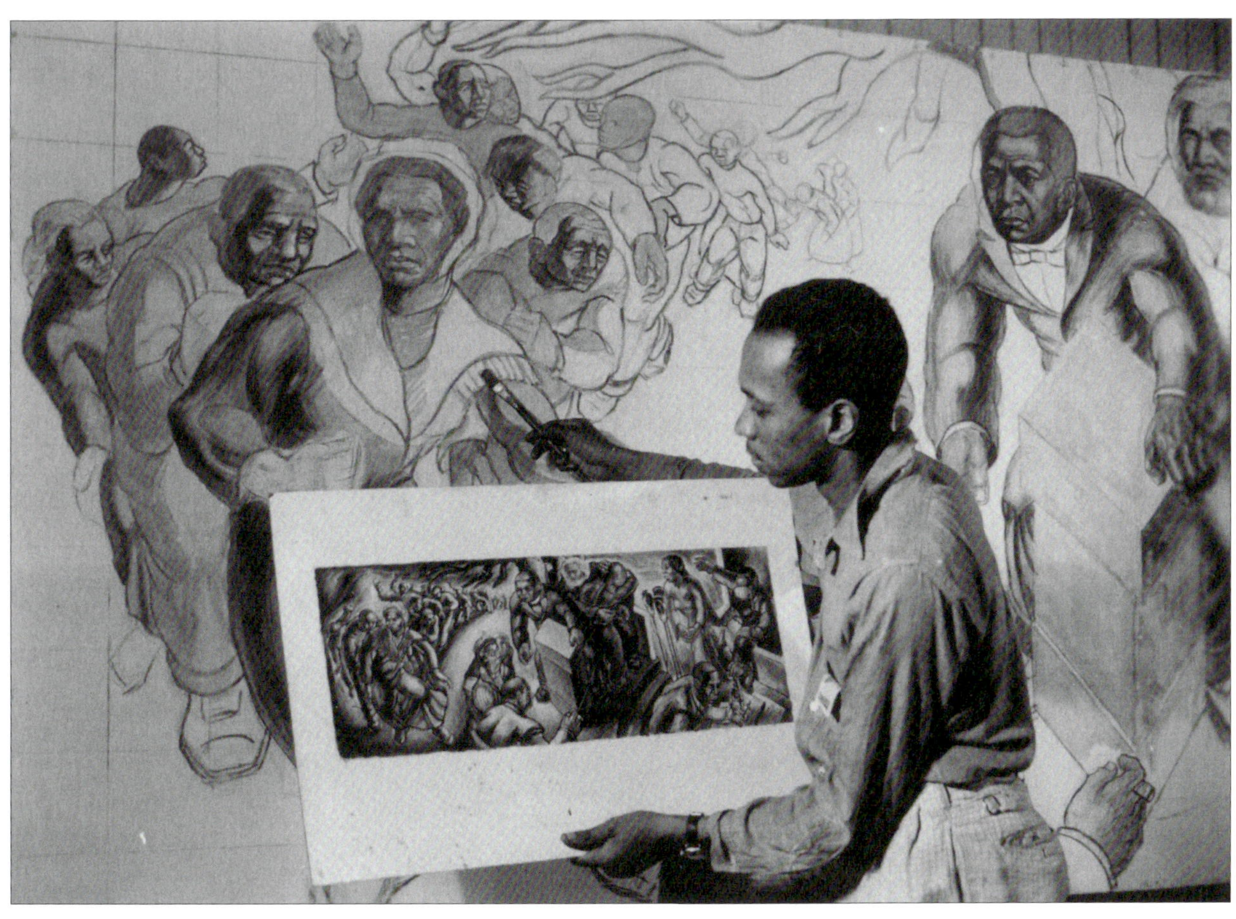

FIG. 4
Charles White working on the mural *Progress of the American Negro: Five Great American Negroes*, 1939. The Museum of Modern Art Archives.

like Walker Evans (1903–1975), Dorothea Lange (1895–1965), Ben Shahn (1892–1969), and later, Gordon Parks (1912–2006), as well as painters including Romare Bearden (1911–1988), Isabel Bishop (1902–1988), Robert Gwathmey (1903–1988), and Reginald Marsh (1898–1954). These artists often sought to democratize art, and their work frequently centered on heroicized historical figures as well as everyday laborers, mothers, and others, with an emphasis on those facing racism, poverty, and other forms of social and political disenfranchisement—qualities that would come to mark White's work.

By the late 1940s, White's figures began to shift from Modernist, Cubist-inspired forms that sometimes evoked thick, rough-hewn blocks of wood, as seen in *Awaiting His Return* (1946, PLATE 5), toward the style for which he later became known: richly-textured figurative works characterized by an overarching sense of movement, emotional tension, a masterful use of complex scale, layered texture, emphatic facial expressions, and massive, meticulously rendered hands.[11] *The Preacher* (1952, FIG. 5), with its exquisite cross-hatching, impassioned gestures, and colossal hands, exemplifies these images. In addition, White's work became increasingly marked by a refined sense of social and political urgency, profoundly and succinctly mining historical narratives and documenting the race- and class-based challenges of his time.

The Workshop of Graphic Art and the *Negro: U.S.A.* Portfolio

The Workshop of Graphic Art issued two important portfolios in the late 1940s. White contributed two lithographs, *Mexican Woman* (1946, FIG. 6) and *Mexican Boy* (1946, FIG. 7), to the Workshop's first portfolio, *Yes, the People! Workshop Prints Number One* published in December 1948. As their titles indicate, both prints were clearly influenced by his time in Mexico, from which he had returned the preceding year. *Negro: U.S.A. A Graphic History of the Negro People in America Workshop Prints No. 2* was issued in 1949 and featured twenty-six prints produced by fifteen artists. These included White's *Our War* and *Head of a Man* (which served as the portfolio's cover image) as well as images by Gwathmey, Leonard Baskin (1922–2000), Roy DeCarava (1919–2009), Antonio Frasconi (1919–2013), Bud Handelsman (1922–2006), Charles Keller (1914–2006), Louise Kruger (1924–2013), Jacob Landau (1917–2001), Al Lass, Jacob Lawrence (1917–2000), Jerry Martin (1926–2017), Leona Pierce (1921–2002), Jim Schlecker, and Edward Walsh.[12]

White's *Head of a Man* is a close-up of the face and neck of a Black male, his visage punctuated by unusually high cheekbones and expressive eyes, and composed of a medley of rounded curves and sharp angles. The figure gazes upward and to his left with a furrowed brow. *Head of a Man* is stylistically linked to White's *We Have Been Believers* (1949, FIG. 8), which features a close-up bust of a male and female couple with similar, seemingly anxious expressions on their faces. With its intricate modeling through extensive cross-hatching and texture, *Head of a Man* also bears similarities to Catlett's sculptural forms.

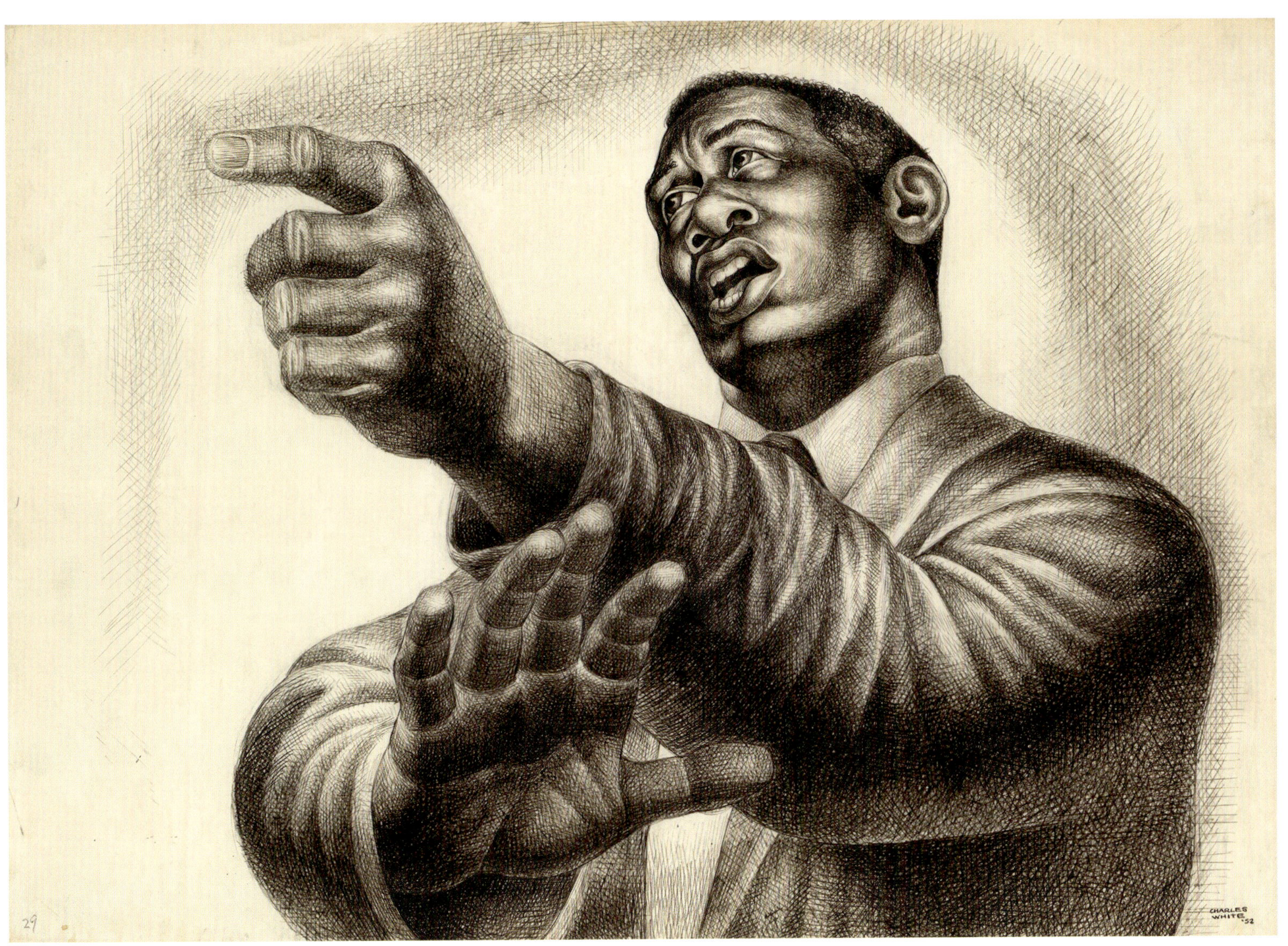

FIG. 5
Charles White, *The Preacher*, 1952.
Pen and ink and graphite pencil on board.
57.9 x 76 cm (22 13/16 × 29 15/16 in.).
Charles White Archives.

White's other print in that portfolio, *Our War*, employs hierarchical scale to great effect, much like the work of both the Mexican Muralists and the Taller. Thematically, *Our War* examines the tragic Port Chicago explosions of JULY 17, 1944, a disaster that highlighted race-based discrimination in the military and culminated in a process of desegregation in the armed forces.[13] At Port Chicago, California, a major ammunition loading facility, African American sailors trained for combat were instead ordered to load six hundred-pound bombs and other munitions aboard two ships while supervised by white officers. The sailors' concerns regarding safety were ignored. The vessels being loaded with ammunition erupted in a series of explosions that resulted in the deaths of three hundred and twenty men, two hundred and two of whom were African American. Nearly four hundred additional men were injured. The surviving sailors received disparate treatment based on race. White officers were provided hardship leaves while Black survivors were ordered to clean up the demolished base, including the remains of the servicemen's deceased colleagues. Later, they were ordered to resume loading munitions at a nearby base. Numerous African American sailors refused. After being threatened with harsh disciplinary action, some of the men returned to service, but fifty resisted. After a military trial, the "Port Chicago 50" were all convicted and received fifteen-year prison sentences.[14]

A tremendous, twisting sense of movement infuses *Our War*, realized by intersecting lines that form blocky, geometric configurations throughout the space, and by the sweeping, expansive gestures of the primary figure, a colossal air raid warden, at left, who grasps a flashlight firmly in his massive right hand, which is positioned at the center of the scene, gesturing to lead people to safety. A procession of individuals retreats into the distance at right. The warden's left hand recedes forcefully into the background, pointing viewers to both the procession of retreating figures and the cornices and other architectural details of the row houses at right. The print's thrusting, lunging sense of motion is reminiscent of the imagery of Muralists including David Alfaro Siqueiros (1896–1974) as well as the German Expressionist bronzes of Ernst Barlach (1870–1938), exemplified by his seminal *The Avenger* (1914). *Our War* also calls forth the work of German Expressionist artist Käthe Kollwitz (1867–1945), whose celebrated *The Peasants' War* print series (1908) was marked by tension through a skillful manipulation of gesture. In some ways, *Our War*'s ominous tone and abstracted, disjointed faces and body parts tilted in various directions also recalls the violent and tragic tableaux in Picasso's mural-scaled *Guernica* (1937), with its sobering anti-war message and condemnation of the Nazis' aerial bombing of the eponymous Basque city during the Spanish Civil War.

It is telling that the Workshop of Graphic Art's logo, featured on the title page of both of the Workshop's portfolios as well as the cover of the first, is a raised fist with a paintbrush and other artists' tools in hand, a visual expression of the collective's belief in the power of revolutionary action through art-making. Equally revealing is the fact that *Negro: U.S.A.* includes a foreword drafted by Marxist historian Herbert Aptheker (1915–2003) and a text by the painter, printmaker, and political cartoonist Charles Keller (1914–2000). Keller, who was affiliated with the collective in 1945 and soon began organizing collaborative projects, stated that the portfolio was produced "in conjunction with the 1949 observances of National Negro History Week, February 6–12."[15] Both portfolios carry out the

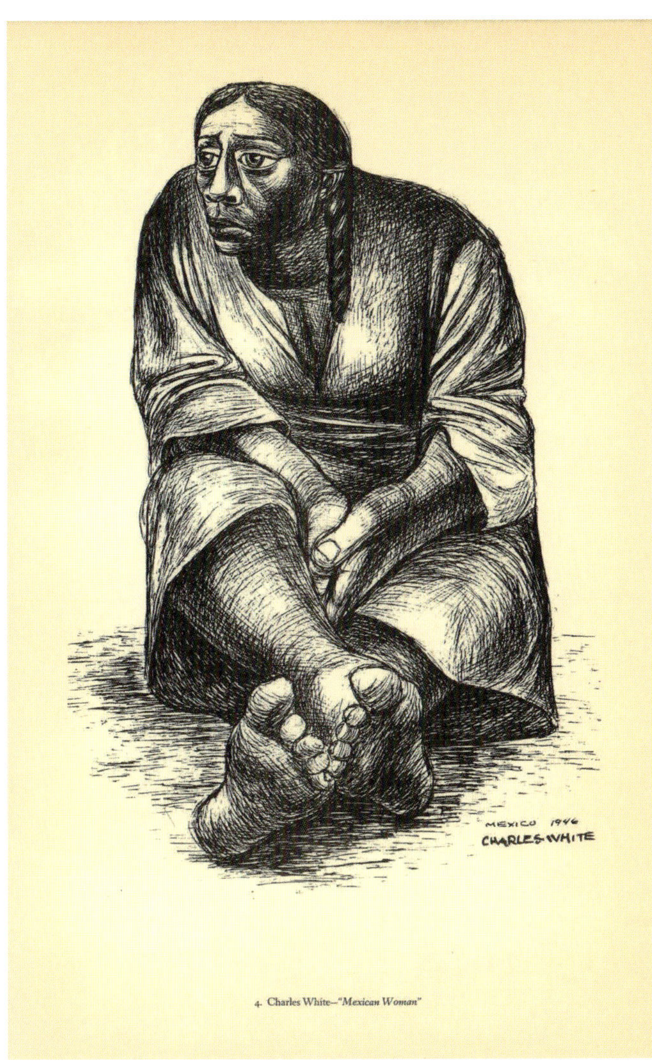

FIG.6
Charles White, *Mexican Woman*, 1948. Offset lithograph. 35.6 × 21.6 cm (14 × 8 ½ in.). The Neverson Collection. Courtesy of Hampton Art Lovers. Charles White Archives.

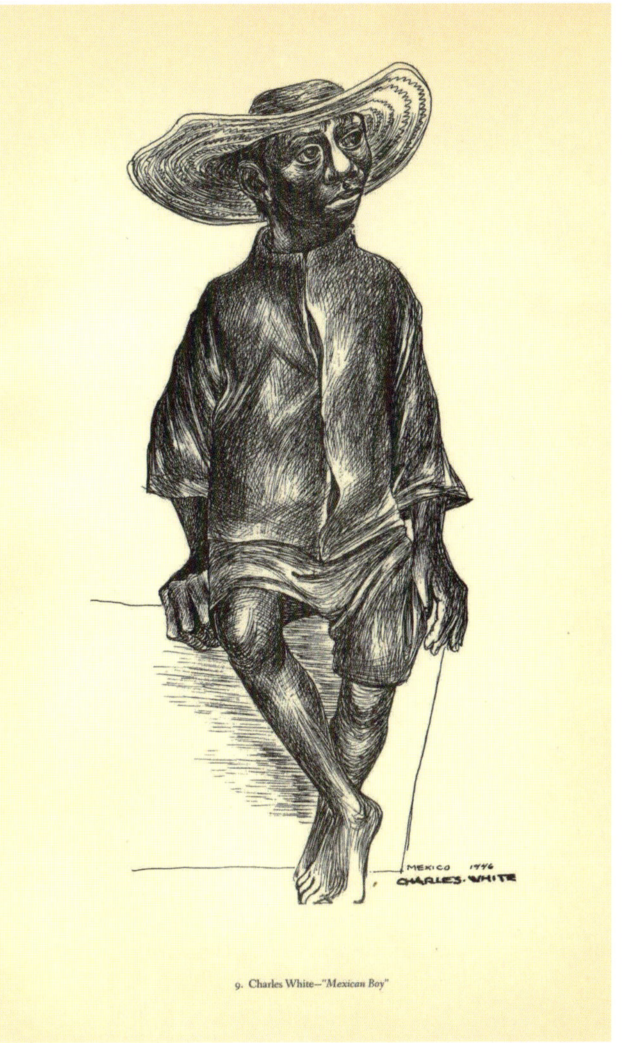

FIG.7
Charles White, *Mexican Boy*. 1948. Offset lithograph. 35.6 × 21.6 cm (14 × 8 ½ in.). The Neverson Collection. Courtesy of Hampton Art Lovers. Charles White Archives.

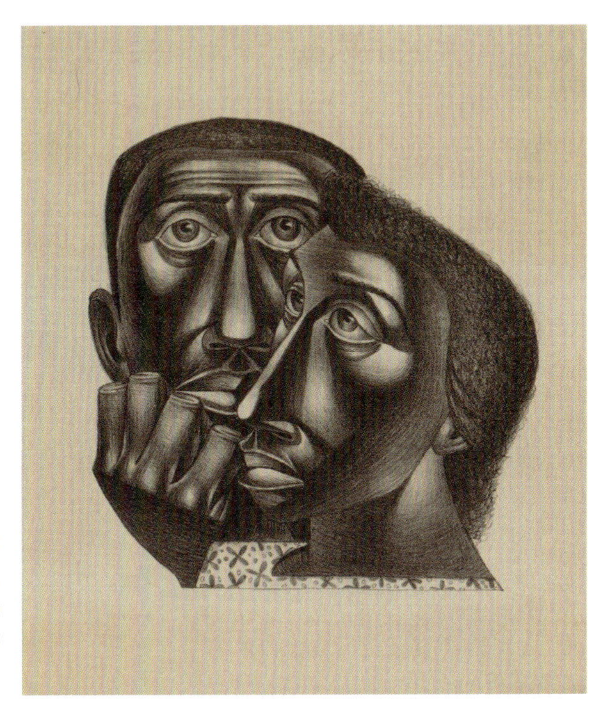

FIG.8
Charles White, *We Have Been Believers*, 1949. Lithograph in black on cream wove paper. 29.5 × 28 cm (11.6 x 11 in.) The Charles White Archives.

purpose of the Workshop, described in Keller's text as "[promoting] art derived from and addressed to the American people, an art which expresses the living content of our democratic fulfillment, peace and abundance." In alignment with its activist convictions, the Workshop produced numerous images for leftist groups during the 1940s and '50s and featured the work of African American and white American artists. Its commitment to "the people" aligned well with those of White's other great sources of inspiration in that period: the Mexican Muralists and the Taller de Gráfica Popular. In considering both *Head of a Man* and *Our War*, the critical relationship between African American artists and Mexican art at this time in general, and White's time in Mexico in 1946–47 in particular, is significant.[16]

Mexico and the Taller de Gráfica Popular

White's work shares conceptual and stylistic linkages with other African American Social Realists working in the 1930s and '40s, including Catlett, Ernest Crichlow (1914–2005), Hughie Lee-Smith (1915–1999), John Wilson (1922–2015), and Hale Woodruff (1900–1980), who greatly admired the Mexican Muralists and the Taller. Art historian Stacy I. Morgan has written of how the Taller served as a restorative space for training in printmaking and a respite of sorts from "Cold War political persecution" for North American artists.[17] In keeping with the values espoused by the Taller, these artists also focused on art that felt accessible, turning again and again to figurative expression and realism, despite the abstraction that was becoming increasingly prominent in much of the art world. They were further linked by a commitment to Marxism and/or Communist Left ideas and a desire to address the needs of "the people" or "the masses" through media like printmaking.

In 1941 White married printmaker and sculptor Elizabeth Catlett, whose renewed Julius Rosenwald fellowship allowed the couple to go to Mexico, where she completed a series of prints dedicated to African American women.[18] In Mexico City, White and Catlett both worked at the Escuela Nacional de Pintura y Escultura (National Academy of Painting and Sculpture), or "La Esmeralda," and at the Taller. For about a year, they resided at Siqueiros's home. White refined his skill in producing linocuts, working with Taller artist Leopoldo Méndez (1902–1969, FIG. 9).

Examining White's work from this period, it is clear that his explosive use of gesture and scale, likely influenced by works like Siqueiros's *Self-Portrait* (1945, FIG. 10), was evolving, as seen in images like White's 1946 political cartoon *Freeport Columbia* (PLATE 6), published in *Congress View* magazine by the Communist-centered National Negro Congress.[19] As White later recalled, "[Mexico] had a tremendous influence on me...the experience of Mexico itself, because of the nature of the kind of stuff I was doing, was more geared to 'social realism'...I found people in Mexico who were also dealing with the same kind of approach (in terms of content)."[20]

White's time in Mexico reinforced his commitment to exploring themes of social change, including race-based struggles. It also solidified his focus on prints as well as his work on series. This period was marked by what art historian Erica Moiah James referred to as "a sharpening synthesis of aesthetic and political ideas."[21]

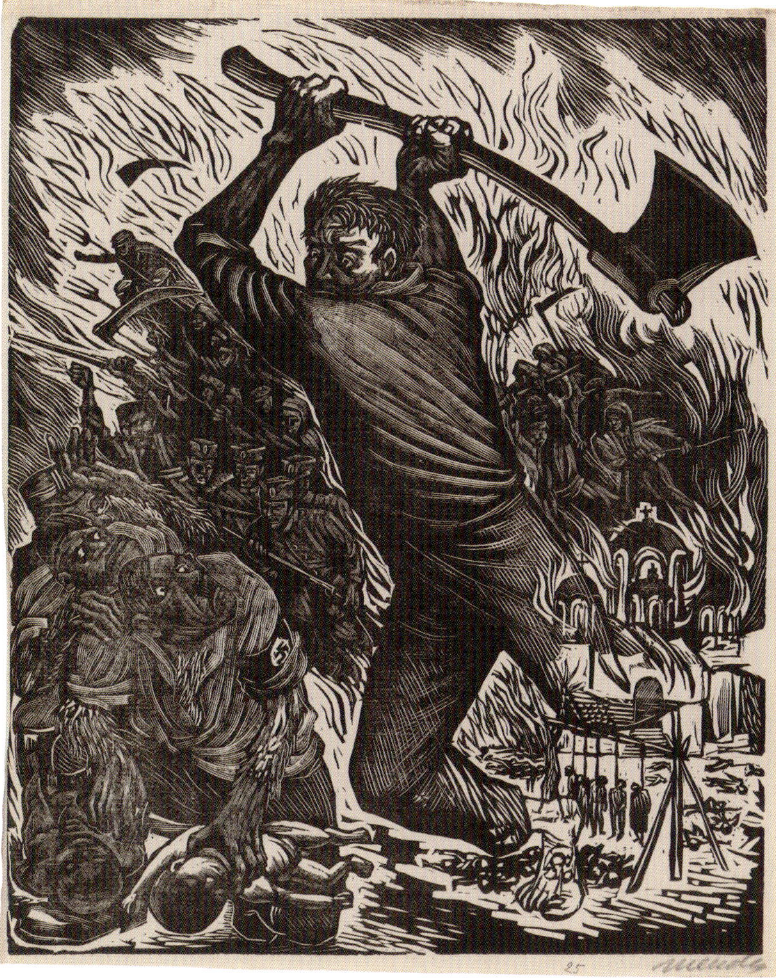

FIG. 9
Leopoldo Méndez, *The Peoples Revenge*, 1943. Wood engraving. 24.8 x 19.7 cm (9 3/4 x 7 3/4 in.) Courtesy Pablo Méndez Hernández / Museo del Estanquillo.

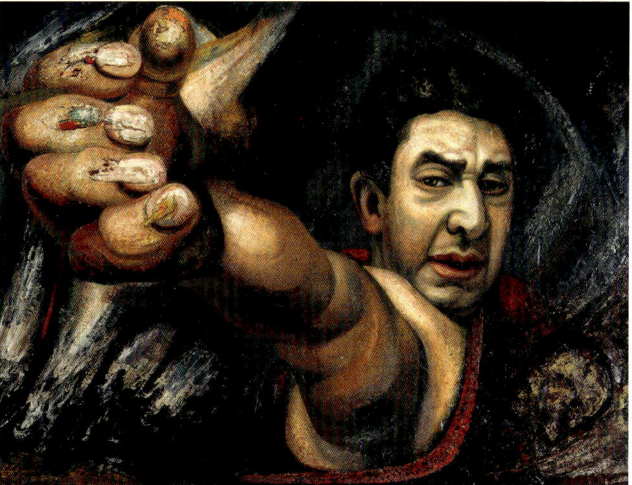

FIG. 10
David Alfaro Siqueiros, *Self-portrait*, 1945. Pyroxilin on Masonite. 91 x 121 cm (35.8 x 47.6 in.). Artists Rights Society (ARS), New York / SOMAAP, Mexico City.

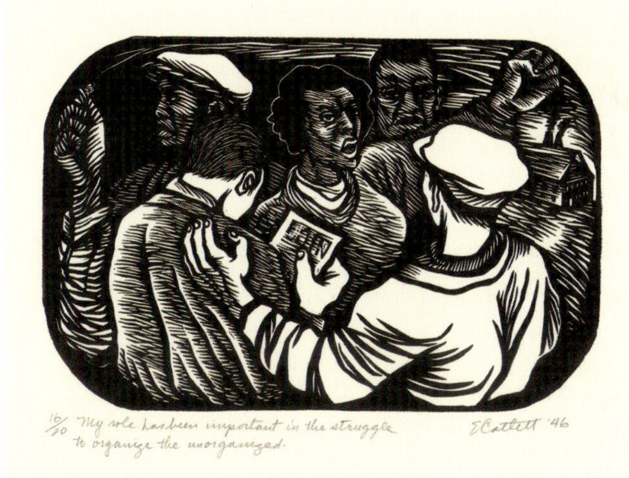

FIG. 11
Elizabeth Catlett, *My role has been important in the struggle to organize the unorganized* (from the Negro Woman series), 1947. Linoleum cut from a series of fourteen linoleum cuts. 15.2 × 22.9 cm (6 x 9 in.). Mora-Catlett Family.

The Influence of Elizabeth Catlett

White's evolving style during the mid- to late-1940s must also be considered in light of his marriage to Catlett. Aside from the very formative trip to Mexico occasioned by her grant, there are multiple ways in which her work likely influenced him. By 1946, Catlett was producing politically charged prints of immense, subtle power, such as the well-known 1947 *Negro Woman* series (FIG. 11). Her oft-reproduced prints as well as her refined, Modernist sculptures, earned her sustained visibility and respect as an artist.[22]

Born in Washington, D.C., Catlett earned a B.S. in art from Howard University in 1935, studying with James Herring (1887–1969), Lois Mailou Jones (1905–1998), and James Porter (1905–1970). In 1940, she became the first student to earn an M.F.A. in sculpture from the University of Iowa, where she studied with American Regionalist painter Grant

Wood. By the mid-1940s, Catlett's lyrical sculptures, in wood, bronze, and marble, had begun to reveal the influence of West African sculptural forms, the art of ancient Mesoamerica (including *chacmool* figures), her studies in the 1940s with Russian-born Modernist Ossip Zadkine (1888–1967) and his Cubist abstractions, and the rugged, explosive force of German Expressionist Barlach's sculptural forms.[23]

In 1945, Catlett received a Julius Rosenwald fellowship, totaling $1,800, to complete "a series of lithographs, paintings, and sculptures on the role of the Negro woman in the fight for democratic rights in the history of America."[24] She requested a renewal of the fellowship in 1946 to complete her print series in Mexico. As she noted in her application, "I would like to strengthen my clarity of approach to art through a visit to Mexico. There I could get at first hand an understanding of the new techniques developed by Mexican artists in painting for and about the people of their country. This would help me...in developing art techniques to reach my own people and others in America."[25]

The celebrated *Negro Woman* series also reveals Catlett's admiration for the German Expressionists Kollwitz and Emil Nolde (1867–1956). According to the art historian Melanie Herzog, Catlett encountered Kollwitz's work in New York, and she "brought several of Kollwitz's prints with her to Mexico."[26] Kollwitz's influence is also evident in Charles White's prints of this period. As with White, the impact of the Mexican Muralists as well as the Taller would become increasingly solidified in Catlett's work over time.[27] Catlett and her second husband, the renowned Mexican artist Francisco Mora (1922–2002), remained members of the Taller through the mid-1960s.[28]

White and Catlett shared many values as well as objectives for what they wished to express through their work. Thematically, Catlett's sculptures and prints centered on images of citizens protesting to achieve equal rights, countering racial and ethnic stereotypes, appreciating the diversity of African physical beauty, and highlighting the everyday and heroic role of African American women. Images of heroic women, whether working women, historical figures, or as part of numerous mother-and-child-themed images featuring African American and Mexican women, figured prominently in her oeuvre.

White's increasing and ongoing focus on female figures, including his many mother-and-child paintings and prints, was very likely inspired by Catlett. White's *I Have a Dream* (1976, plate 42) exemplifies these works. As previously mentioned, Catlett's influence may also be seen in the near-sculptural quality of prints like White's *Head of a Man*, with its close-up, bust-like presence, sharply delineated cheekbones, cross-hatching, and use of light that mimics the sheen of black marble. When reproduced for the cover of *Negro: U.S.A.*, the portfolio's title appears to serve as a plinth. *Head of a Man* may be compared to Catlett's sculptural works like her 1947 piece *Head* (FIG. 12), and these stylistic and thematic linkages deserve additional scholarly examination.[29]

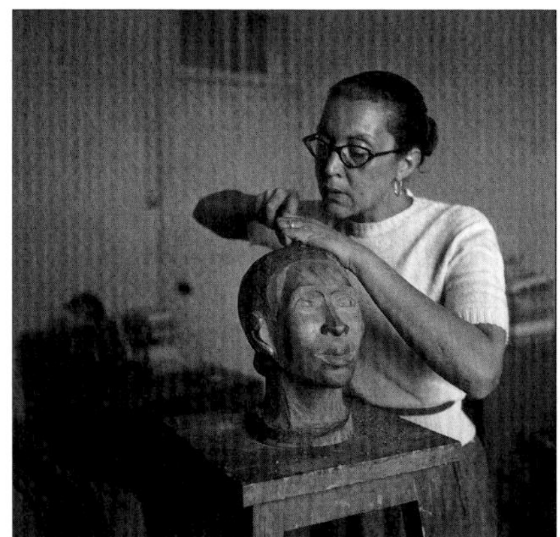

FIG. 12
Elizabeth Catlett in her studio, 1947. Bernice Kolko, photographer. Bernice Kolko ©Fundacion Zuñiga Laborde A.C. (Mexico). Mora-Catlett Family.

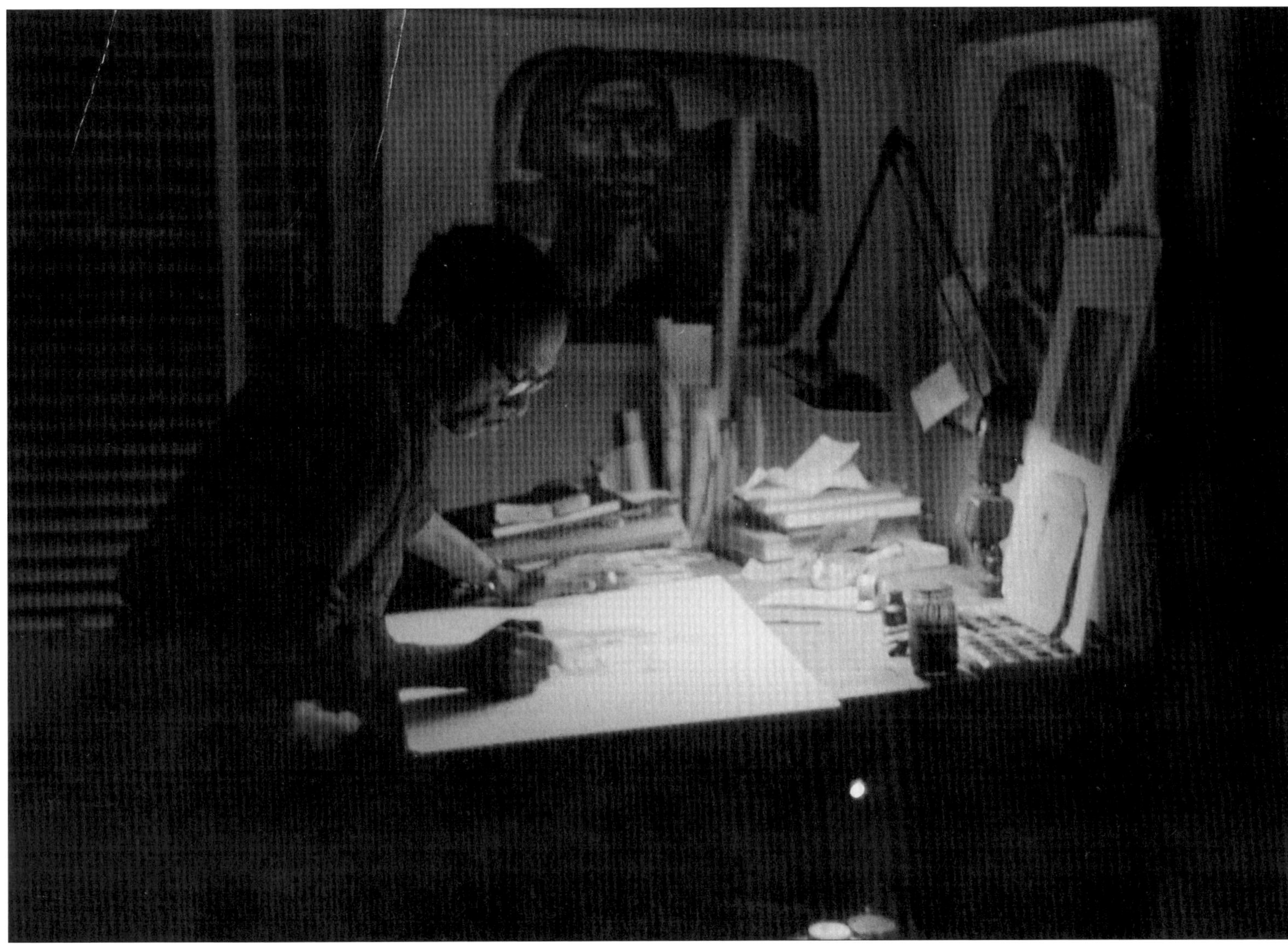

FIG. 13
Charles White in the home studio of his 24th Street apartment in New York City, ca. 1951–52. The Charles White Archives.

A Moment in Mexico that Resonated

White's time in Mexico proved to be a pivotal moment in the artist's early career, as evidenced by the *Negro: U.S.A.* portfolio prints and other works produced in the late 1940s and beyond (FIG. 13). This moment was marked by a striking confluence of networks, or waves of influence, including White's early interest in the Mexican Muralists and involvement with the IAP, his lengthy engagement with leftist, Chicago-based artists, his association with Catlett and her signature styles as well as her social and political thematic preferences, and both White and Catlett's involvement with the Taller, initially as a couple, and then later as individual artists. As noted, White referred to this time in Mexico as "a milestone," a space in which he was able to witness, and participate in, a vision of artists, both individually and collectively, producing "an art about and for the people." It was also a moment that affirmed, for him, the critical, highly active role that artists, and artists working together, might play in documenting and illuminating a path toward progressive change.

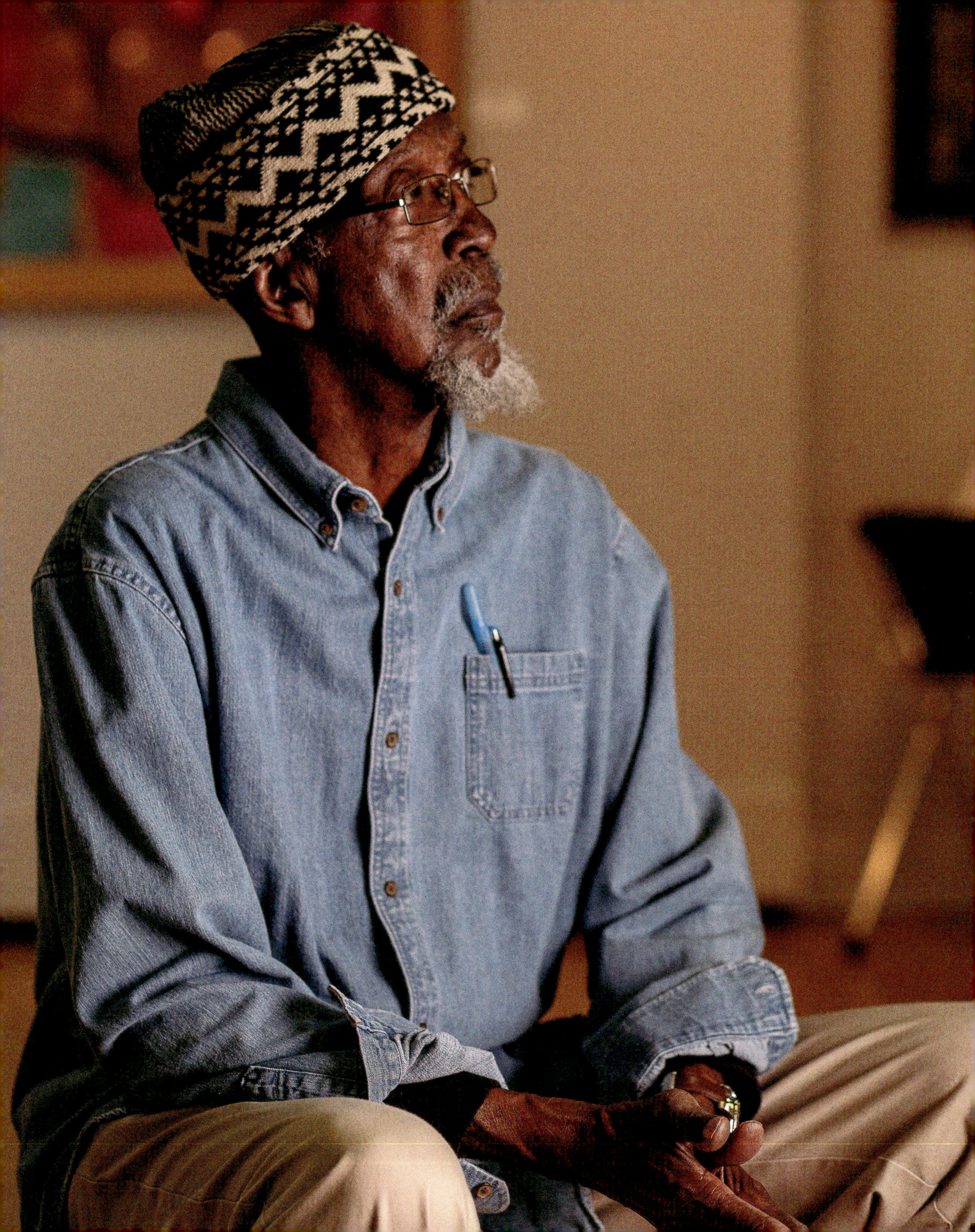

ON CHARLES WHITE: HIS VISION WAS HIS OWN

Willis "Bing" Davis in conversation with Will South

Some people are huggers, others are not. I am definitely not. So it was a shock when I spontaneously hugged Bing Davis after introducing him to a large audience at the Columbia Museum of Art several years ago. When questioned about this unprecedented and very public display of affection, all I could say was, "It felt natural." Simply *knowing* Bing feels natural. You never talk to Bing, or at him, but always with him. He is a marvel of calm wisdom, concern for community, and artistic inspiration.

Willis "Bing" Davis (B. 1937) is an artist, curator, arts educator, gallery owner, and cultural leader. He met Charles White in 1968, when he invited White to teach young students in an arts program in Dayton, Ohio, as he recounts in this conversation, which took place via telephone in October 2021.

Davis has exhibited his work at and curated shows for museums and galleries around the country and internationally, including the Schomburg Center for Research in Black Culture, The Studio Museum in Harlem, the Smithsonian's Anacostia Community Museum, and the American Craft Museum. He has served multiple organizations, including positions as president, co-chair of the board of directors, and acting treasurer of the National Conference of Artists; president of the National Alliance of Artists from Historically Black Colleges and Universities; and chair of the art department and director of the Paul Robeson Cultural and Performing Arts Center at Central State University in Wilberforce, Ohio.

His forty-plus-year career in arts education included teaching at the elementary, high school, and university levels, founding multiple programs, and being recognized with many awards. After he retired from teaching in 1998, he established the Davis Art Studio and EbonNia Gallery.

During our conversation about Charles White, I was reminded once more of Bing's expansive warmth, charm, generosity, and the depth of his knowledge.

Will South: Bing, when I think of Charles White, you always come to mind. The two of you were artist/activists from the very start, each with a focus on Black America, despite having two completely different approaches. Your focus is abstraction and he was a traditional realist. Yet, you both had the same goal—to elevate a people. Why don't we start with when you met? It was decades ago, when you were a young teacher in Dayton, Ohio, and you brought Charles White to town to expose kids to the very best in African American art. That was in 1968, the year Bobby Kennedy was assassinated in

Bing Davis, 2021.
Photograph © Shon Curtis.

June, following the assassination in April of Dr. Martin Luther King Jr., and there were the riots in Los Angeles and riots at the Democratic National Convention in Chicago, to name just two among the scores of riots across the country. America was on fire in 1968. So, tell me: Why Charles White just then, and what were you hoping to achieve by working with him?

Bing Davis: Yes, those were turbulent times. But hopeful times, too. In 1967, here in Dayton, the Living Arts Center was founded, and I was the art director. This was a special Title 3 program in public schools that provided funds to open up a studio-gallery complex that dealt with art, music, dance, drama, creative writing, and the humanities. In 1966, one hundred Daytonians on various committees worked with the Dayton Public Schools to write up a special proposal where we would utilize the arts to enhance not only the arts, but also human development. I'm still using the arts to bring light and understanding and appreciation. We all believed then, and still do, that art can change lives.

WS: You were a high school art teacher. Did you have to give up your job teaching high school for the Living Arts Center?

BD: Yes. We didn't have benefits through the Living Arts program, but it was exciting enough to me that I felt I could leave the stability of the public school and shift over to this very special program. I was in the visual arts, and there was someone to head up music, someone for drama, someone for creative writing, someone for dance, and we all involved ourselves in the humanities. We had funds to refurbish a warehouse for an after-school and weekend program, too. Each of us had a pot of money we could use to bring in professional artists to supplement the work we were doing. I had a seen an article that Charles White had illustrated in *Ebony* magazine and got the idea he would be perfect as a visiting artist for our program. I don't know what to call it, but I was foolish enough to write him a personal letter.

WS: I would call it ambitious in the best way. And you're talking about the illustrations that would eventually be in the book *The Shaping of Black America,* right?

BD: Yes, by the noted historian Lerone Bennett Jr.

WS: Well, Bing, this is one of those moments in life where a great circle appears—those illustrations, all of them, are featured in this exhibition [*Charles White: A Little Higher*], and here you are, providing context for their appreciation.

BD: Wow—that's amazing!

WS: I know. I had to mention it. But let's get back to your bringing Charles White to Ohio.

BD: I had been teaching art in the Dayton Public Schools since graduating from college in 1959. Working in an urban area, I was always looking for ways to incorporate African and African American art and culture into my classes. As I was saying, I sent a letter in care of Mr. Ben Horowitz at the Heritage Gallery in Los Angeles—he was White's dealer. I described the Living Arts program and asked, respectfully, would Mr. White consider coming to Dayton, Ohio, for a week to interact with young people in the arts. I couldn't believe it, but Charles White

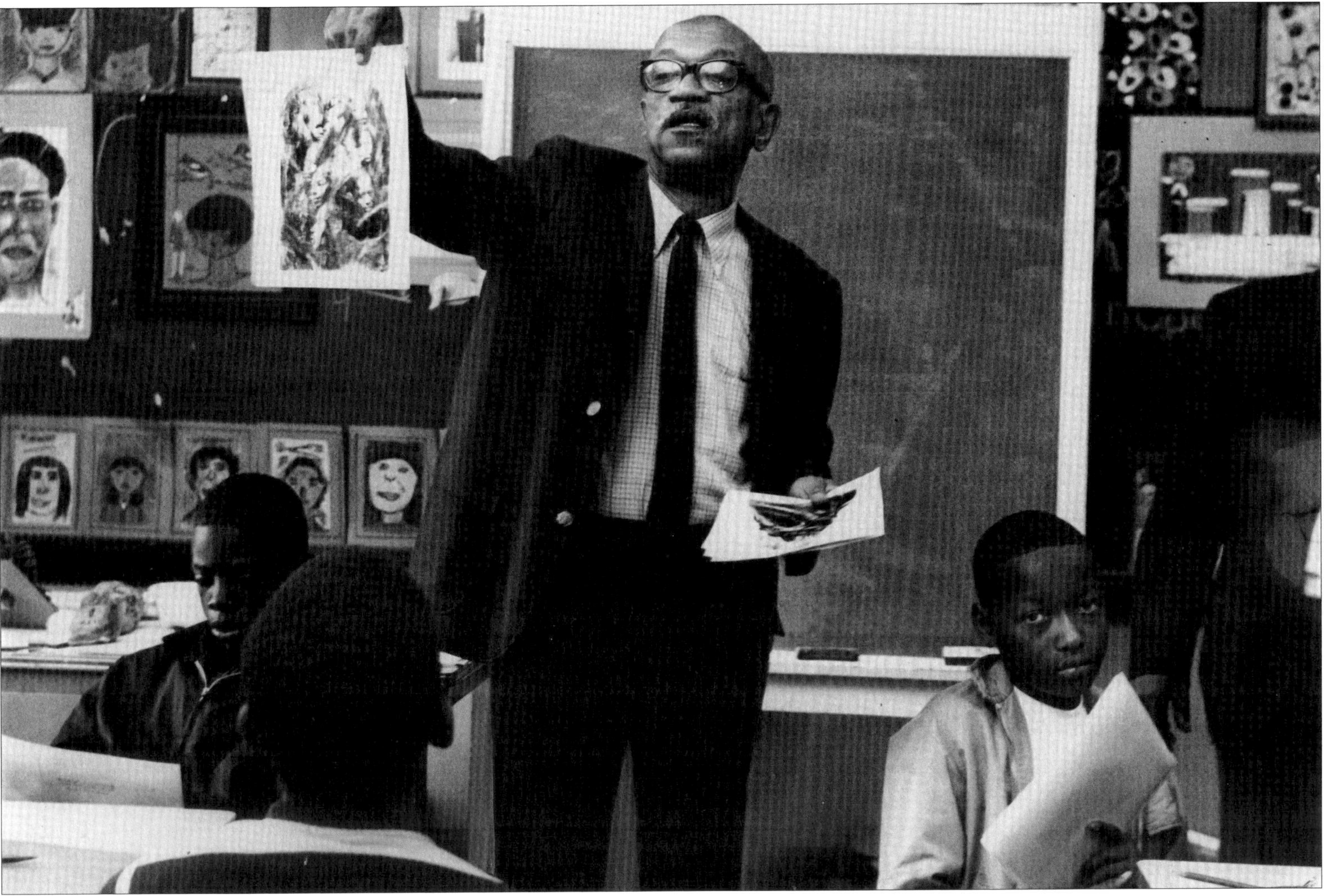

Charles White with students during his time as a visiting artist with the Living Arts Center program. "Artist's Job: Giving Things Beauty, Meaning," *Dayton Daily News*, May 22, 1968.

answered me: "Where in the hell is Dayton?" But seriously, he was very open, warm, and receptive. Working with Mr. Horowitz, we booked him in town for a week. During the day, I would take him to schools on all the sides of town, north, south, east, and west. Then, after school, students who were involved in the Living Arts program had direct contact with an artist of the highest caliber, Charles White.

WS: A half century later, that seems unbelievable.

BD: Yes. Then, on Friday, we had a public opening in a little gallery in this warehouse where we had installed a small exhibit of his works prior to and during the time he was here. At that time, people in Dayton were able to come and acquire Charles White's original work. It was inspiring to have a person of his standing respond to a little unknown high school art teacher who was trying to do something.

WS: Something good.

BD: Yes, well, I knew he could have asked for so much more than he did, and when he was here, he was the most gracious and giving person. He shared so much with our young people, and it was an amazing experience. All the kids of different ages opened up to him. He was inspirational to the kids and the teachers. It was so successful, the whole experience, that we were able to then invite other artists who came because Charles had done it. Artists like Richard Hunt, A. B. Jackson from Virginia Commonwealth, Edgar Tafur, who is the artist who studied in Colombia, South America, and Joe Overstreet from New York.

WS: What was White's method of teaching? He couldn't simply say, "Do what I do," because no one could have done that.

BD: He shared with students the why and how of art without belaboring the point. He talked about the beauty of the figure, and for me every day was like going to church. The teachers were well prepared for his visit as we had sent them all informational packets, including images of his work, ahead of time. This allowed them to ask questions, too, and it prepared them to support the students' efforts. Charles White, like many other great artists, was a natural teacher. He shared his artistic vision relative to subject matter, his medium, and his approach to drawing and painting. His teaching at Otis College of Art and Design in Los Angeles is praised by his students. He did a little demonstration of drawing, plus his work in the gallery gave everyone a chance to see his work up close.

WS: Did he draw in front of the students? Did he give demonstrations?

BD: Yes, yes, he did a little bit of demonstrating in addition to the students being able to see his work at the center.

WS: Although your art is abstract and White's work is figurative, clearly White made an impression on you. Can you talk about whether White's art affected you and affected the people who saw it, and if so, how?

BD: The most meaningful part of what he was doing was portraying African American people in everyday and common kinds of situations, whether it was a preacher or whether it was a mother or whether it was a child, and every image was always well done and well-crafted. And importantly, all of White's art was positive and uplifting, in contrast to the stereotypical kinds of images that were derogatory in terms of how they were drawn. His art was totally the opposite of the negative images of Black people that came out of the commercial experience, images like Aunt Jemima and Uncle Ben and the Gold Dust Twins. His work gave you *pride.* His images were always strong, virile, and positive, nothing mean or negative, and you understood that visually, no words needed. His work was inspiring on that unspoken level, but he also obviously had a fully African American perspective and a knowledge of African art as well. Although his figures were so realistic, he was aware that even those who worked abstractly, like myself, could still draw on the same inspiration of a positive Black experience.

WS: So as artists, although one was figurative and one abstract, you didn't see yourselves in two different worlds?

BD: No, not at all.

WS: Two sides of the same coin, maybe?

BD: Exactly.

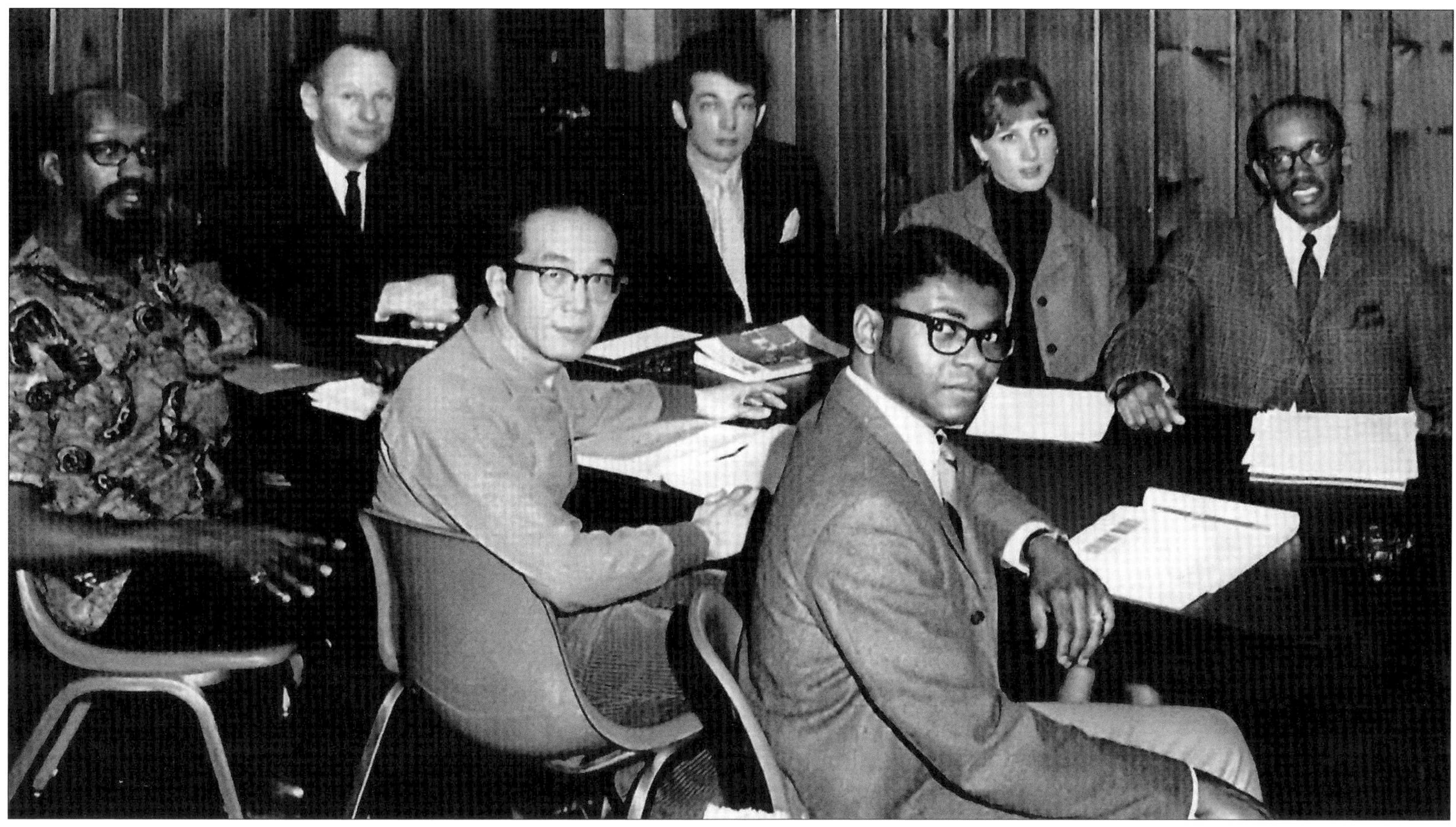

Living Arts Center staff members, 1967–70. Bing Davis is far left. Courtesy Bing Davis.

WS: I want to talk about his focus on the figure in the 1960s. In the 1950s, and you'll remember this well, Abstract Expressionism was on the rise, and then in the 1960s it was [Andy] Warhol and that whole phenomenon of Pop Art, of commercial art becoming fine art. None of that had anything to do with Charles White and his type of work. The attention was focused on artists like [Jackson] Pollock or [Willem] de Kooning or Warhol. How did Charles White feel about that? I imagine he must have felt at odds with the art world.

BD: Oh, no. He was aware of all of that. But I heard him speak, and what you learn is that there were other artists that inspired and validated African American artists. Pollock, Warhol, and de Kooning, they had their niche, certainly, but for Black artists there were [José Clemente] Orozco and [David Alfaro] Siqueiros and [Diego] Rivera, and all of the Mexican Muralists. Remember, White went to Mexico for a while. White was aware of the strong figurative tradition that came out of the Muralist movement, and that gave reinforcement to him and to others. There were, of course, Black artists who explored the Abstract Expressionist form and others, like Jacob Lawrence, who stayed true to their styles despite what was going on around them in America. They had a confidence and strength in their artistic vision, and like them, White never questioned his emphasis on the figure. Whatever was in the press and whatever was selling in galleries did not sway him. His vision was his own.

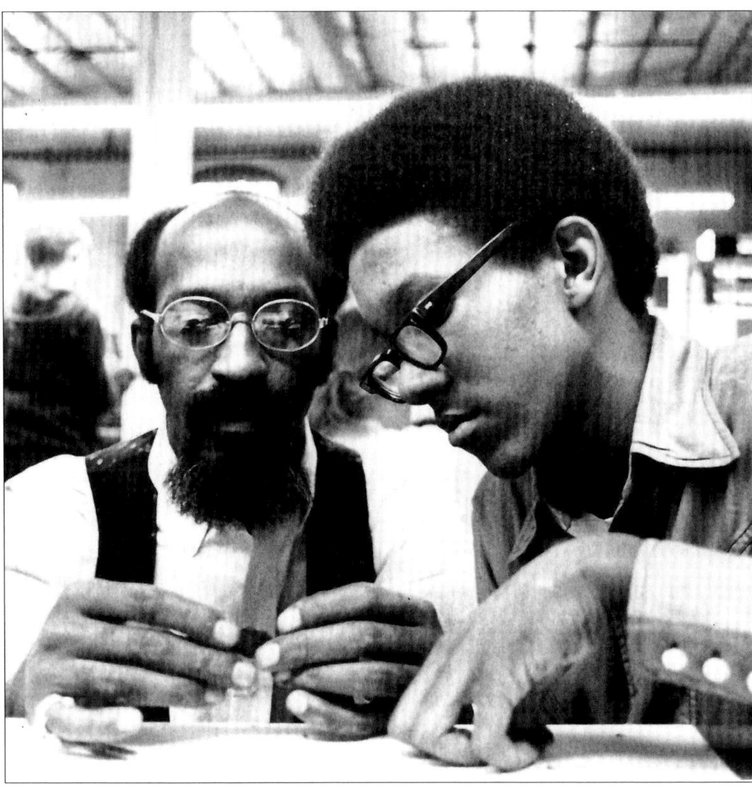

Bing Davis helping a student with a jewelry project, Living Arts Center, 1968. Courtesy Bing Davis.

WS: He doesn't even seem to have experimented with abstraction. I don't think I've ever seen any dabbling in that direction.

BD: A lot of artists like White understand that when they look inside the figure they can see the same kind of fluidity and the gesture and motion that's in an abstract piece, but it's in a figurative form.

WS: Did White ever talk about the significance or the influence on him of Renaissance artists like Michelangelo, who excelled in the figurative? In Michelangelo, many artists have found that fluidity and movement you mention. I feel there's clearly a relationship between White's work and those long-ago, big, beefy figures, and how each artist finds movement and grace.

BD: Oh yes, as a matter of fact he talked with me about those artists many times. He had experienced and been exposed to the European masters that established the foundation for classical drawing. But here's also something to understand about White: He *enjoyed* drawing. He loved pencil and paper. He could smear a piece of paper with his finger and know how the paper would react. He never tired of drawing or looking at the work of others who excelled at drawing, like Michelangelo. At the same time, he looked at the beautifully made lithographs of the American printmaker Stow Wengenroth, little remembered now but a fine draftsman and an influence on White.

WS: I want to go back to something you said a bit earlier, which was that as a Black American, White's work gave you pride. As we've discussed, when you first met White it was a turbulent time in American history. Did you two ever talk politics?

BD: Politics were woven into his entire existence. Even with the youngest of people, he didn't talk politics specifically, but he talked about family and community. When he talked with young people, he didn't get uptight or aggressive, but you *heard* what he was saying, and you knew that that he had a worldview, a pan-African understanding, and it came out naturally, not forced. It was even in the way he carried himself; it was all there. His body language was open and confident, poised and personable.

WS: He was very far left in his politics. He made illustrations for both the *Daily Worker* and the *New Masses*—as left as it got then. Do you recall him talking about or mentioning anything that caused him trouble? We know that in 1952 the House Un-American Activities Committee had its eye on him.

BD: You know, many of our great leaders came through that. You remember the difficulty this country gave Paul Robeson, for example, confiscating his passport, suspending travel privileges, and ultimately calling him to testify before Congress. We know that McCarthyism caused numerous stresses, and even going to Mexico to study with the Muralists made Charles White suspect. He didn't speak directly about any particular situation, but he was conscious of it all.

WS: During the 1960s, there was a sense among civil rights activists that if your art was abstract, it couldn't help the cause. And additionally, if it wasn't aggressive and explicit, it couldn't be helpful. How did you respond to that? And do you know how White responded to that?

BD: There have always been individuals who would choose their own particular way of making a stand or making a statement. What was important was to be true to oneself. You could not try to be something that you were not, even when some others wanted a certain kind of protest. I would imagine that most artists at some point have to deal with the question: What is going to be the form of my vision and my expression, and what is the best route for me? I was questioned as to whether or not I was really a part of the struggle because my work took an abstract point of view. But I learned from looking at African art that while it implied function, it also contained within itself expressive ways of working and of expressing oneself, including abstract ways.

WS: Charles White had this incredible output during his career, and he died when he was just sixty-one years old. Recently, in 2018–19, he was the subject of a major retrospective organized by the Museum of Modern Art in New York, the Art Institute of Chicago, and the Los Angeles County Museum of Art. But that was thirty-five years after he died. Do you think that his legacy of great figurative art in the service of elevating Black people has received the recognition that it's due?

BD: That recognition is still to come. I'm continually amazed by how many individuals fear the human body. It's almost unspoken. So that phenomenon is still there. So yes, the full recognition is still to come. I think what is happening and what has been happening in the last couple of summers has brought a new interest and commitment to trying to rectify that lack of full appreciation of the artistic expression that comes out the Black experience. There are more positive opportunities being presented and developed that I hope will add to the advancement of the struggle for real progress and understanding and for a fuller appreciation of the Black experience. And I think creative artists like Charles White have given us a visual message that will stand the test of time and that will always be a beacon of leadership.

WS: When we talk about Charles White and his legacy, we agree he had an impact and he's still having an impact today, but we also agree that he's not as well known as he should be. However well known he is or is not, what is the core message of his legacy? Is it to challenge other artists to continue the traditions of skill and craft and close observation? Is it to use art in the service of others?

BD: The legacy of Charles White is to search for artistic and creative excellence. More than anything else, that's what the legacy of Charles White means to us as artists. He chose to hone and develop his craft to its highest levels and to use that craftsmanship and skill to celebrate African American people. He will always be an inspiration to many of us because of that commitment. The work of Charles White lifts the value and validity of the African American experience from his chosen viewpoint of the human figure.

WS: Bing, that's so beautifully stated, so clear and meaningful. You touched on the idea early in this conversation that he drew and painted everyday people, regular people, and made them feel good about themselves. I think White was prescient in a way because now there's this twenty-first century body-positive movement that advocates against discrimination based on body type, or hair style, or any type of so-called "unconventional" appearance. White saw the humanity in every kind of body, in every kind of face, yes?

BD: Right, as did many Black artists. The great African American artists recognized that *all* aspects of the Black experience are worthy subject matter. They didn't suffer from that Eurocentric concept of beauty where only the idealized body is thought to be beautiful. Beauty was and is all around us, in everybody.

WS: That statement alone is a great introduction to Charles White. You two must have kept up with each other, yes?

BD: Charles White and I stayed in touch after his visit to Dayton. I was honored to get on his Christmas card list. He invited me to visit him and his family in Altadena, California. I graciously accepted, and with my wife at the time, visited him where we had the opportunity to meet his wife, Fran, and their two children, Ian and Jessica. We had a warm and wonderful dinner after which I had the joy of seeing his home studio and work that was in progress. This was prior to my sending him funds that I had been saving up to purchase a piece of his work. As a high school art teacher and newlywed and buying a home, I saved up from a couple of art sales and sent it to him at his home rather than to his gallery and asked him to send me any piece of his art that my funds could afford. I did not know that I should have been contacting Ben Horowitz at the Heritage Gallery in Los Angeles, who handled his work. Being "green" when it came to buying and selling art, I nonetheless got the best two pieces that I could have ever hoped for. I also had the opportunity to see him a couple of times at conferences.

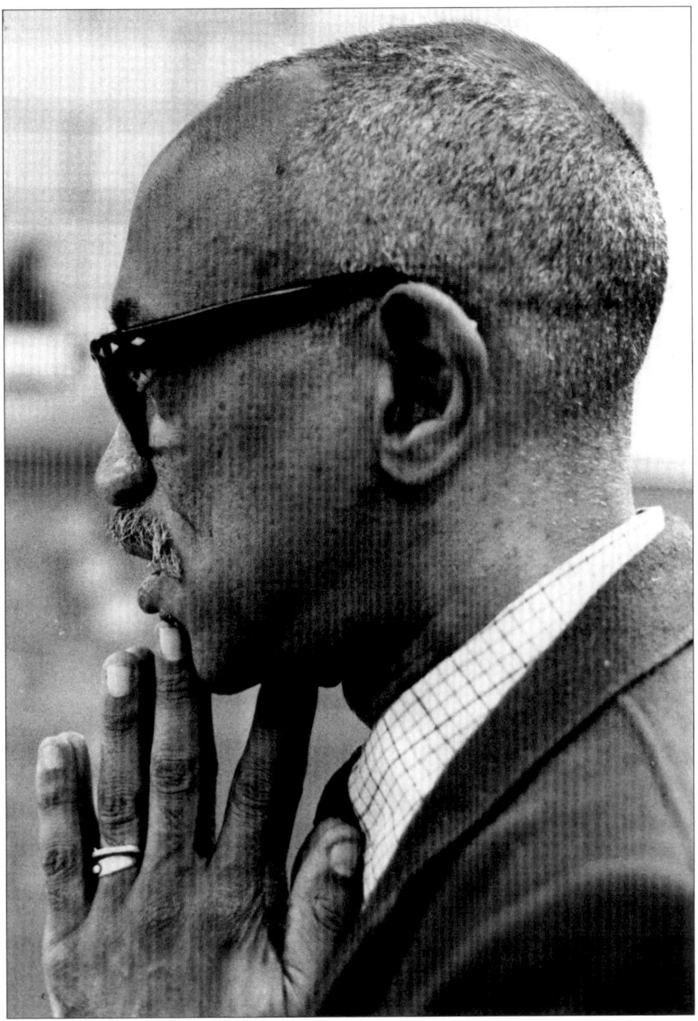

Charles White during his time as a visiting artist with the Living Arts Center program. "Artist's Job: Giving Things Beauty, Meaning," *Dayton Daily News*, May 22, 1968.

WS: Is there anything else you would like to add?

BD: As a role model and icon, Charles White stands as a giant among giants because of the art he created during his lifetime and because of the commitment he had to the Black experience and to his craft.

WS: Bing, it's been my great privilege to talk to you and benefit from your insights into Charles White. Many, many thanks.

BD: Thank you, and thanks to all the organizations and institutions that have come together to make this possible. I am so pleased to see what is going on with him and his work. Charles White would have been proud to know that his art, his ideas, and his message are continuing to be heard. He knew justice would take time, but that the dream would endure. And so it does.

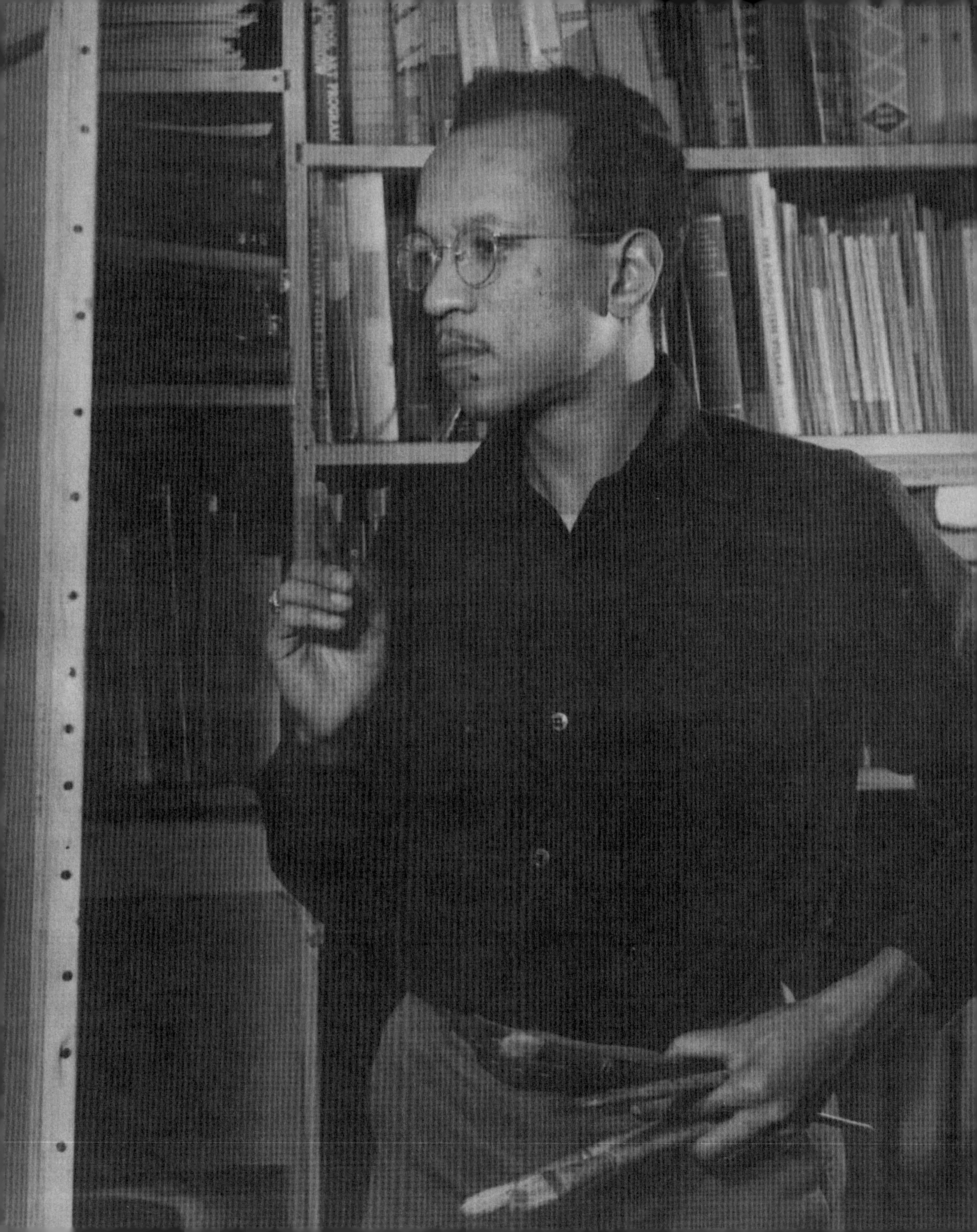

THE MISEDUCATION OF CHARLES WHITE

Nijah Cunningham

Imagine the artist at work: pencil in hand, or perhaps a brush, or an etching needle (FIG. 1). Maybe he is reaching for a piece of graphite after unfurling a sheet of architectural vellum, preparing to draw a primary composition that he will later transfer onto paperboard (e.g., *Study for Pope X* [CA. 1960, PLATE 12]). Now imagine his ink-stained hand brushing charcoal dust across the surface of one of his cartoons to create the darkness in which a Black veteran of the U.S. Armed Forces raises a torch to reveal the venality that hides in the shadows (PLATE 6). Now watch him dilute oil paint with turpentine to produce the burnt umber that he painstakingly layers to create the different shades that compose his monochromatic drawings such as *Black Pope (Sandwich Board Man)* (1973) or the images commissioned for Lerone Bennett Jr.'s 1975 book *The Shaping of Black America* (PLATES 29–40). Years later, a student of his will come across the source image for *Black Pope (Sandwich Board Man)* in Leonard Freed's seminal photojournalistic study *Black in White America*, published in 1968. Imagine opening the artist's copy to see how "the spread is marked by a folded corner and is heavily stained with brown fingerprints."[1] Dog-eared and tarnished, these pages carry traces of his art-making and intellectual labors. Through these markings we are able to glimpse, or at least imagine, the artist at work. They are testaments, small tokens he left behind that attest to the philosophical ambitions that animate his creative endeavors.

There is something marvelous that happens when Charles White shifts between book and brush. Certainly, like any artist, White's practice extends beyond his ways of drawing, painting, etching, and other creative modes. However, there are subtle aspects of his approach that reflect not only the profound rigor and commitment to social justice that are characteristic of his aesthetic sensibility but also convey a unique style of intellectual engagement.[2] This essay details and explores the creative strategies and techniques Charles White deploys that are essentially modes of thought. Allowing for the possibility of visual art as a thinking form enables us to cultivate innovative ways of seeing and approaching the artist's figurative and representative art. It is from this perspective that we can glean the decomposition and recomposition of concepts and ideas that unfold in his treatment of the physical plane of the picture as he makes his art.

This unfolding often takes place in a particular space in White's studio. His "think room," as Frances Barrett White explains in her biography of her husband, was the place that "would house the collection of art books and periodicals that were as much a part of his life as the pencil and brush."[3] There are various explicit and less explicit ways to link

FIG. 1
Charles White at work, n.d.
Charles White Archives.

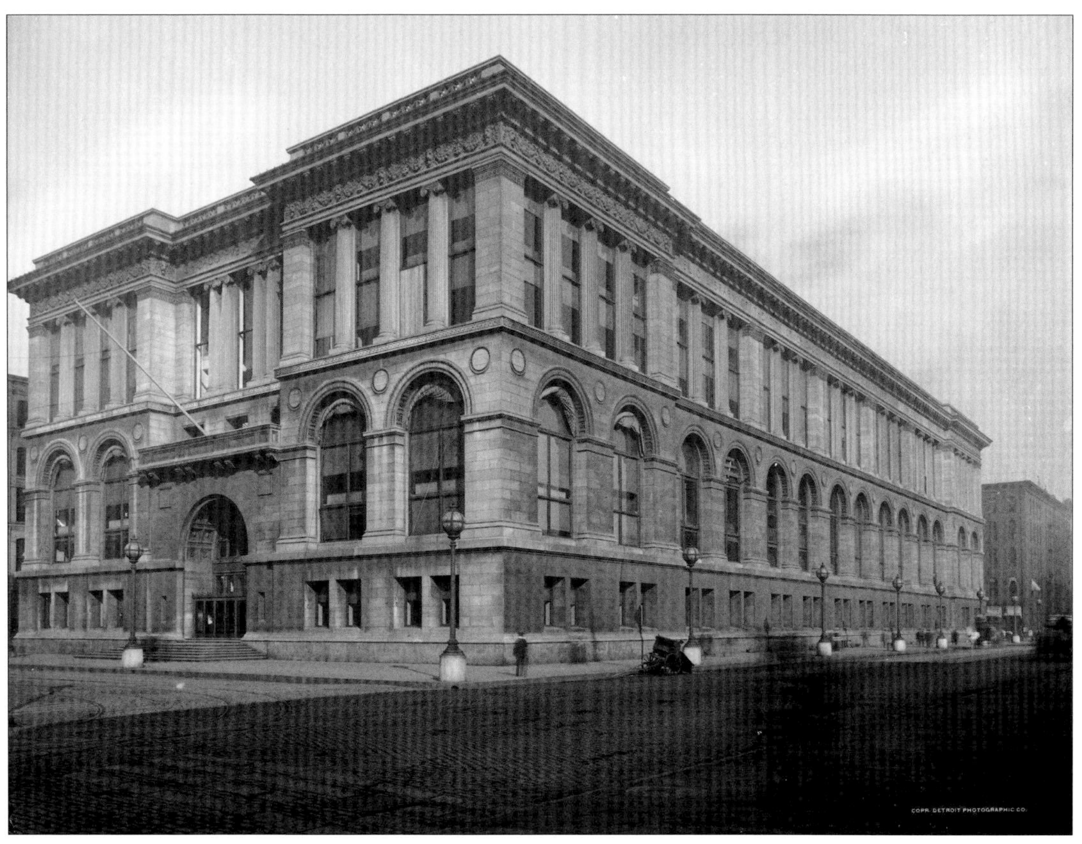

FIG. 2
Central Library, Chicago, 1900.
Courtesy of the Library of Congress.

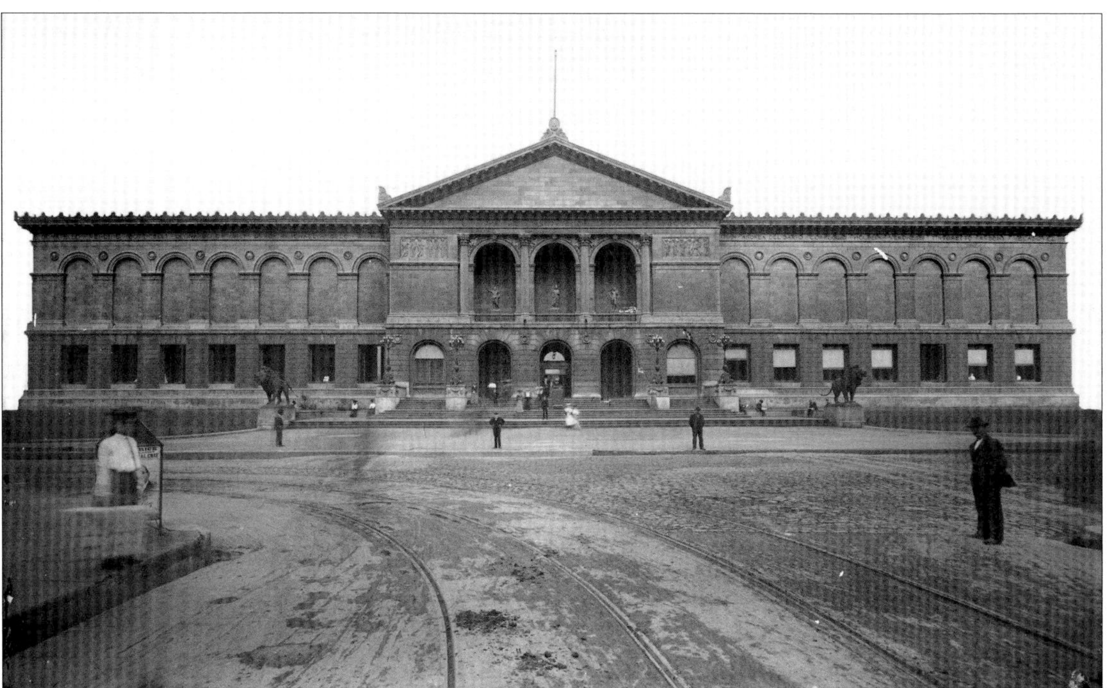

FIG. 3
Art Institute of Chicago, ca. 1892.
Barnes-Crosby Company, photographer.
Chicago History Museum, ICHi-019219.

White's art-making practice to his collection of books, magazines, and other periodicals. One way of exploring the link is by focusing on the ways his personal library functioned for him not only as an archive or a repository but also as a *site of memory.*[4] Unlike public libraries and university collections, a personal library is a source of tumult and wonder, replete with vague impressions and half-remembered truths that cling to each object. All that is assembled releases a "spring tide of memories" that surges toward the collector.[5] Of particular interest are the tides of Black memory that once flooded White's think room. Flowing from the art books and periodicals, poetry and pamphlets, anthologies and catalogues stacked in his studio space, these tides collapse the past into the present, creating a wake that inundates his art with a sense of mystery and enchantment.[6]

Art historians frequently note that as a young child in Chicago, White spent many of his days at the public library while his mother was at work (FIG. 2). That is where he first encountered what he later called the "secret life." He would often stumble across books with information he was not taught in school. "For a while I kept this new-found knowledge to myself," he explains. "It became a kind of secret life, a new world of facts and ideas in diametric opposition to what was being taught in the class rooms and text books as unquestionable truths."[7]

One can imagine a young Charles White getting reprimanded by teachers for distracting himself with "farfetched" stories and "irrelevant" details about Black folks and their contributions to arts, culture, and the making of the modern world more generally. His dislike of school was exacerbated by the fact that he frequently found himself on the verge of being expelled. But, like many outsiders, he knew of the thin line between education and subjugation. What is both terrible and beautiful about his story is how the loneliness and despair brought on by this ostracization drove him to art: "Playing truant, I would go to the Art Institute of Chicago and wander about its galleries, looking at paintings, and dreaming of becoming an artist" (FIG. 3).[8]

His truancy was not only a momentary escape—his refusal to attend class was also his way of marking the systematic negation of Blackness that sent him looking elsewhere for the secret life, which if he wished to be perceived as educated he must disavow. This secret life was much more than his refuge from the classroom where "[e]very characteristic of Negro culture was isolated and distorted into an object of hilarity."[9] His wandering through art galleries was his way of resisting that negation and an enactment of a kind of "unrestrained philosophical desire," which, as scholar Sarah Jane Cervenak might argue, emerges out of a tradition initiated by Sojourner Truth, reformulated by the likes of Harriet Jacobs, and that found its expression in the general strike of Black labor that brought American slavery to its end.[10] What might come across as childlike defiance was, in fact, an unruly way of knowing and being that is diametrically opposed to what goes unquestioned. White's absenting of himself from the regime of "truth" enshrined in his textbooks and classroom instruction resonates with the waywardness that moves throughout the history of the modern world like an almost imperceptible hum or a murmur that is capable of being heard and felt as the history of Black struggle.

Such waywardness characterizes White's aesthetic sensibility but is repeatedly overlooked in analyses of his figurative and representational art. In his art there is a secret life invoked for the viewer to embrace, a diffuse formation that strays from what is permissible as truth within the racial order that structures modernity. This secret life is like a gift he could never possess but that is given over to the viewer, wrapping itself around those who encounter his art and openly embrace the "poetic vision" with which it is endowed.[11]

Think Room

White's think room was, in part, a counter-archive that refuted the textbooks that demeaned Black culture and the teachers who struck the struggles and achievements of Black people from the historical record.[12] No matter the subject matter, the materials he acquired and added to his collection were animated by his desire to remember what had been ignored and forgotten by history.

He had stacks of books in his studio. Poetry, novels, history books, pamphlets, exhibitions catalogues, and art books. Faces, bodies, themes that appeared in his work, you would find some of them there, somewhere among *The Fire Next Time; From One China to the Other; The Unchanging Hopi; The Negro in the American Theatre; Kunst ist Waffe im Kampf für den Frieden; Portrait of Latin America As Seen by Her Print Makers/Retrato de la América Latina por sus artistas gráficos; In Battle for Peace: The Story of My 83rd Birthday; 12 Million Black Voices; Art of Russia; Rembrandt: A Novel;* issues of *US Camera; In Person, Lena Horne: As Told to Helen Arstein and Carlton Moss; Journal of Residence on a Georgian Plantation in 1838–1839; Brown Girl, Brownstones; Beautiful Junk; Ghana: The Autobiography of Kwame Nkrumah; Dogon World; A Catalogue of Art and Myth for You to Complete; Eleventh Annual of Advertising Art...*[13]

"[T]he collector's passion borders on the chaos of memories," Walter Benjamin writes. "More than that: the chance, the fate, that suffuse the past before my eyes are conspicuously present in the accustomed confusion of these books. For what else is this collection but a disorder to which habit has accommodated itself to such an extent that it can appear as order?"[14] For Benjamin, there is "profound enchantment" that a personal library engenders for its collector. No matter how the materials are organized and arranged, it is impossible to maintain the order of time and space, as fantasies and recollections fuse and comingle on the shelves.[15] Whatever chance or fate that led items to White's library imbues these objects with a sense of mystery and wonder that recalls the secret life he discovered as child. In the artist's think room, a longing to retrieve what has been lost and forgotten permeates his artistic practice. Through the creative strategies and techniques that he deploys, he conjures another mode of thought from the "chaos of memories." If his figurative and representative art generates a "poetic vision... composed of powerful images of stunning people of African ancestry," White's approach and orientation toward the picture plane sketch out a "blueprint for disorder" that point to alternative ways of knowing and being.[16]

Wanted Poster Series

White's devotion to the secret life that endures within the gaps and silences of history shapes both his intellectual style and art-making. This becomes apparent when we consider his description of his self-invented oil wash technique: "I very often abuse a surface harshly since I scrub into it with rags and a lot of tools. For instance, in my monochromatic oil drawings, I use Q-tips, Kleenex, rags, balsa wood, brushes, and a whole slew of other things besides—all in one given work."[17] As part of his oil wash technique, White takes up a wide variety of instruments to apply and blot diluted oil paint on paperboard. What results are the shades of burnt umber, textured surfaces, and the "faceted effect" seen in his monochromatic drawings from the late 1960s and 1970s.[18] This "abuse" verges on "*ab*-use"—an aberrant way of doing or a purposeful departure from purposefulness—as when he deploys this technique in his *Wanted Poster* series (PLATES 21 and 22) to interrogate the production of historical knowledge and conjure the secret life buried in the records of the past.

The fourteen oil wash drawings and seven lithographs that make up White's *Wanted Poster* series were inspired by a cache of antebellum newspapers he acquired from his friend Edmond Gordon.[19] While it is not unusual for an artist to draw inspiration from historical records and artifacts, the monochromatic drawings in this series suggest that White was not simply moved by what he encountered in the pages of these documents. The painstaking layering and scrubbing he carries out transforms the surface of the pieces into historical documents. Each work features a sepia-toned background in which the contrast of different shades of burnt umber produces folds and creases that create the illusion of a crumbled piece of paper. What results from the way he "abuse[s] a surface" are backgrounds that strikingly resemble nineteenth-century handbills that advertised slave auctions and offers of rewards for those who had escaped captivity.

In *Wanted Poster #5* (FIG. 4, PLATE 21), magnificent portraits of three Black women appear faintly against a faceted surface. In addition to the names "Ida," "Clotel," and "Edmonia" stenciled below, the numbers "1619" and "19??" are printed just above their heads on opposite side of the composition. Whereas White's use of portraiture conveys the beauty and significance of the lives he represents, the names printed below tell very little of the women who appear in the painting but allude to remarkable Black women (real and fictional) in history. The ambiguous status of the women pictured in this work is intensified by the numbers, which suggest that they reside in the slave past and its unending afterlife. White's use of portraiture conveys a level of admiration and esteem for these figures that must contend with the debasement and brutality inscribed in the background. The three figures face in different directions and recall the side-view and front-view photos in a mugshot. This aspect of the work, along with the appearance of the dates, links the legacy of slavery to the persecution of Black radical activists in the late 1960s by overlaying antebellum placards with more contemporary wanted posters.

"Appropriating these historical documents," Ilene Susan Fort suggests, "White reinforced the layering of time and place by situating them in his own lifetime, thereby suggesting that injustices suffered in the past still occur in the present."[20] The crumpled background produced by White's painstaking layering and scrubbing of diluted oil paint is suggestive of a critical engagement with history that he enacts through his artistic practice. In *Wanted Poster #5,* White's longtime interest in "the visual possibilities of folds and fabrics" transforms the surface of the image into a site of memory where the unspeakable horrors of the past press their weight onto the present.[21] The downcast eyes of the figures pictured in this work refuse the viewer's gaze, gesturing to the stories withheld in the historical record that remain untold. As Kellie Jones argues, "[t]hese are not the history paintings that White was known for at the beginning of his career—featuring heroes from an earlier moment with much to tell us about our own time—but works where the past and present inform each other on the physical plane of the picture itself."[22]

Head of a Man and *Congress View* Cartoon

While White's use of his oil wash technique in *Wanted Poster #5* conjures the absent presences that haunt us to this day, there are other examples of his *ab*-use of the surface of the image found in work from earlier in his career. In his work from the 1940s and 1950s such as *Head of a Man* (1948, PLATE 7), included in the portfolio and used as the cover of *Negro: U.S.A: A Graphic History of the Negro People in America Workshop Prints No. 2*, as well as the cover art and illustrations he contributed to progressive magazines such as the *Daily Worker* and *Masses & Mainstream*, White confronts the racist depictions that circulated in the public imagination during the postwar era. For instance, consider how the dark tones and sharp angles featured in *Head of a Man* reconfigure the historical relationship between the Blackness and modern art. At the turn of the twentieth century, Primitivism's valorization of the exotic "other" reified racial difference and espoused the opposition of Black culture and modernity. Whereas Alain Locke called for an earlier generation of African American artists to claim as their aesthetic inheritance the same African masks from which European artists drew their inspiration, White carves out a trajectory from Primitivism to its successor, Cubism, through the sharp lines and geometric angles that draw out the facial features of the Black figure in this work.[23] Here, the visual vocabulary of Cubism enables White to instill a sense of interiority and capture the dilemmas of Black personhood through the figure's raised eyebrows, tight mouth, and averted gaze. Just as Frantz Fanon showed how racialization occurs through inscription of social and historical narratives onto Black flesh, White's subtle nod to Cubism reveals how the surface of the image operates as a potent site for defining and reimagining the meaning of Blackness.

The cartoon *Freeport Columbia* (1946, PLATE 6), in the March 1946 issue of the National Negro Congress publication *Congress View* (FIG. 5), is another demonstration of the intellectual labor that White enacts on the surface of the image. In this work, his use of movement and the play of shadow and light expose the venality of the U.S. justice system. A Black veteran reaches out over a scene of carnage, his right hand thrusting forward an object similar to the iconic torch of the Statue of Liberty, which shines a light on three white men standing together in the foreground: a judge, a police officer, and a Klansman holding up the other end of the severed noose that is around the Black figure's neck. The illuminating gesture reveals the document in their hands, which reads, "Permit to Kill Negro Vets and Civilians." The white figures peer at the legal document with gleeful expressions of gratification, with their backs to the scene of terror and violence behind

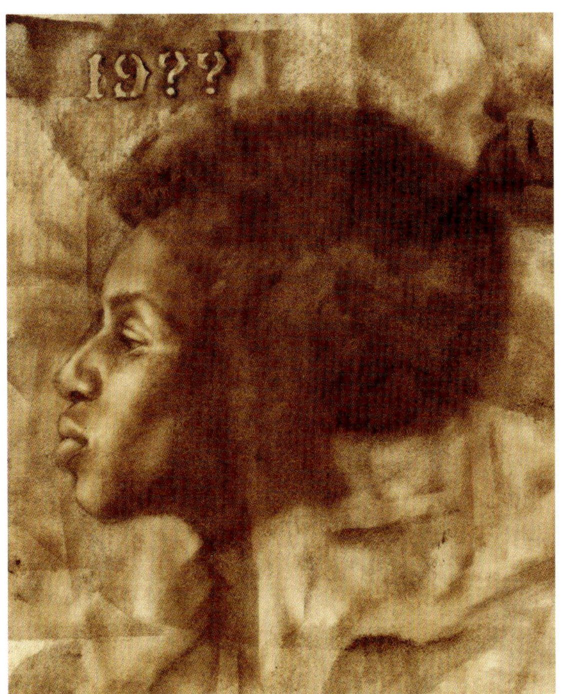

FIG. 4
Charles White, *Wanted Poster #5*, 1969, detail (see plate 21).

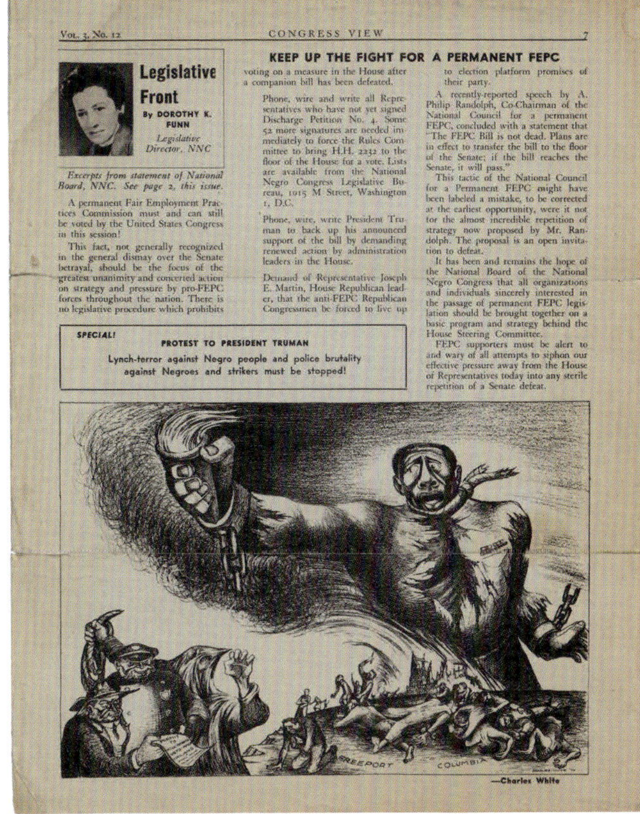

VOL. 3, NO. 12 — CONGRESS VIEW — 7

KEEP UP THE FIGHT FOR A PERMANENT FEPC

Legislative Front
By DOROTHY K. FUNN
Legislative Director, NNC

Excerpts from statement of National Board, NNC. See page 2, this issue.

A permanent Fair Employment Practices Commission must and can still be voted by the United States Congress in this session!

This fact, not generally recognized in the general dismay over the Senate betrayal, should be the focus of the greatest unanimity and concerted action on strategy and pressure by pro-FEPC forces throughout the nation. There is no legislative procedure which prohibits voting on a measure in the House after a companion bill has been defeated.

Phone, wire and write all Representatives who have not yet signed Discharge Petition No. 4. Some 52 more signatures are needed immediately to force the Rules Committee to bring H.H. 2232 to the floor of the House for a vote. Lists are available from the National Negro Congress Legislative Bureau, 1015 M Street, Washington 1, D.C.

Phone, wire, write President Truman to back up his announced support of the bill by demanding renewed action by administration leaders in the House.

Demand of Representative Joseph E. Martin, House Republican leader, that the anti-FEPC Republican Congressmen be forced to live up to election platform promises of their party.

A recently-reported speech by A. Philip Randolph, Co-Chairman of the National Council for a permanent FEPC, concluded with a statement that "The FEPC Bill is not dead. Plans are in effect to transfer the bill to the floor of the Senate; if the bill reaches the Senate, it will pass."

This tactic of the National Council for a Permanent FEPC might have been labeled a mistake, to be corrected at the earliest opportunity, were it not for the almost incredible repetition of strategy now proposed by Mr. Randolph. The proposal is an open invitation to defeat.

It has been and remains the hope of the National Board of the National Negro Congress that all organizations and individuals sincerely interested in the passage of permanent FEPC legislation should be brought together on a basic program and strategy behind the House Steering Committee.

FEPC supporters must be alert to and wary of all attempts to siphon our effective pressure away from the House of Representatives today into any sterile repetition of a Senate defeat.

SPECIAL!
PROTEST TO PRESIDENT TRUMAN
Lynch-terror against Negro people and police brutality against Negroes and strikers must be stopped!

FIG. 5
Charles White, political cartoon in magazine *Congress View* 3, no. 12, 1946. Charles W. White papers, 1933–1987. Archives of American Art, Smithsonian Institution (see plate 6).

them. Below a pile of dead bodies, the words "Freeport" and "Columbia" are inscribed in the ground. Where the white figures remain affixed to the letter of the law, the large and courageous Black figure illuminates the pervasive atmosphere of anti-Black violence that links the police killing of two Black men in Freeport, New York, and the attack on Black veterans by a white mob in Columbia, Tennessee, that occurred the month before the cartoon's publication. Writing in the March 1946 issue of *Labor Action* under the pseudonym J. R. Johnson, Black radical thinker C. L. R. James draws out the significance of the link that White's cartoon renders visible:

> It must not be thought that the incidents and their repercussions are confined to Freeport or Columbia. Negro communities all over the country are seething with indignation. The NAACP and other Negro organizations are as usual protesting mightily but doing nothing to mobilize the great masses of the Negro people in demonstrations which can give effective force to the rage which consumes them.[24]

For both White and James, to think that the incidents in Freeport and Columbia were not connected would be to inhabit the perspective of the white figures that remain ignorant of or indifferent to Black suffering. The veteran figure, with a tattered noose, broken handcuffs, and a torn uniform, is suggestive of a kind of political enlightenment forged from the experience of racial terror that the eyes of the law refuse to see. Arguably, White's cartoon visualizes the untapped potential of the Black masses in his rendering of a claim to freedom born from the quotidian experience of state-sponsored brutality and the rage that it engenders. White's cartoon is his contribution to a broader intellectual project to envision "the social and political significance of the independent Negro struggle for democratic rights."[25]

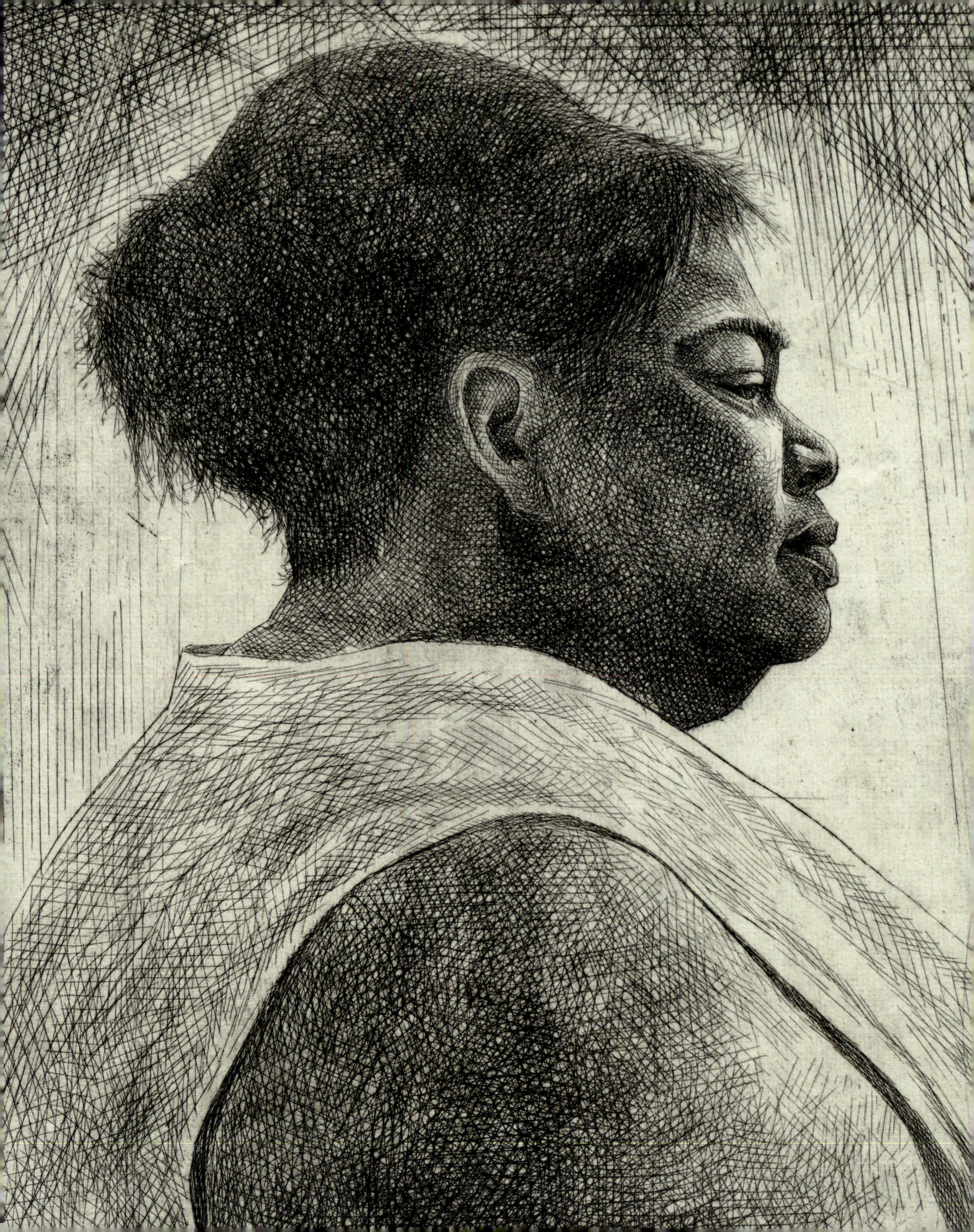

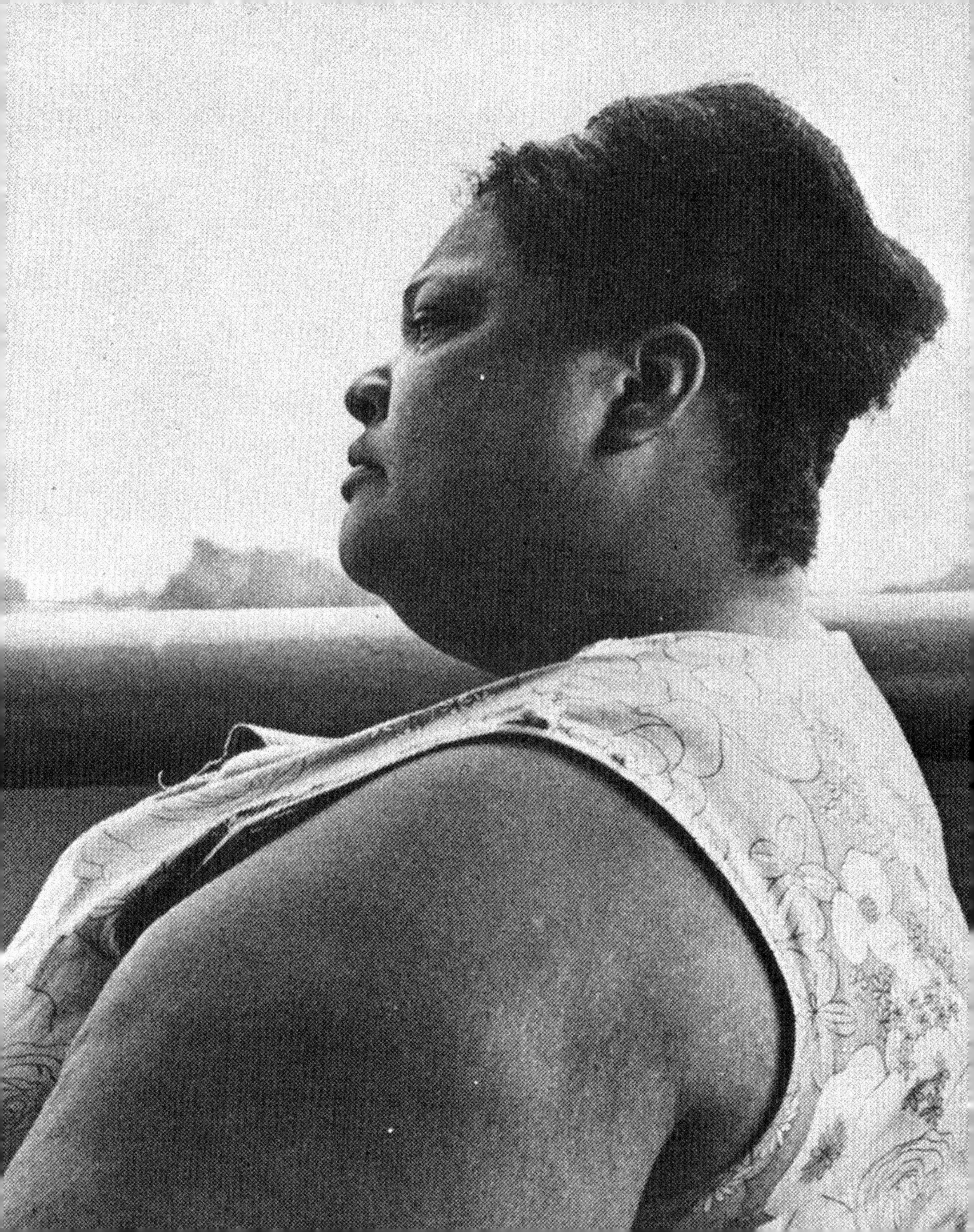

PREVIOUS SPREAD

FIG.6
Charles White, *Missouri C*, 1972, detail (see plate 25).

FIG.7
Alwyn Scott Turner, *Passengers. Boblo boat*, 1970, detail. From Turner, *Photographs of the Detroit People* (USA: Alwyn Scott Turner, 1970), 46.

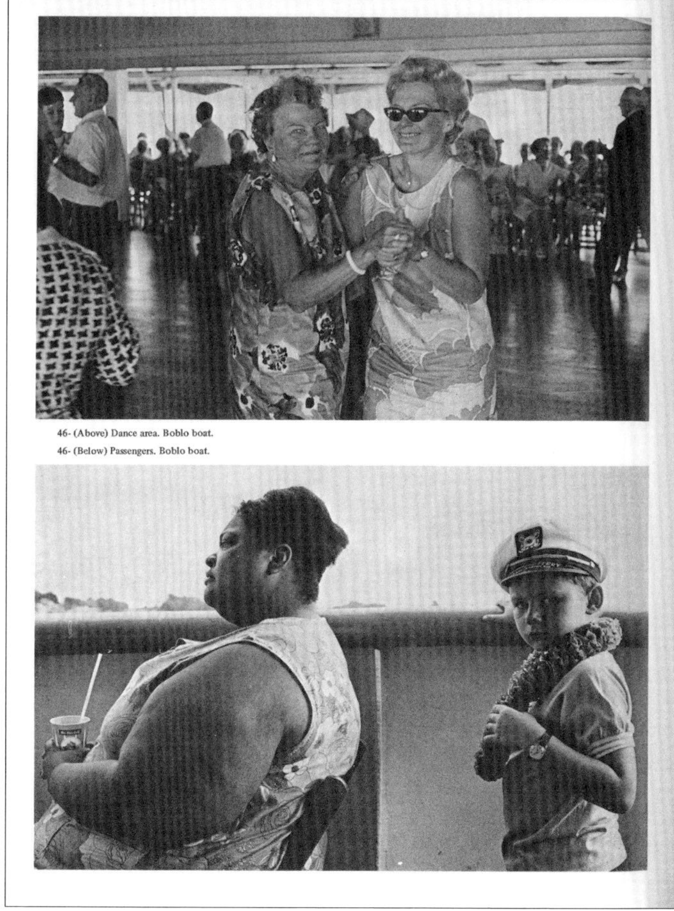

FIG.8
Alwyn Scott Turner, *Dance area. Boblo boat* and *Passengers. Boblo boat*, photographs. From Turner, *Photographs of the Detroit People*, 46.

Missouri C

In 1967, Harry Belafonte famously celebrated White's commitment to realism: "In a period when many artists have deserted reality for the various schools of nonobjectivity and abstractionism, Mr. White has continued to work for broader horizons of human expression and to explore deeper dimensions of truth and reality."[26] White's rejection of abstraction and the nonobjective is well documented and serves as a useful vantage point for analyzing his art. However, in one of his later works, we find the artist attending to what escapes realism's grasp.

Printed at Joseph Mugnaini's (1912–1992) Altadena, California, studio in 1972, White's *Missouri C* (FIG. 6, PLATE 25) uses a dry-point etching technique to focus on a single figure against an empty backdrop.[27] White drew the source image for *Missouri C* from Detroit-based photographer Alwyn Scott Turner's self-published book *Photographs of the Detroit People* (1970), which Turner describes as a "documentary on the people of Detroit."[28] Turner's photograph captures a Black woman (FIG. 7) seated beside a boat railing while, to her back, a young white boy wearing a captain's hat and a lei around his neck turns to stare at the camera (FIG. 8).[29] The woman seems indifferent to the presence of both photographer and child. Turner includes an unremarkable caption to this curious image that reads "Passengers. Boblo Boat."

The peculiarity of this scene reflects the style of social documentary photography that Turner deploys to create a sober depiction of everyday life in this midwestern city. As part of his project, the photographer uses his layout to create story lines and juxtapositions to reveal the social problems and injustices that linger through the city. As one critic writes, "the relatively dispassionate nature of the snapshot esthetic makes it possible for [Turner] to record their individual weirdnesses without resorting to distortive techniques."[30] The "weirdness" of the scene in which we encounter the Black woman and white child is articulated by Turner's decision to place the photograph just under an image of two white women happily dancing together in a crowded dance area below deck. On the page, the Black woman is situated away from the scene of revelry, a pairing that suggests the enduring legacies of racial segregation in Detroit through her relative position at the margins of the scene of amusement.

White's dry-point technique for *Missouri C* counters the "dispassionate nature of [Turner's] snapshot esthetic."[31] White creates intricate crosshatchings that reveal a scene of calm where the viewer encounters a single figure with downcast eyes. Parallel and intersecting lines fill the space surrounding the figure and create shadow and depth. White draws out a sense of solitude from the alienation that Turner sought to capture. The "burr" created by White's incisions on the copper plate result in a "velvety and rich effect" that stands in stark contrast to Turner's detached gaze.[32] The creases beneath her eye contribute to a tenderness enhanced by other details of the print, such as the soft contours of the figure's face and chin, the way the fabric of her garment gathers along her side, how her skin folds at her underarm, and the strands of hair that peek out from her bun.[33] The work is named after White's Aunt Missouri, whom he would see during his trips as a child to visit relatives in Mississippi.[34] According to Andrea Barnwell, "White's close relationship with his family, especially his aunts and mother, informed and shaped his art in meaningful ways as his work matured and evolved."[35] In *Missouri C*, White's childhood memories transform the image in Turner's photograph, imbuing it with a warmth and intimacy as if he were to reach out and claim the unknown woman pictured as his kin.

That the Black woman was even a passenger on the boat is significant, as years earlier the Michigan Supreme Court found the Bob-Lo Excursion Company to be in direct violation of the State Civil Rights statute for adopting the policy of "excluding so-called 'Zoot-suiters,' the rowdyish, the rough and the boisterous and...excluding colored."[36] That is in part how she ended up in the pages of a softbound photography book, and then in Charles White's think room. For the photographer, she's a passenger who bears the burden of representing the flaws of society. But in the think room, she's a stowaway, a presence buried in someone else's vision of reality. To Charles White, she is more than mere evidence or a representation of the persistence of racism as a social problem. The artist's social realism is far from dispassionate. He wants to communicate a relationship, the hidden weave of Black social life to which he remains passionately attached. She is not Aunt Missouri. But he holds her in regard as if she were his own. His etching of her aims to convey not what she represents but the inner life she refuses to disclose. Her solitude is a revaluation of an interiority otherwise reduced to sociological data. Hers is the secret life that is hidden in plain sight. She teaches us a similar lesson to the one White enacts through his art-making process. That is, the surface of the image is more than where the eye does its work. It is where the given is disordered and knowledges that were never meant to be known are gained as our collective miseducation.

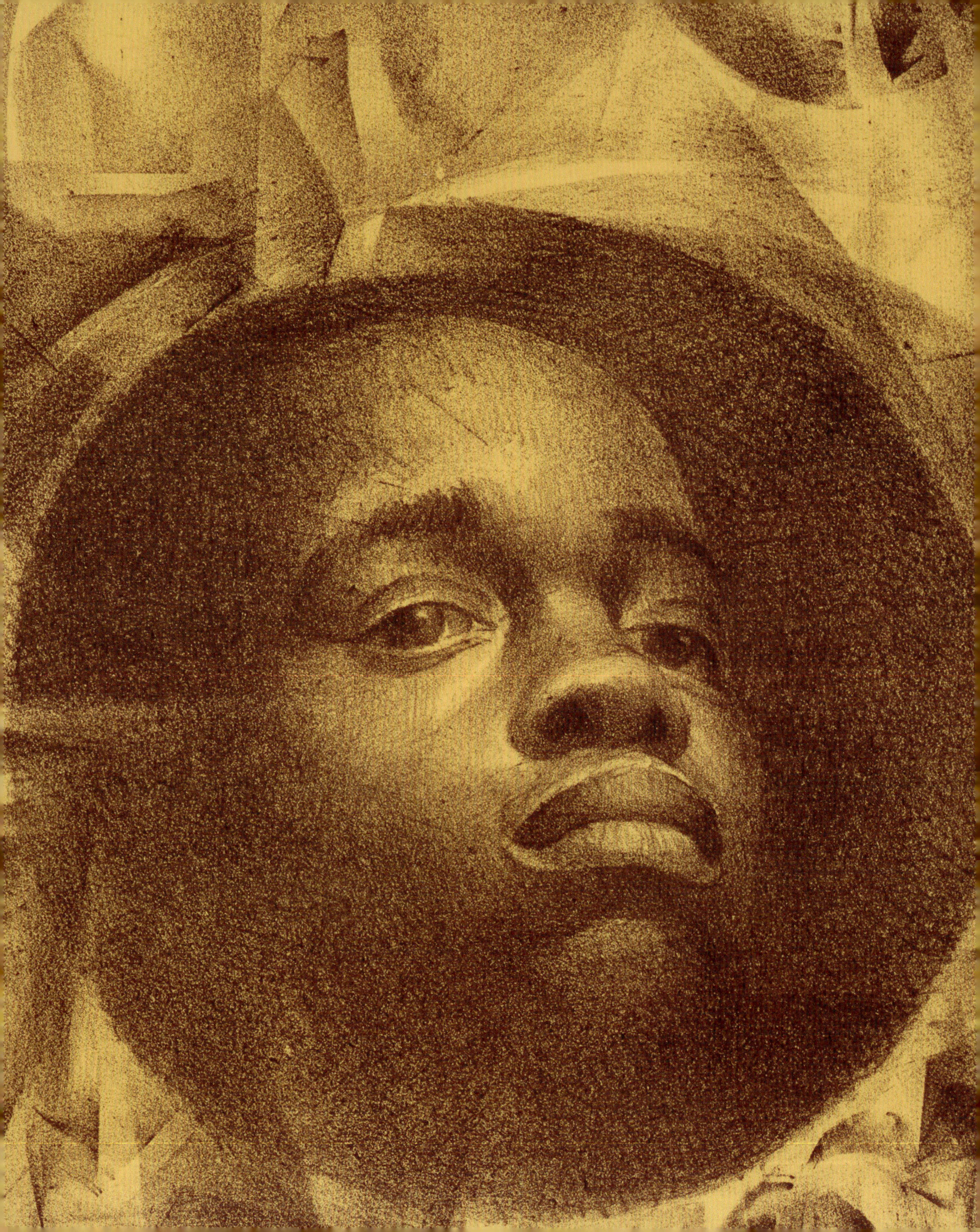

PLATES

Texts by Jill Deupi

PLATE 1

Children in the Snow, ca. 1938–42

Gelatin silver photograph
17.78 x 22.86 cm (7 x 9 in.)

This charming photograph showcases White's admiration for the work of Gordon Parks (1912–2006), Dorothea Lange (1895–1965), Walker Evans (1903–1975), and others hired by the Farm Security Administration (FSA) between 1935 and 1946 to document farmers, sharecroppers, and seasonal workers across America. Its documentary style relates to these photographic commissions while simultaneously channeling the Social Realist concerns and the refined, yet spontaneous, compositional approach that would come to characterize White's paintings and works on paper. *Children in the Snow* is also an apt reminder of White's long friendship with Parks, who moved with his wife and children to Chicago in 1940 and set up a darkroom in the basement of the South Side Community Art Center, a federal Works Progress Administration–funded organization with which White was deeply involved.

White and Parks were kindred spirits, united by similar backgrounds and motivated by a shared commitment to progressive activism. Naturally drawn to one another, they walked the streets of their segregated urban community together, comparing notes and seeking inspiration. As art historian and curator Kellie Jones notes: "The friends' early vision as creators came from visiting South Side neighborhoods, experiencing poverty, and seeing that, through the modes of social realism and related documentary photography, they could offer important perspectives on 'the lives of ordinary people in a politically engaged manner.'"[1]

Children in the Snow also speaks to White's work as an amateur photographer, his aesthetic impulses, and his intellectual priorities, which included carefully observing and deftly capturing all facets of the human experience by locating the extraordinary in the ordinary. Though this photograph is not associated with a finished drawing or painting, White used photographs (both from his personal archive of the more than three hundred pictures he took as well as images drawn from books, periodicals, and other publicly available sources) as source images for several of his works.

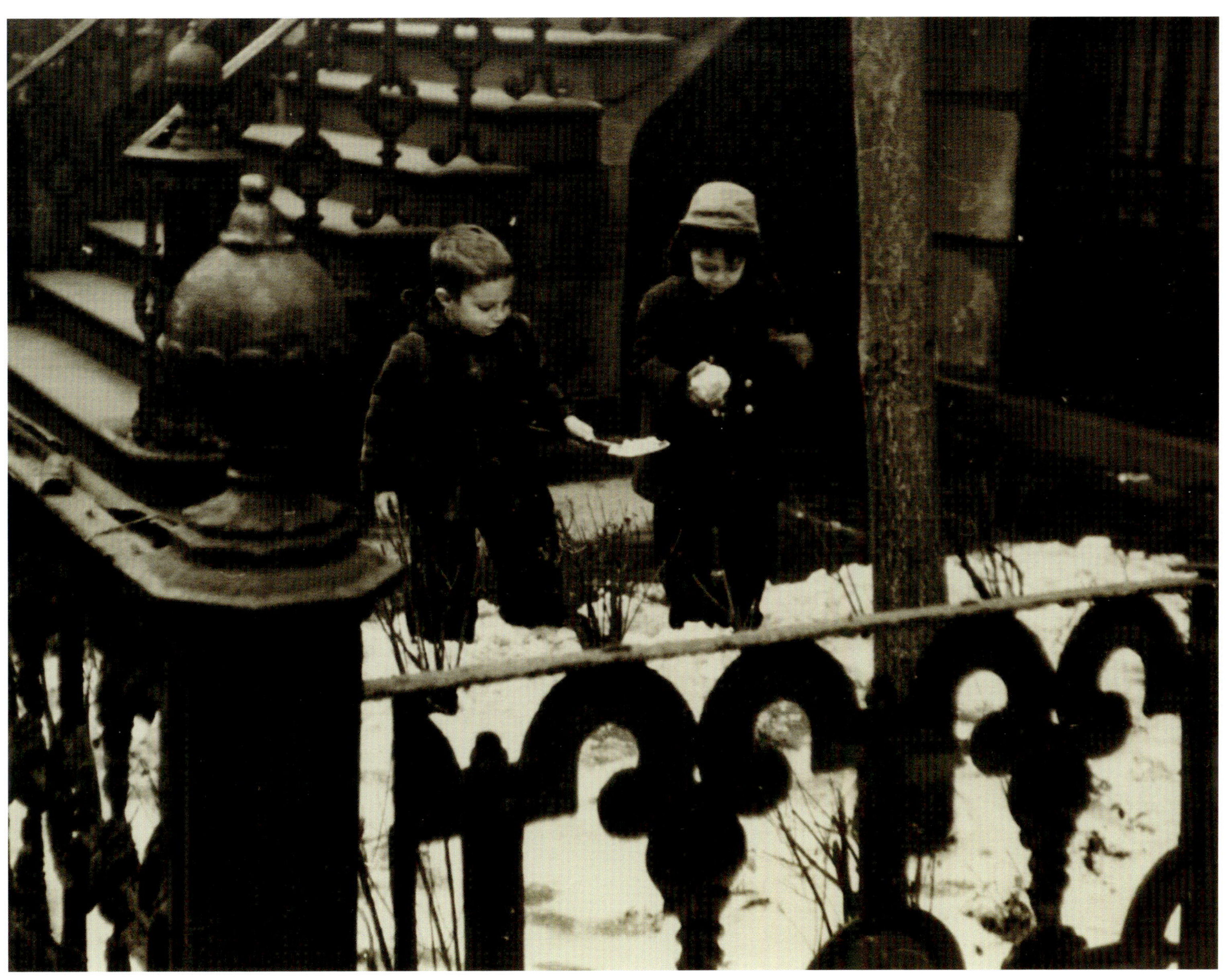

PLATE 2

Boy with Accordion, 1939

Charcoal on paper
70.17 x 46.83 cm (27 5/8 x 18 7/16 in.)

White went to work for the Illinois Art Project (IAP), a state affiliate of President Franklin D. Roosevelt's New Deal Federal Art Project (FAP), in 1938. He completed several murals under IAP commission in the five years that followed, including *Progress of the American Negro: Five Great American Negroes* (1939–40, Howard University School of Law, Washington, D.C.), *Techniques Used in the Service of Struggle* (1940–41, incomplete and now lost), and *The Contribution of the Negro to Democracy in America* (1943, Hampton University, Hampton, Virginia). It was during this time that the young artist began working with more seasoned painters at the IAP, such as Mitchell Siporin (1910–1976) and Edward Millman (1907–1964), both of whom were enthralled with the work of the Mexican Muralists. The latters' abiding devotion to bold gestures, monumental figures, and pointed social commentary clearly impacted White both in his own mural-making and in his stand-alone images from this period, including *Boy with Accordion*.

Executed in charcoal on paper, White's drawing features a young African American male immersed in music-making. The downturned corners of the protagonist's eyes and mouth, like his furrowed brow, convey a sense of worried anguish; a mood fueled, perhaps, by the song he plays, his life circumstances as a Black youth navigating the troubled waters of systemic racism in America, or some combination of these (and potentially other) factors. White leavened his image with deft roseate touches, which add warmth and dimensionality to the work. He also energized lines that graphically hug the youth and telegraph a clear sense of movement.

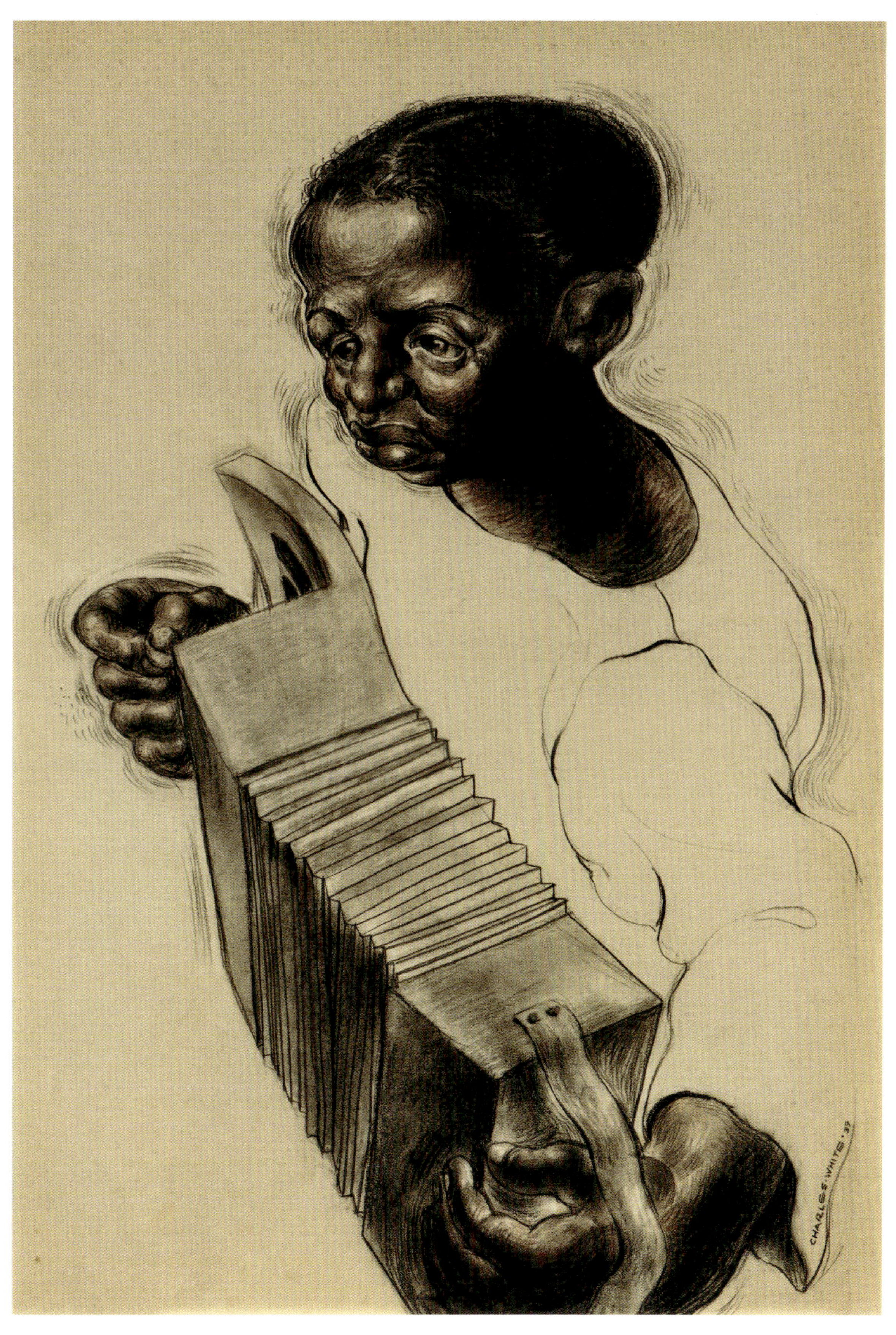
CHARLES WHITE '39

PLATE 3

The Soldier, ca. 1940

Pen and ink on paper
18.42 x 24.13 cm (7 1/4 x 9 1/2 in.)

Created during a period when White was working for the Illinois Art Project (IAP), a state affiliate of President Franklin D. Roosevelt's Federal Art Project, *The Soldier* marks a sharp departure from the style for which the young artist was developing a reputation. Unlike the bold and stylized figures that are the hallmarks of his IAP mural commissions and related works, this image is fluid and loose. White has conjured his protagonist—a bivouacked soldier—in wispy, curving lines, some of which double back on themselves to give the illusion of shadow and depth. Given the work's spontaneity and lack of finish, it is reasonable to assume it is a sketch, used by White to capture a fleeting impression or idea. Although no subsequent, finished work has been associated with this image, he did return to the subject of the servicemen in the early 1940s as exemplified in works like *Soldier* (1944) and *Our War* (1948, PLATE 8). The same year that he completed the former, White himself was conscripted into the US Army, service that would effectively end just months later, when he contracted tuberculosis while sandbagging the flooded Mississippi and Ohio Rivers.

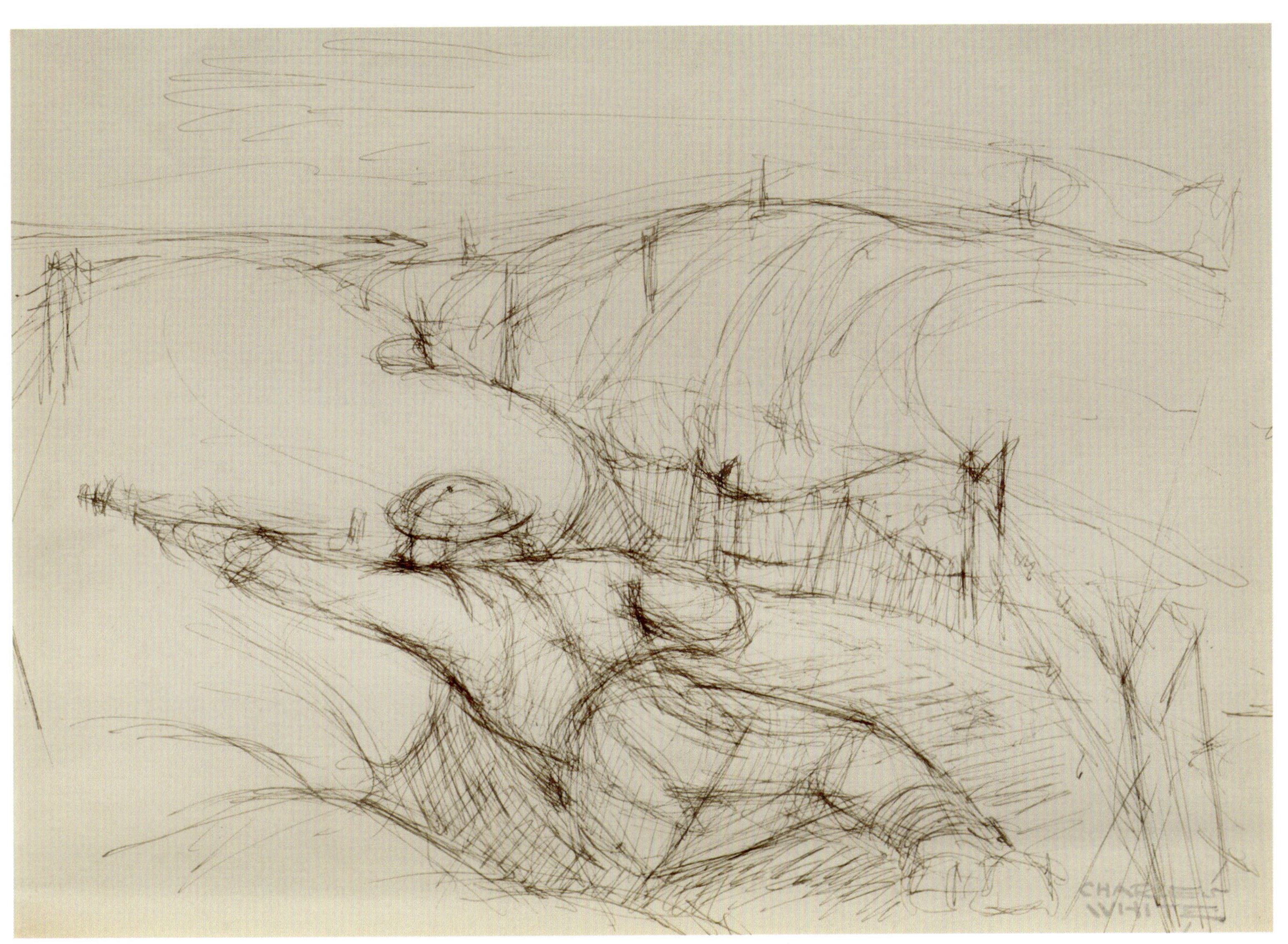
CHARLES
WHITE

PLATE 4

Working Man, ca. 1940

Pen and ink on paper
22.86 x 17.78 cm (9 x 7 in.)

Like *The Soldier* (PLATE 3), *Working Man* conveys White's early interest in line, form, and the human figure. Depicted in an overcoat, collared shirt, and tie, the subject of this loose pen and ink sketch is a man in motion. The title suggests that his destination is work-related, but it is unclear where he is going: The office? Home? A meeting? A meal? Though we may not know his destination, the subject's slumped shoulders and glum expression make clear that, wherever he is headed, he will arrive there depleted of both enthusiasm and energy. Like White's other works from this period, *Working Man* reflects the young artist's interest in both Social Realism and American Regionalism, which—though having distinctly different political aims—emphasized easily legible, content-driven narratives that heroized the disenfranchised and members of the underclass, including agricultural workers (in the case of the former) and the working poor (in the case of the latter).

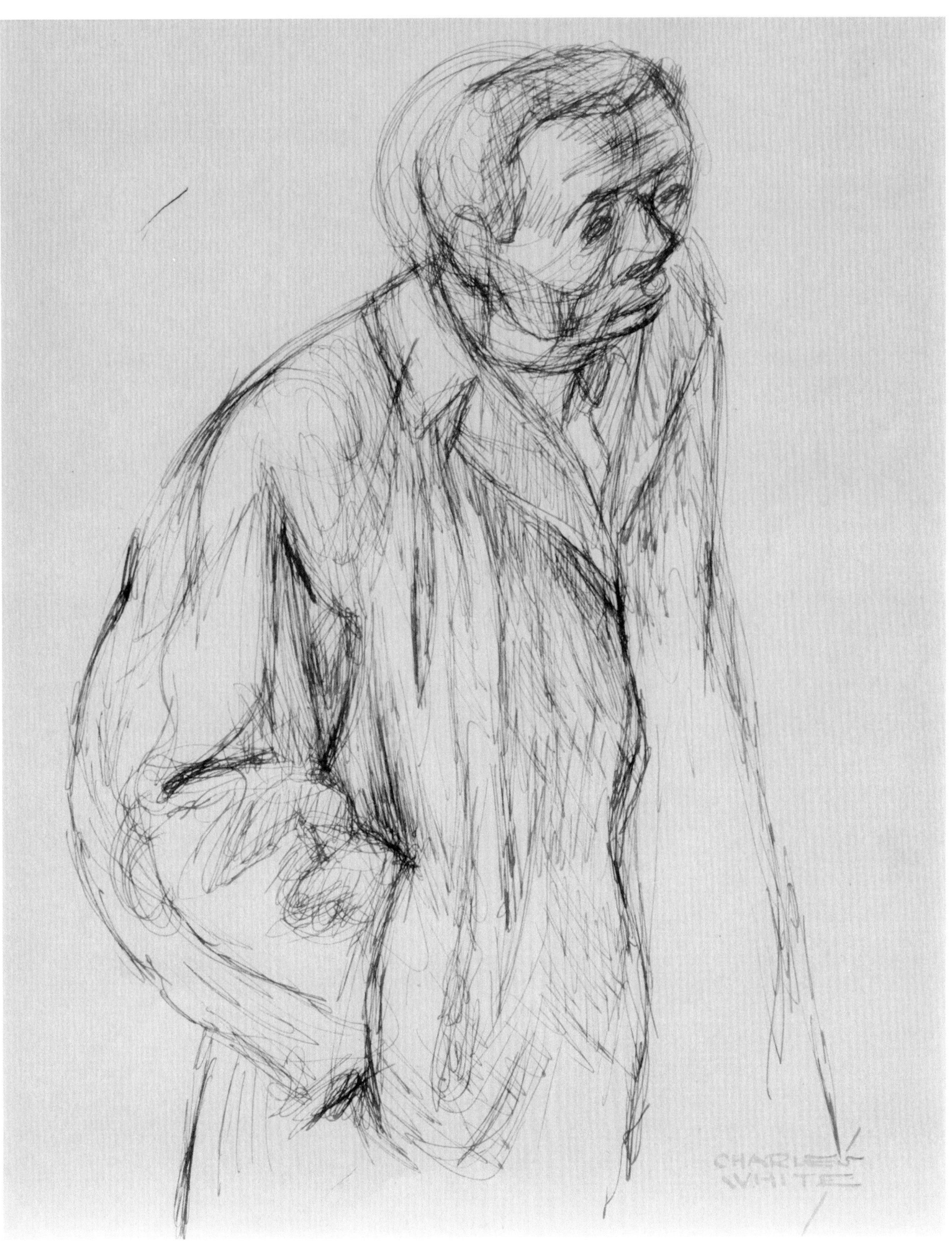
CHARLES
WHITE

PLATE 5

Awaiting His Return, 1946

Lithograph
40.01 x 31.12 cm (15 3/4 x 12 1/4 in.)

Marked by strongly faceted, blocky forms, this work reflects White's early interest in Cubism. Its clarity and directness also remind us of the young artist's admiration for the Mexican Muralists, whom he met in 1946 (the year he created this work) when he and his first wife, the artist Elizabeth Catlett (1915–2012), spent several months in Mexico thanks to a renewed Rosenwald Fellowship she had won. White's protagonist—a lone, seated woman—is constructed from sharp angles and geometric curves. Her sculpted solidity visually connects her to the wooden table at which she is seated, suggesting both were hewn from the same ligneous material. This visual consonance is heightened by the woman's posture: She sits firmly rooted in her chair and inclines the right side of her face heavily against the base of her palm. The woman's left forearm rests before her, but her bearing is not one of repose. Rather, her large eyes stare anxiously into an unseen middle distance, her gaze emphasized by the directionality of her left hand and arm. The set of the woman's jaw also telegraphs worried unhappiness, an unease emphasized by the balled fingers of her hand, against which she leans. The cause of her concern is revealed by the Blue Star Service Banner hanging on the rear wall, for this is the unofficial flag of families whose loved ones are on active military duty. White's protagonist, then, is anxiously awaiting the return of someone near and dear to her. Created in the same year that the artist's marriage to Catlett began to fray (they divorced in 1947), this powerful lithograph perhaps reflects White's own dark mood at the time.

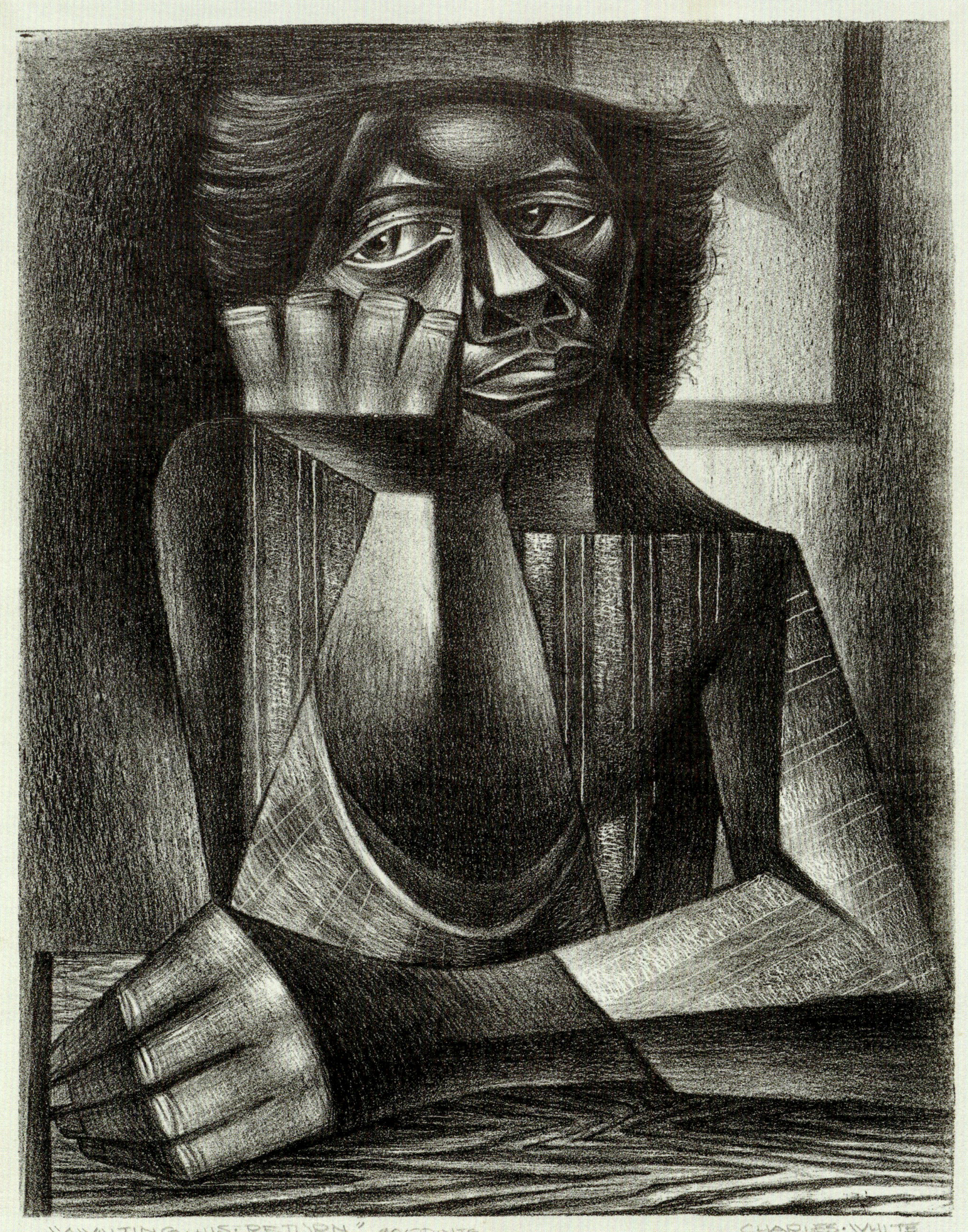
"AWAITING · HIS · RETURN" 20/PRINTS
CHARLES · WHITE '46

PLATE 6

Freeport Columbia, 1946

Ink and charcoal on paper
37.78 x 53.34 cm (14 7/8 x 21 in.)

A visceral commentary on the treatment of Black military veterans by white America, *Freeport Columbia* melds two harrowing events. On February 5, 1946, serviceman Charles Ferguson and his brothers, Alfonso, Joseph, and Richard, approached the Freeport, New York, bus terminal after an evening out to celebrate Charles's re-enlistment in the US Army. They were stopped by Joseph Romeika, a provisional officer with the local police, on grounds of disorderly conduct. Matters escalated and Romeika shot and killed the uniformed Charles as well as Alfonso, in addition to injuring Joseph. The policeman was found guilty of no crimes despite eyewitness accounts reporting that Romeika's shots were unprovoked and the fact that the Fergusons, who were Black, were later confirmed as having all been unarmed. At the close of that same month (February 25–26, 1946), a race riot broke out in Columbia, Tennessee. Precipitated by the incarceration of James Stephenson (who was also Black and a veteran of the US Navy) and his mother, Gladys, following a brief altercation with William Fleming (a white store clerk), the Columbia Race Riot culminated with law enforcement officials carrying out warrantless raids and weapons seizures in the town's predominantly African American business district. One hundred Black men were arrested, twenty-five of them on charges of attempted murder.

White's forceful image speaks to these horrific abuses of power and race-based violence, leaving no doubt about the predations visited upon people of color in the United States. A strong diagonal axis cuts through the pictorial field from upper left to lower right, drawing our eye to the mass of battered, brutalized, and murdered Black bodies peppering the middle ground. Behind them, a raging storm of urban chaos and destruction gives way to the towering figure of an African American man in uniform. His military shirt—identifiable by the service bars above his breast pocket—is tattered and torn, while a noose with cut and fraying ends encircles his neck and manacles circumscribe his wrists. The chains of bondage on his right hand are loose, enabling the man to hold aloft a torch (a symbol of justice and truth). His left hand, however, remains bound and in visible tension with the chain that restrains him. Beneath the billowing clouds that threaten to consume the figure are three white men: a judge, an officer of the law, and a member of the Ku Klux Klan. The latter is particularly menacing as he raises his claw-like left hand in anguished frustration while grasping the broken lynching rope—the terrifying puzzle piece that links him to the noose above—in his right. Meanwhile, his companions smirk as they read a printed announcement emblazoned with the unthinkable words: PERMIT TO KILL NEGRO VETS AND CIVILIANS.

White's use of explosive gesture and scale in this ink and charcoal drawing speak to his ongoing interest in the Mexican Muralists, many of whom he would meet later that same year when he and his first wife, artist Elizabeth Catlett (1915–2012), embarked on an extended stay in Mexico. The work also evinces his commitment to political activism, as *Freeport Columbia* was published in the March 1946 edition of *Congress View* under a banner that read: "PROTEST TO PRESIDENT TRUMAN. Lynch-terror against Negro people and police brutality against Negroes and strikers must be stopped!" This work is also related to the cover illustration White created for a 1946 pamphlet titled *Dixie Comes to New York: Story of the Freeport GI Slayings*, published by the *Daily Worker*.

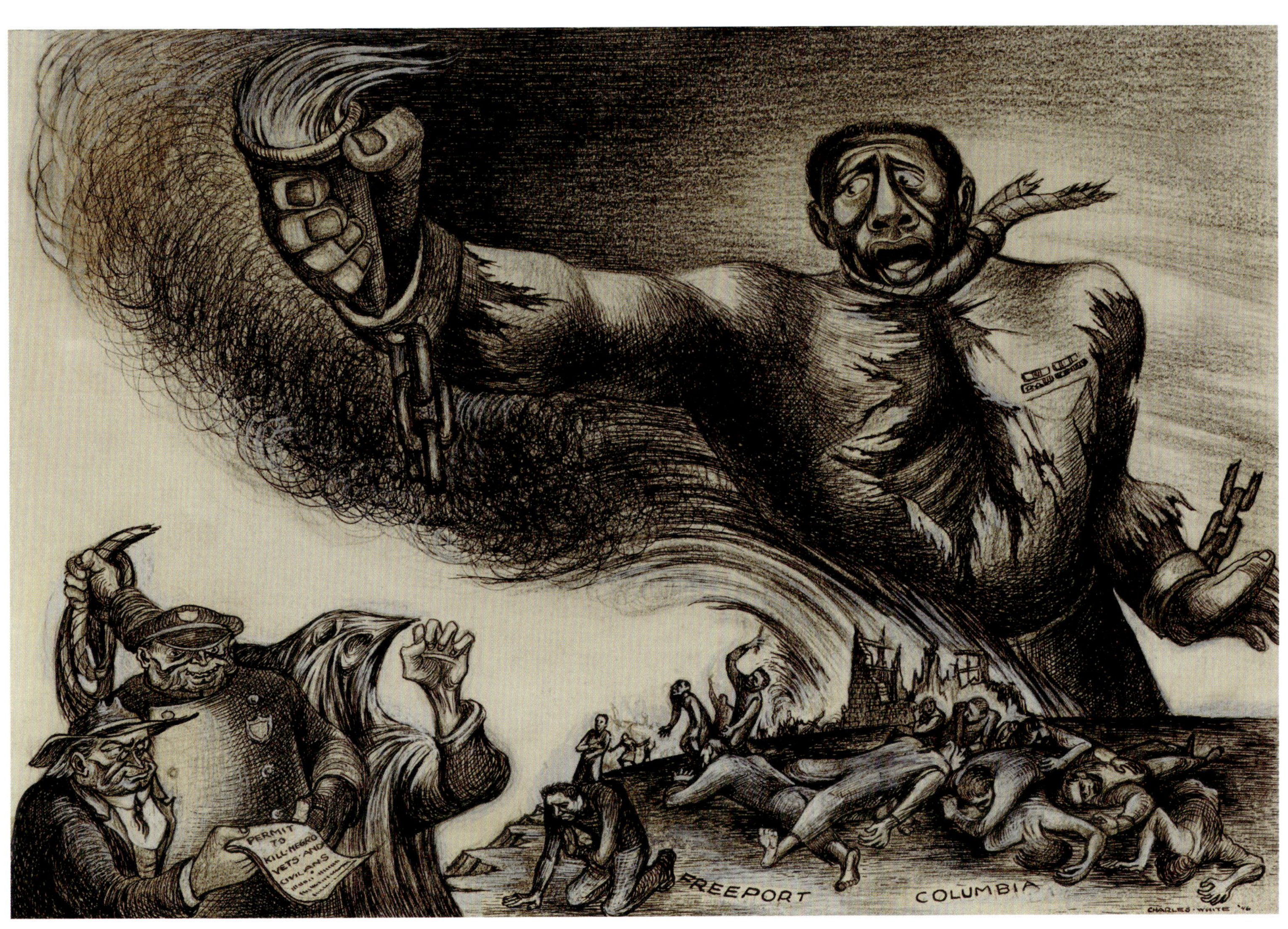
PERMIT
TO
KILL·NEGRO
VETS·AND
CIVILANS
FREEPORT
COLUMBIA
CHARLES·WHITE '46

PLATE 7

Head of a Man, 1948

(From the portfolio *Negro: U.S.A. A Graphic History of the Negro People in America Workshop Prints No. 2*)
Offset lithograph
34.29 x 22.86 cm (13 1/2 x 9 in.)

Head of a Man—like *Our War* (PLATE 8)—was created by White for *Negro: U.S.A. A Graphic History of the Negro People in America Workshop Prints No. 2*, a 1949 portfolio of twenty-six prints by fifteen artists issued by the New York City–based Workshop of Graphic Art in observance of National Negro History Week (February 6–12, 1949). An interracial group of Social Realist artists, the Workshop produced numerous images for leftist groups during the 1940s and 1950s. Its logo—a raised fist grasping a paintbrush and other artists' implements—affirmed the consortium's belief in the revolutionary power of art. This philosophy not only tracks closely with White's own outlook but also informs this powerful work. With tremendous graphic economy, the artist created an impactful image of a man's head and neck. Tightly cropped and pushed close to the front of the picture plane, his elongated face is punctuated by remarkably high cheekbones and sorrowful eyes. He gazes upward and to his left, his brow deeply furrowed. The figure's anonymity renders him a symbol for Black Americans, his humanity a lesson for us all. White's expert use of hatching and cross-hatching endows the work with a dimensionality reminiscent of sculpture and evinces his mastery of lithography.

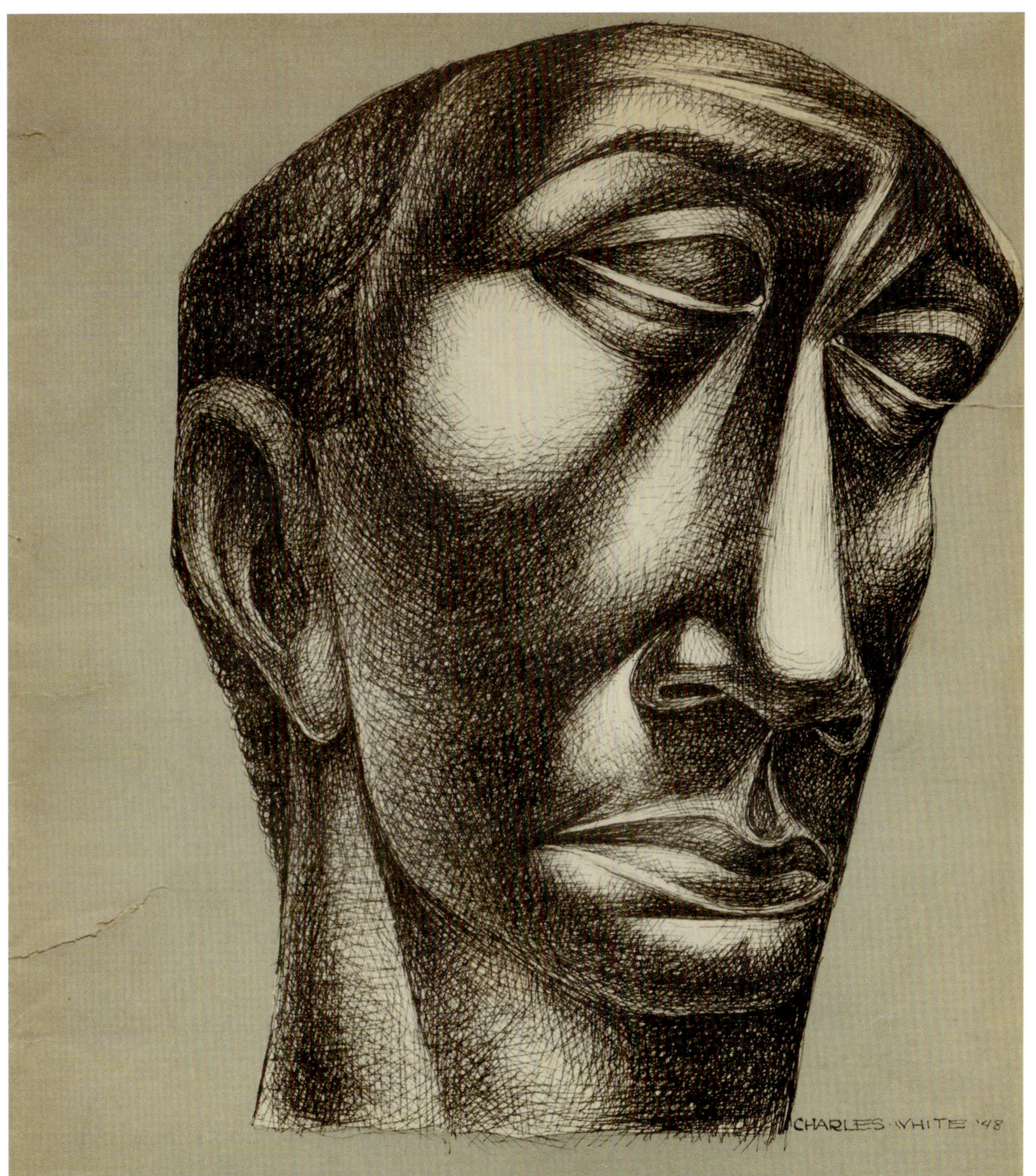

NEGRO: U.S.A.

THE GRAPHIC WORKSHOP • • • WORKSHOP PRINTS No. 2

PLATE 8

Our War, ca. 1948

(from the portfolio *Negro: U.S.A. A Graphic History of the Negro People in America Workshop Prints No. 2*)
Offset lithograph
17.78 x 21.59 cm (7 x 8 1/2 in.)

Our War—like *Head of a Man* (PLATE 7)—is one of two lithographs created by White for *Negro: U.S.A. A Graphic History of the Negro People in America Workshop Prints No. 2*, a 1949 portfolio of twenty-six prints published by the New York City–based Workshop of Graphic Art. The subject of White's visceral work is the 1944 Port Chicago (California) explosion in which three hundred and twenty servicemen were killed and another four hundred injured, two-thirds of them African American sailors reassigned to unload munitions without protective measures. The disaster threw the U.S. military's discriminatory practices into high relief and led to strident calls for desegregation and equal treatment.

White's visual retelling of this tragic event is gripping. At left, a uniformed warden's outsized right hand punches through the foreground and into our space. He firmly grasps a flashlight and gesticulates vigorously in an effort to lead those behind him to safety. A knot of figures behind him beats a hasty retreat, leading our eye through the middle ground and toward an unseen horizon, where San Francisco (located twenty miles from the explosion) is referenced with great visual economy. Blocky yet scenographic, the distinctive urban row houses are an apt visual complement to the sweeping, expansive gestures of White's figures. The image's thrusting sense of motion is reminiscent of the work of Mexican Muralists, notably David Alfaro Siqueiros (1896–1974), with whom White was acquainted, as he and his first wife, Elizabeth Catlett (1915–2012), briefly lived with Siqueiros while in Mexico in 1946.

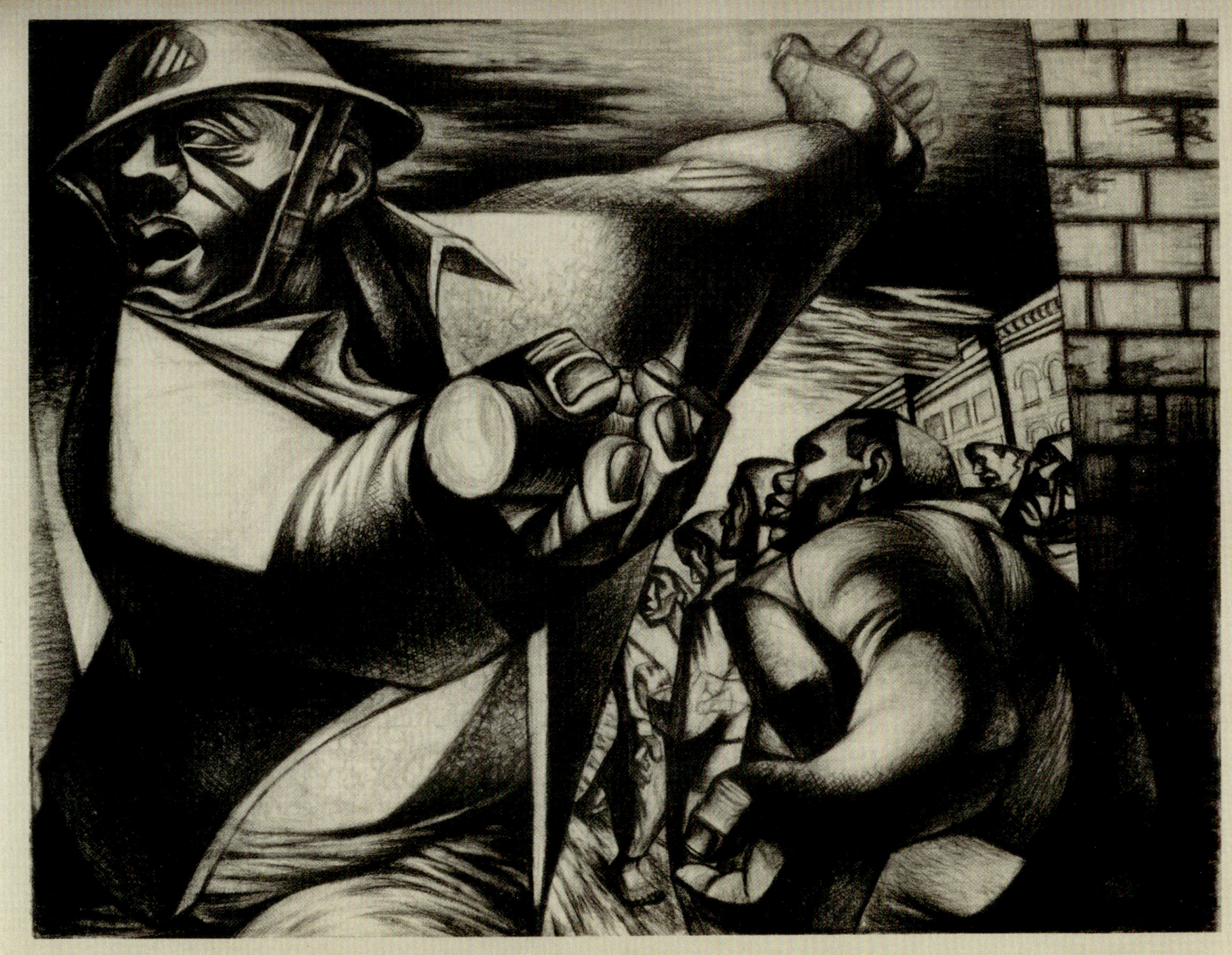

Our War Charles White

PLATE 9

Abraham Lincoln, 1952

Wolff crayon and charcoal on paperboard
82.55 x 40.01 cm (32 1/2 x 15 3/4 in.)

Reflecting on his work, White noted: "I use Negro subject matter because Negroes are closest to me. But I am trying to express a universal feeling through them, a meaning for all men."[2] This statement encapsulates the artist's commitment to both his fellow African Americans as well as to humanity writ large, a sentiment reflected in White's 1952 drawing of President Abraham Lincoln (1809–1865). Executed in a photorealist style, this image is based on one of five portraits taken by the Civil War photographer Alexander Gardner (1821–1882) on NOVEMBER 15, 1863, just days before Lincoln delivered his Gettysburg Address. As with Gardner's photo, White's drawing telegraphs the sobriety of the moment, a time when the United States was deeply divided over the issue of slavery and rent by internecine warfare. It equally communicates the grit and determination of Lincoln, who engages our gaze directly with an unflinching stare and firm set of jaw. Lincoln, like the white abolitionist John Brown (1800–1859), was one of the artist's very few Caucasian subjects, a reflection of his admiration for both men's commitment to equity and racial justice. This work was also included in a 1952 portfolio of six of White's lithographs published by the leftist journal *Masses & Mainstream*.

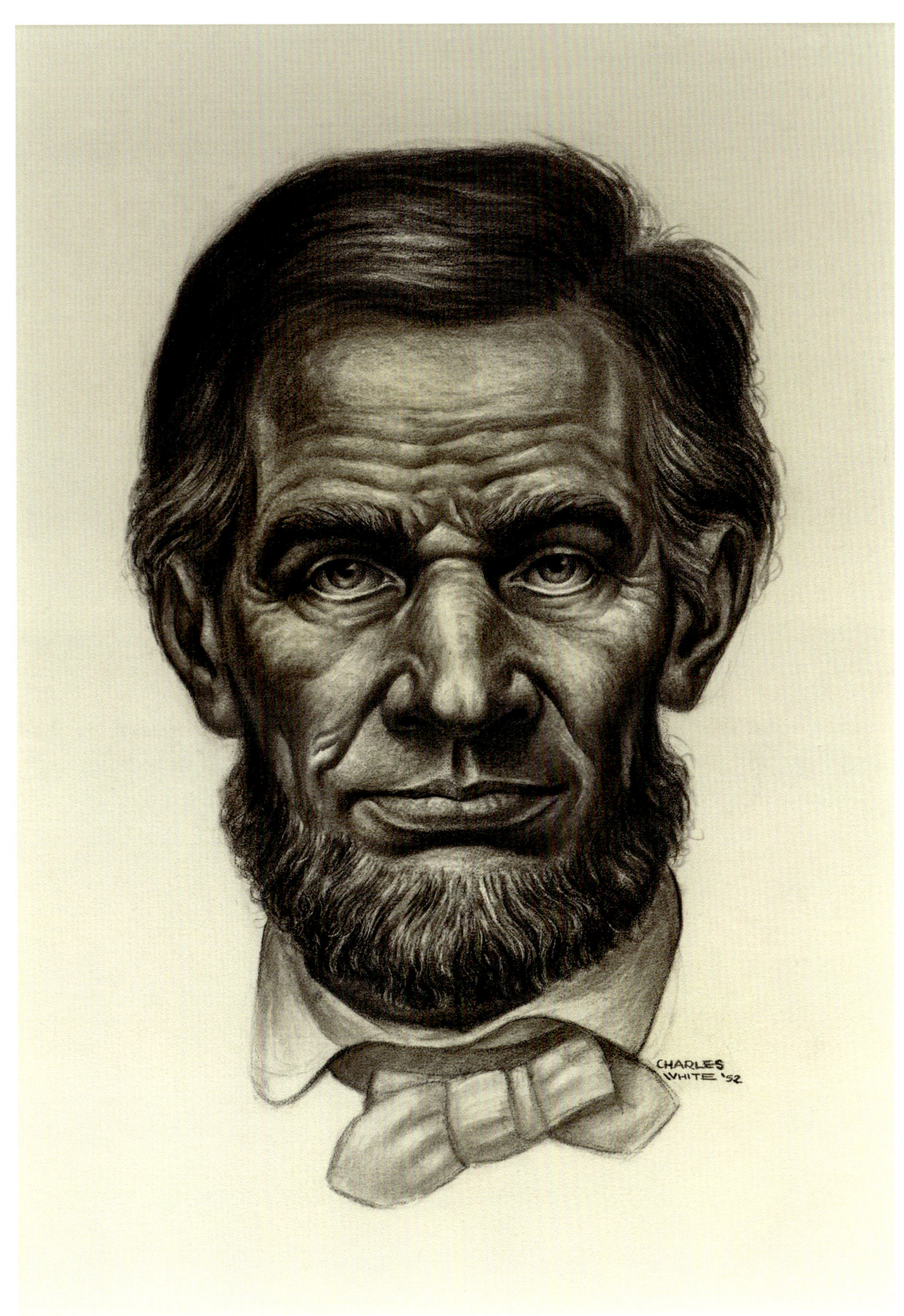
CHARLES
WHITE '52

PLATE 10

Jazz Flute, 1955

Pen, ink, and gouache on paper
71.76 x 54.29 cm (28 1/4 x 21 3/8 in.)

White, who was given a violin by his mother when he was nine and later confessed to having "scratched away on the [instrument] for about seven years," was not a natural musician.[3] He did, however, harbor a lifelong interest in music and a profound admiration for performers. Beyond creating lasting friendships with professional entertainers such as Paul Robeson (1898–1976), Sidney Poitier (1927–2022), and Harry Belafonte (B. 1927)—some of whom he featured in his paintings and graphic works—he painted powerful images of singers like the iconic Mahalia Jackson (1911–1972) and Bessie Smith (1894–1937). Music was also the subject of his *Gospel Singers* (1951) and *Goodnight Irene* (1952) in addition to figuring prominently in some of White's murals, such as *Progress of the American Negro: Five Great American Negroes* (1939–40, Howard University School of Law, Washington, D.C.), which features the contralto singer Marian Anderson (1897–1993).

Misidentified in the past as *Jazz Clarinet*, this delicate pen and ink drawing is composed of only two elements: the hands of a musician and the flute they hold. The result is not spartan or spare, however. Rather, White used deft cross-hatching to create dimensionality in the hands, whose graphic density contrasts sharply with the instrument, which—represented with the barest of outlines—is as light and airy as the music it will be used to produce. Despite the verisimilitude of *Jazz Flute*, this image (which was likely related to commissions White received from the Vanguard record label to illustrate album covers for the Sam Most Sextet in the 1950s) was clearly not drawn from life since both the number of keys and their disposition on the flute's body are incorrect.

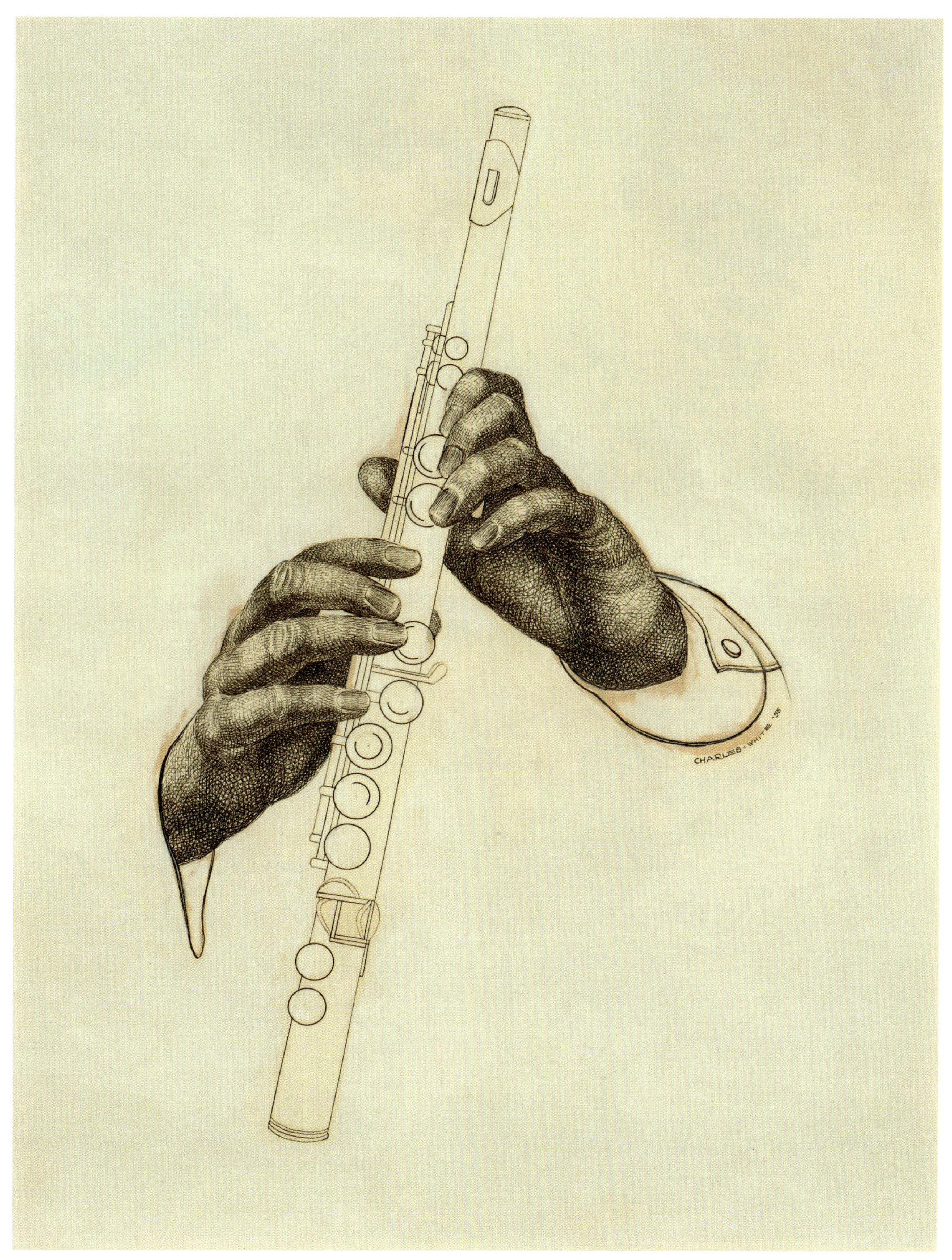
CHARLES • WHITE '56

PLATE 11

Solid as a Rock (My God is My Rock), 1958

Linocut
99.70 x 36.83 cm (39 1/4 x 14 1/2 in.)

David sang to the Lord the words of this song when the Lord delivered him from the hand of all his enemies and from the hand of Saul. He said: "The Lord is my rock, my fortress, and my deliverer; my God is my rock, in whom I take refuge, my shield and the horn of my salvation. He is my stronghold, my refuge, and my savior—from violent people you save me."
—King James Bible, 2 Samuel 22:1–3

On Christ, the solid Rock, I stand; All other ground is sinking sand.
—Edward Mote, "My Hope is Built on Nothing Less" (Christian hymn), 1834

White produced this large linocut two years after he and his wife, Frances Barrett White, relocated to greater Los Angeles. Though it took the couple some time to adjust to suburban living after the hustle and bustle of New York City, L.A. afforded them not only a better climate (the catalyst to their move, given the artist's chronic pulmonary issues) but also more space. For the first time in his career, White had access to a proper home studio, which fueled his creativity. Writing a few years after their move, he noted: "Working becomes more and more exciting each day. Picking more challenging themes and probing deeper into the meaning of life, people and culture, I am trying to communicate in simple, yet more meaningful symbols."[4]

Such concentrated potency is evidenced by this work, which is richly allusive despite its apparent simplicity. A master of linocut (a printing technique in which images are cut into a block of linoleum that is then inked before being pressed onto a support [generally paper]), White unleashed his skills on this oversized sheet to create a single, full-length figure. Slightly androgynous in appearance, the individual—whose discreet bustline suggests she is a woman—is attired in an ambiguous garment with a pleated yoke and cascading folds. Despite his subject's remarkable solidity, her stance is activated. She bears her weight on her left leg as she pulls her far shoulder slightly away from the picture plane. Her right leg and foot appear ready to move in the same direction as her gaze, causing her to turn her head to the left, thereby presenting us with her dignified profile. The figure's left hand, too, is energized as she grasps the side of her gown and pulls it up into the ball of her fist. So, too, is her mouth, which seems to be mid-speech or, perhaps, mid-song. The energy she telegraphs is heightened by the dynamism of White's mark-making: His expert gouges into the linoleum block result in radiating patterns of light that suggest movement and flow while the untouched surfaces (which appear black when inked and printed) create deep pockets of contour and shadow. Despite the kinetic energy she embodies, White's protagonist has a staid monumentality that calls to mind the work's title. Clothed in the robes of a chorister, she speaks not only to the strength White admired in Black women and his love of music (including gospel music) but also to the role of the Church in Black America as a place of communion, fellowship, sanctity, salvation, and safety.

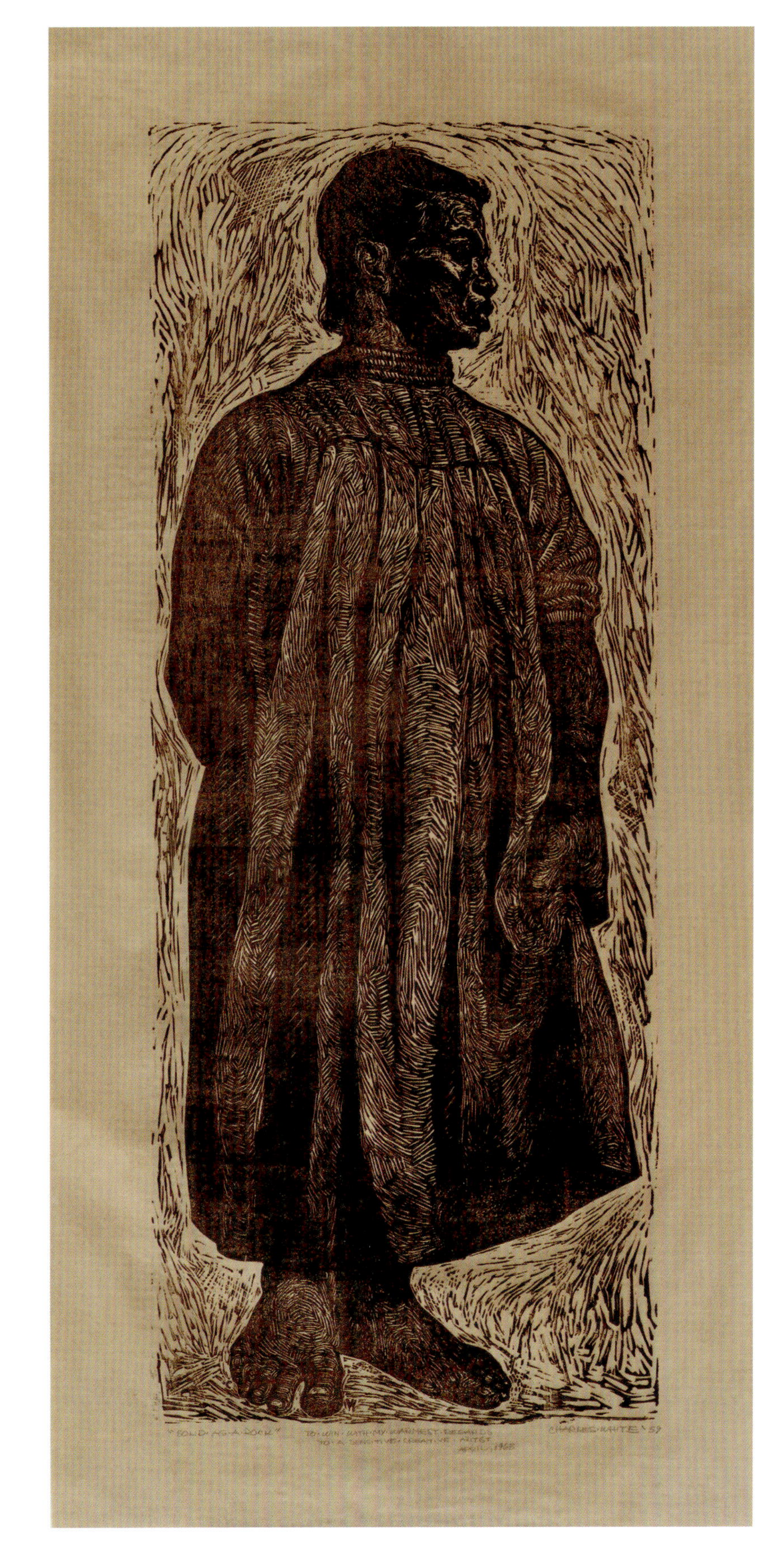

PLATE 12

Study for Pope X, ca. 1960

Graphite on architectural vellum
81.60 x 111.13 cm (32 1/8 x 43 3/4 in.)

White depicted Black preachers multiple times over the course of his career. *Study for Pope X* sees the artist taking this theme to a higher allegorical plane by melding the titular head of the Catholic Church with a modern-day African American man. The symbolism with which he vests the work reflects the artist's steadfast commitment to equity and social justice as well as contemporaneous discourse centered on the possibility of a Black man ascending the throne of Saint Peter. Executed in graphite on delicate vellum, *Study for Pope X* depicts a man shown half-length and in a relaxed, seated position. White's protagonist wears a nondescript ecclesiastic chasuble together with a distinctive miter (the ceremonial hat reserved, in the Catholic tradition, for bishops and the pope). In an interesting sartorial twist, he also wears sunglasses, a nod to White's desire to make his pope—who bears more than a passing resemblance to Dr. Martin Luther King Jr. (1929–1968)—a man both for *and of* the people. Swiftly but carefully sketched (note, for instance, how the artist has included proportional guides for the face to ensure mimetic accuracy), White's drawing has a compelling dynamism and lyrical sense of movement heightened by his sure pencil and strong composition. This study may have been inspired by the great Spanish Baroque painter Diego Velázquez's (1599–1660) iconic *Portrait of Innocent X* (CA. 1650) and Francis Bacon's (1909–1992) *Study after Velázquez's portrait of Pope Innocent X* (1953). It is also thematically related to White's later *Pope X* (PLATE 26).

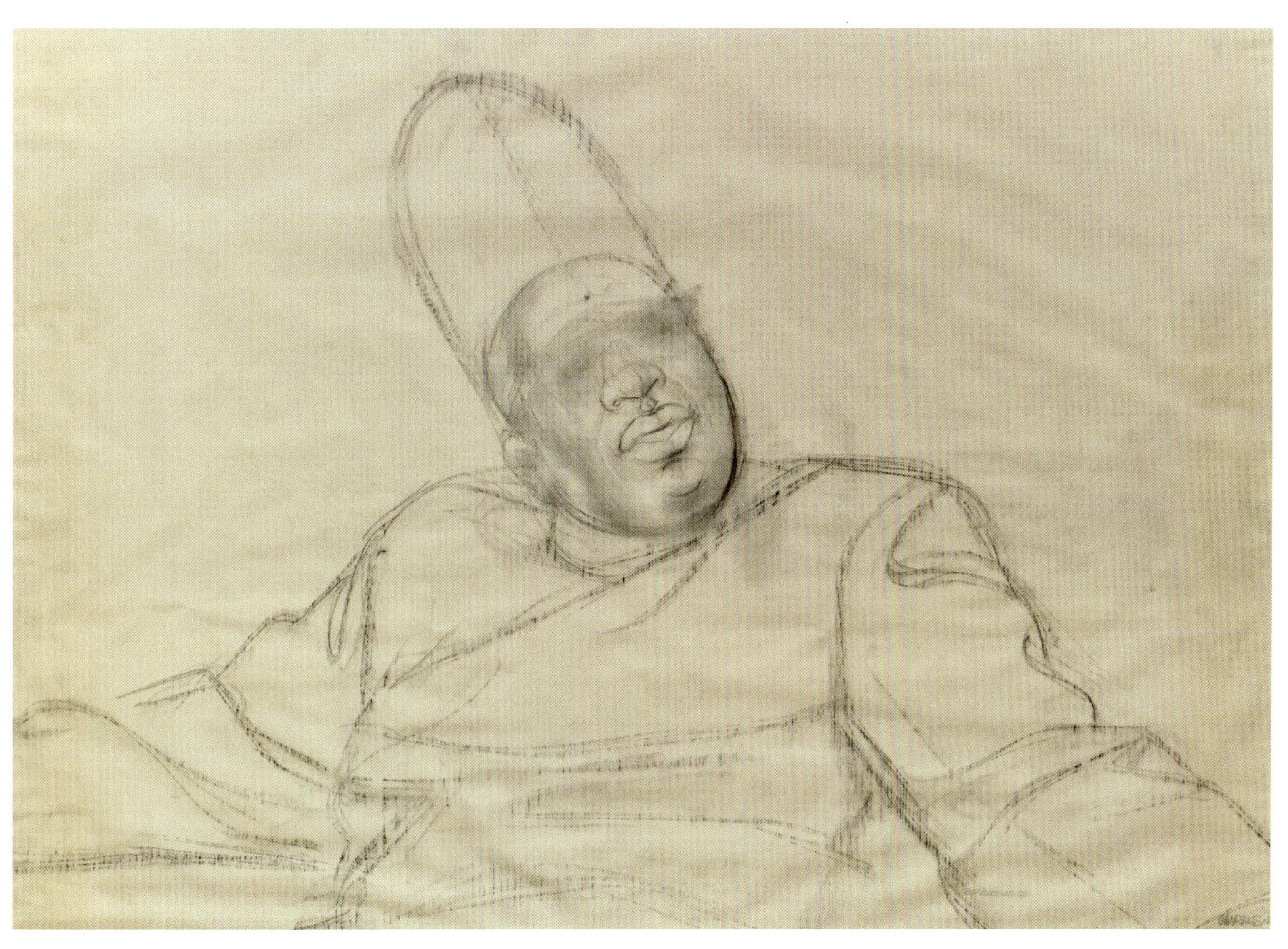

PLATE 13

Micah, 1964

Lithograph
40.96 x 30.48 cm (16 1/8 x 12 in.)

White created two works dedicated to the Old Testament Prophet Micah in 1964; this lithograph and an ambitiously scaled linocut (PLATE 14). Given that the artist was not known to be a particularly religious man, his choice of subject bears further consideration. White scholar Andrea Barnwell's comments are instructive in this regard: "During the early to mid-1960s, many African American preachers, most notably Dr. Martin Luther King Jr...relied on verses from the Old Testament Book of Micah when he delivered his message of nonviolent change to convey the harsh treatment that all people repeatedly and unconsciously inflicted on one another."[5] Barnwell concludes, "White's reference to the highly cited prophet was especially relevant during that time of ongoing strife and racial conflict."[6]

In this treatment of the subject of the eighth-century BCE Biblical figure, White aptly conveys the sobriety of Micah's denunciations of covetousness, dishonesty, idolatry, and greed as well as his predicted fall of Samaria and Jerusalem. His prognostications were not all grim, however, for Micah also foretold the reestablishment of the Judean state as well as the birth of the Christian savior Jesus Christ. His, then, is a message of redemption through righteousness. White effectively conveys Micah's stalwart energy and spiritual conviction in this compact image, which depicts the protagonist walking through the darkness and into the light, a clear metaphor for salvation. In doing so, he reminds us that the road to a life of peace, prosperity, and tranquility is one paved with justice, integrity, and equity.

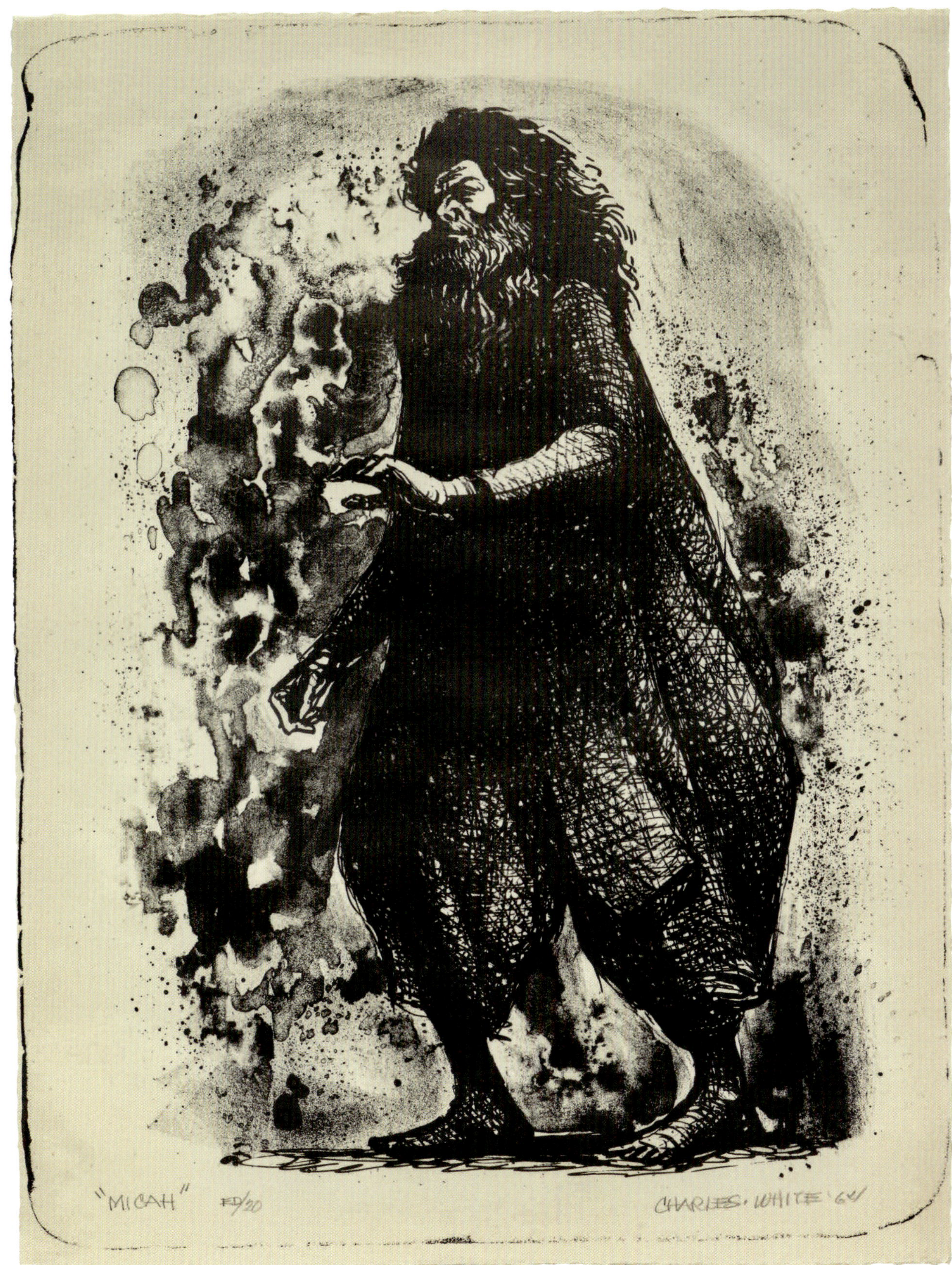
"MICAH"
CHARLES · WHITE '64

PLATE 14

Micah, 1964

Linocut

123.19 x 62.55 cm (48 1/2 x 24 5/8 in.)

Like his other work bearing this same name and also created in 1964 (PLATE 13), White here depicts the Old Testament Prophet Micah. Monumental in format, this linocut is equally powerful in its visual articulation. The eighth-century BCE biblical figure is turned at a forty-five-degree angle from the picture plane, his gaze firmly locked on a scene not visible to us. White has endowed Micah with a colossal, Moses-like presence. His full-length robes swirl around him, conveying an energy that parallels the prophet's heightened sense of purposeful, yet agitated emotion. This same sensibility is communicated in his full beard and thick mane of hair, which, like his garment, pulse with expressive vitality. His oversized hands, too, are tense with emotion and embody the fervor and sobriety of Micah's prophecies, which foretold the downfall of ancient kingdoms in the face of humanity's sinful, impious behavior. His message warns against the dangers of dishonest rulers, false idols, corruption, and greed, and invites us to prepare for the birth of Jesus Christ (which he foretold) as well as the renewal of Judea. Thus, Micah extols us to live a life of rectitude in fellowship with others in our quest for salvation, a message Civil Rights leaders such as Dr. Martin Luther King Jr. (1929–1968) explicitly incorporated into their own writings, sermons, and speeches.

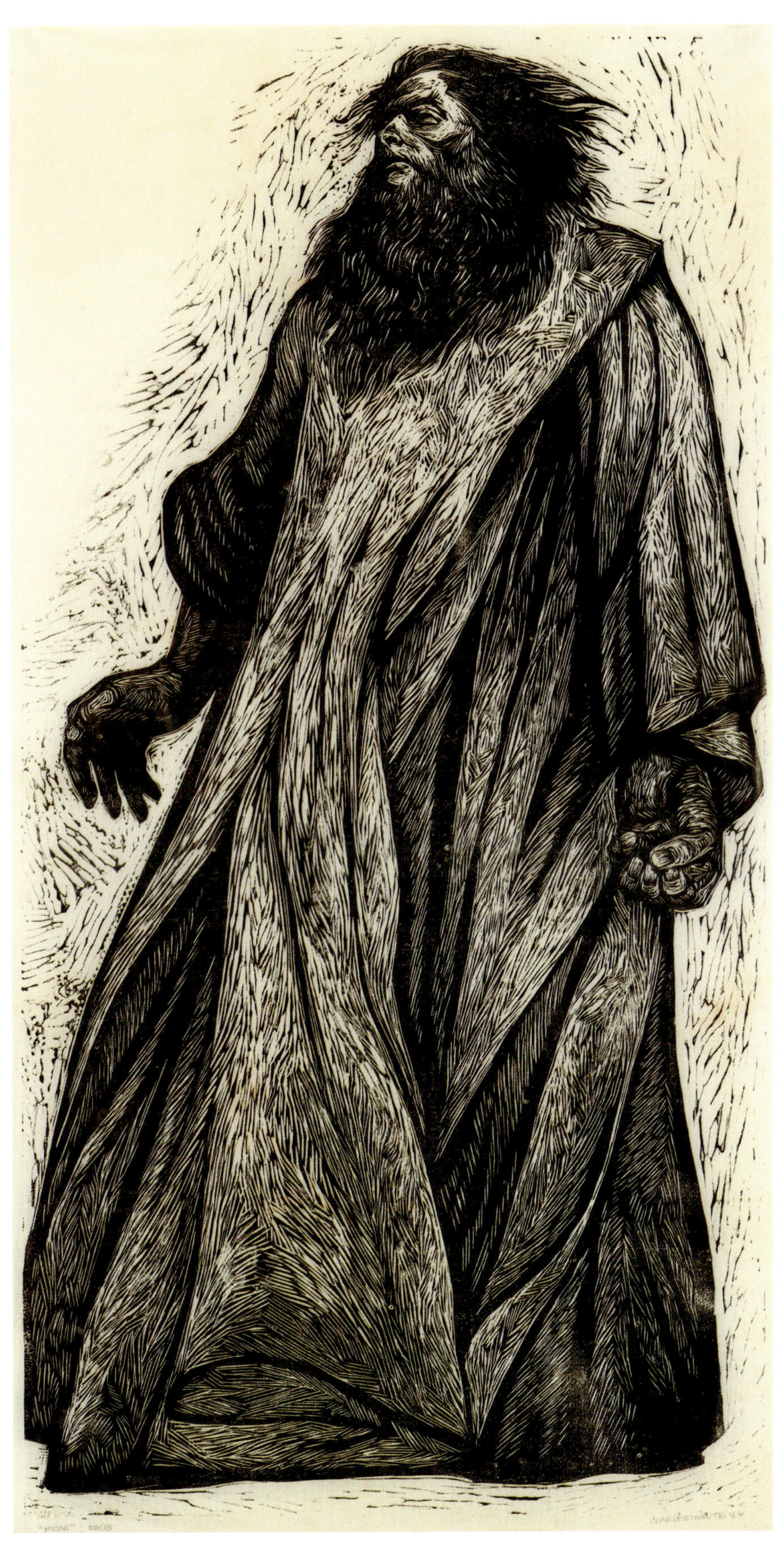

PLATE 15

J'Accuse #2, 1965

Charcoal on paper
81.92 x 57.79 cm (32 1/4 x 22 3/4 in.)

On January 13, 1898, the French writer Émile Zola (1840–1902) published an open letter to Félix Faure, President of France's Third Republic, on the front page of the Socialist newspaper *L'Aurore*. The headline read, simply: *J'Accuse* ("I accuse"). In his impassioned polemic, Zola defended Alfred Dreyfus, a French artillery officer who, in 1894, had been sentenced to a lifetime of solitary confinement on Devil's Island (a penal colony in French Guiana that was just as miserable as its name suggests). Perhaps more significantly, he accused France's government and military of complicity, duplicity, fraud, and corruption. The author also drew attention to the fact that Dreyfus was Jewish, and lobbed allegations of institutionalized anti-Semitism in France, claims that would soon divide the nation. White was very clearly referencing this well-known incident through the title of this work, one of a dozen images bearing the title *J'Accuse* (followed by a sequential number) that White executed in charcoal in 1965. The grouping was not envisioned as a seamless whole from the start, however. Rather, the artist made a spontaneous decision to change the works' titles and unite them under a shared nomenclature shortly before they were shown in his solo exhibition at the Heritage Gallery that year. As Erica Moiah James has argued, "[w]hile no one is certain what sparked the artist's change in titles...[the latter] expressed White's crisis of faith in the capacity of his politicized aesthetic to do the work he intended it to do."[7]

Of White's *J'Accuse* works, Ilene Susan Fort has observed that they are "transitional" in terms of the artist's "fluid yet representational technique that became a signature style."[8] She further notes that the works evidence the artist's commitment to surfacing socioeconomic and social injustices—such as poverty, housing insecurity, and the demands of physical labor—while also delivering messages of hope and dignity. This same duality is encapsulated in the final passages of Zola's fervent letter, in which he writes: "I have but one passion, the search for light, in the name of humanity which has suffered so much and is entitled to happiness. My fiery protest is simply the cry of my very soul."

In this image, nine distinct faces circumscribe a lozenge shape. They emerge from an abstracted background that seems to move and sway, like aquatic plants animated by the current, licks of flames, or even rising smoke. Though the figures' expressions are varied, all are marked by a seriousness that, in some instances, veer toward worry or anxiety (as indicated by pronounced furrows between certain individuals' eyes). Each is bathed in light, indicating an unnatural—or supernatural—source of illumination, suggesting that each one has been touched by the divine. The image field itself is a highly unusual rectangle with an arched top; a shape that harkens back to Western European altarpieces and that may also call to mind a grave marker or tombstone.

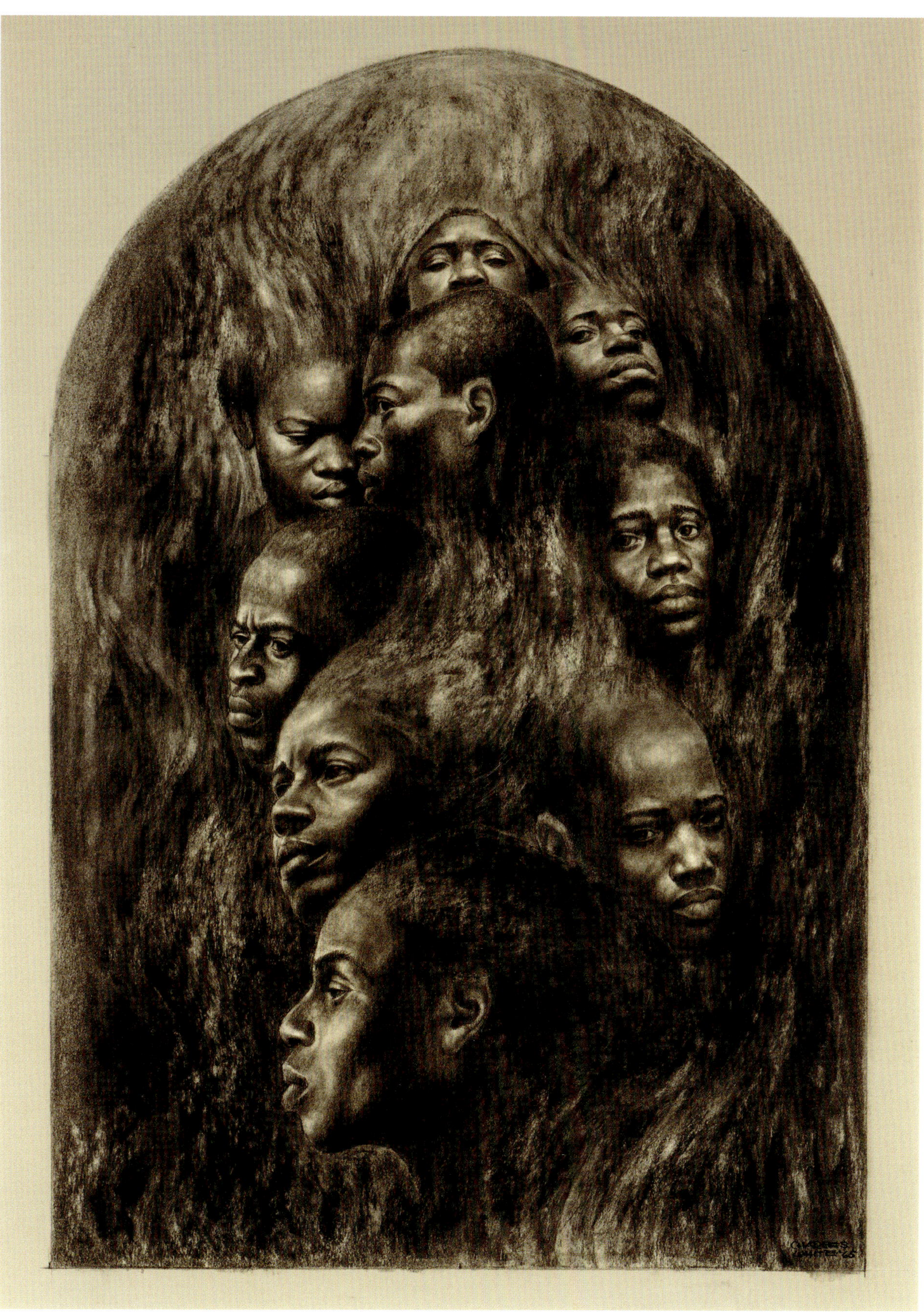

PLATE 16

Lazarus (Black Cowboy), 1965

Charcoal on paper
Image: 100.33 x 74.30 cm (39 1/2 x 29 1/4 in.)

Created the same year White began teaching at Otis Art Institute (now Otis College of Art and Design), the deftly executed *Lazarus (Black Cowboy)* speaks to White's persistent interest in both realism and the figure. His subject is a man who, seated atop a mule, dons what appears to be a Kepi (distinctively shaped caps worn by soldiers fighting for both sides—Union and Confederate—during the Civil War). His unbuttoned jacket, too, bears more than a passing resemblance to an enlisted man's sack coat, despite the modern collar and suggestion of a turtleneck worn beneath. The artist's protagonist holds a shotgun firmly in his right hand as he fixes his gaze on a point on the horizon, a gaze paralleled by the direction of his gun's barrel. Though the background is abstract, the knee-high grasses and lack of visible trees evoke the Great Plains. It is his mount and his attire, however, that point to the work's subtle yet potent allegorical richness. Subtitled "Black Cowboy" (a name recorded on a Heritage Gallery label dated August 1965 on the work's verso, indicating that the title was, if not assigned by White, certainly approved by him), the drawing invites us to wonder why this man is attired more like a solider than a cowboy and why he rides a beast of burden and not a horse. A partial interpretive key may lie in the secondary name by which this work is sometimes referred: "Buffalo Soldier," a term thought to have been coined by North America's Indigenous Peoples when, during the American Frontier Wars (1609–1924), they encountered individuals of African descent whose hair was said to remind them of the fur between the horns of buffaloes (the strength and fearlessness of which Black men were also said to embody). A more straightforward account points to the buffalo-skin overcoats that Black soldiers (who typically were posted to locales with the harshest, most extreme conditions) donned in winter. Whatever its origin, this phrase was later adopted as a sobriquet for African American soldiers serving in the all-Black 9TH and 10TH Cavalries as well as the 24TH and 25TH Infantries, peacetime units formed by Act of Congress in 1866 specifically to keep the armed forces segregated. Treated as second-class soldiers, the members of these units were typically given the most dangerous assignments, the poorest provisions, and the worst mounts (including mules in place of horses). The work's proper title, *Lazarus*, is equally potent, as it alludes to African Americans' and Indigenous Americans' melding of Christian saints, prophets, and martyrs with their own ceremonies and religious writings, rites, and rituals as a means of preserving their own identities under the guise of (forced) assimilation. Like Moses, Lazarus—a brother of Martha and Mary who was resurrected by Jesus Christ from the dead four days after his death—was a particularly popular syncretic symbol, as he represented a journey through the darkness into light, guided by faith. Lazarus, then, was the perfect metaphor for the survivors of what scholar Joanna Brooks has referred to as "the crushing legacies of slavery and colonization [as well as] the chaos of war, epidemic, resettlement, exile, and the political uncertainties of the new nation."[9] This sense of hope in the face of despair is suggested by the celestial light that seemingly bathes the man from above.

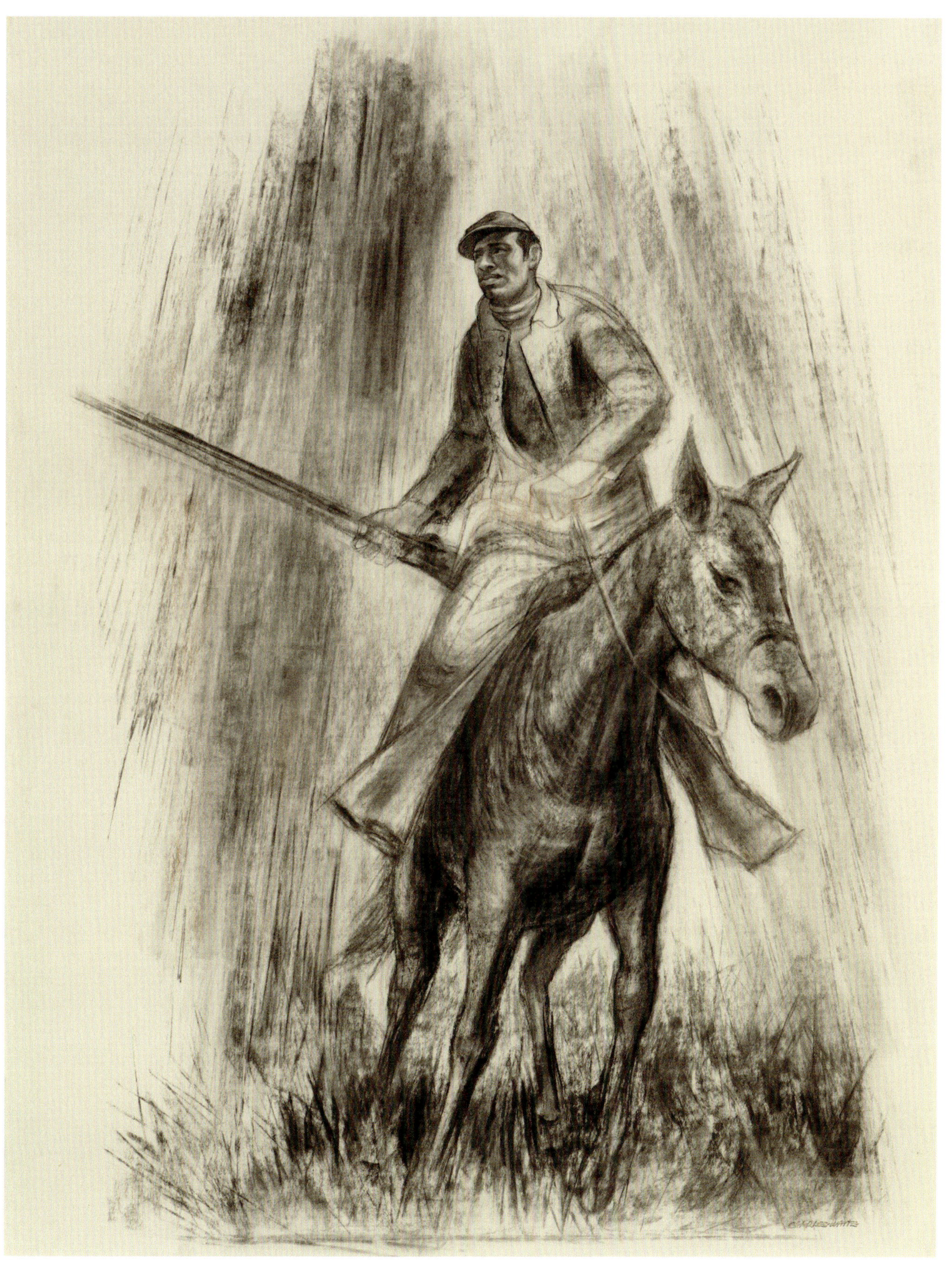

PLATE 17

Emancipation Proclamation, 1965–67

Ink and collage on paper
45.09 x 56.20 cm (17 3/4 x 22 1/8 in.)

This work was part of a commission White received in the mid-1960s to provide illustrations for Philip Sterling and Rayford Logan's *Four Took Freedom: The Lives of Harriet Tubman, Frederick Douglass, Robert Small and Blanche K. Bruce* (1967). Written for a young adult audience, the book profiles four Black individuals who, born into slavery, went on to not only emancipate themselves but also emerge as leaders in the fight for freedom and justice for all African Americans. Executed in ink with white heightening (used by White to camouflage edits and adjustments to his illustration rather than to emphasize particular passages), the work also features a single collaged element: a fragment of a piece of paper on which the words "BY THE PRESIDENT OF THE UNITED STATES OF AMERICA *A Proclamation*" are printed. The latter is a reference to President Abraham Lincoln's implementation of the Emancipation Proclamation by executive order on JANUARY 1, 1863. The presidential mandate declared "that all persons held as slaves within [states rebelling against the Union], are, and henceforward shall be free; and that the Executive government of the United States, including the military and naval authorities thereof, will recognize and maintain the freedom of said persons." A figure, shown from the rear with the short hair and strong arms of a man, holds this news aloft while raising his head (presumably so that he can read the proclamation but also to underline a renewed sense of hope and dignity). His foil is a woman who balances the left side of the composition while further animating the work by extending her arms in the air in a posture of both jubilation and relief. She, too, holds an oversized document in her raised left hand; a reference, one can imagine, to the printed news of Lincoln's monumental order. The abstracted garment she wears is reminiscent of a chorister's gown, signaling the importance of faith, shared worship, and community in Black American churches. The text that this image accompanies provides some interpretative insights into White's work. Referencing the Emancipation Proclamation, Sterling and Logan write:

> There was rejoicing in the South wherever the word reached the enslaved. There were public celebrations in the big cities of the North. In Boston's Tremont Temple a capacity crowd waited from early evening until well past ten o'clock when a man rushed in shouting, "It's on the wires!" From his place on the platform Douglass could see the emotions of three thousand people turn on. The scene was wild and grand. He could hear the hallelujahs and the sobs. He could see the tears of thanksgiving. Nowhere did the news stir a greater storm than in the heart of Frederick Douglass—a storm of sadness for the past, triumph for the present, dreams for the future, and love for his people.[10]

The drawing's fragmented and fractured background not only gives it a modern sensibility but also speaks to the heightened emotion of this pivotal moment in American history.

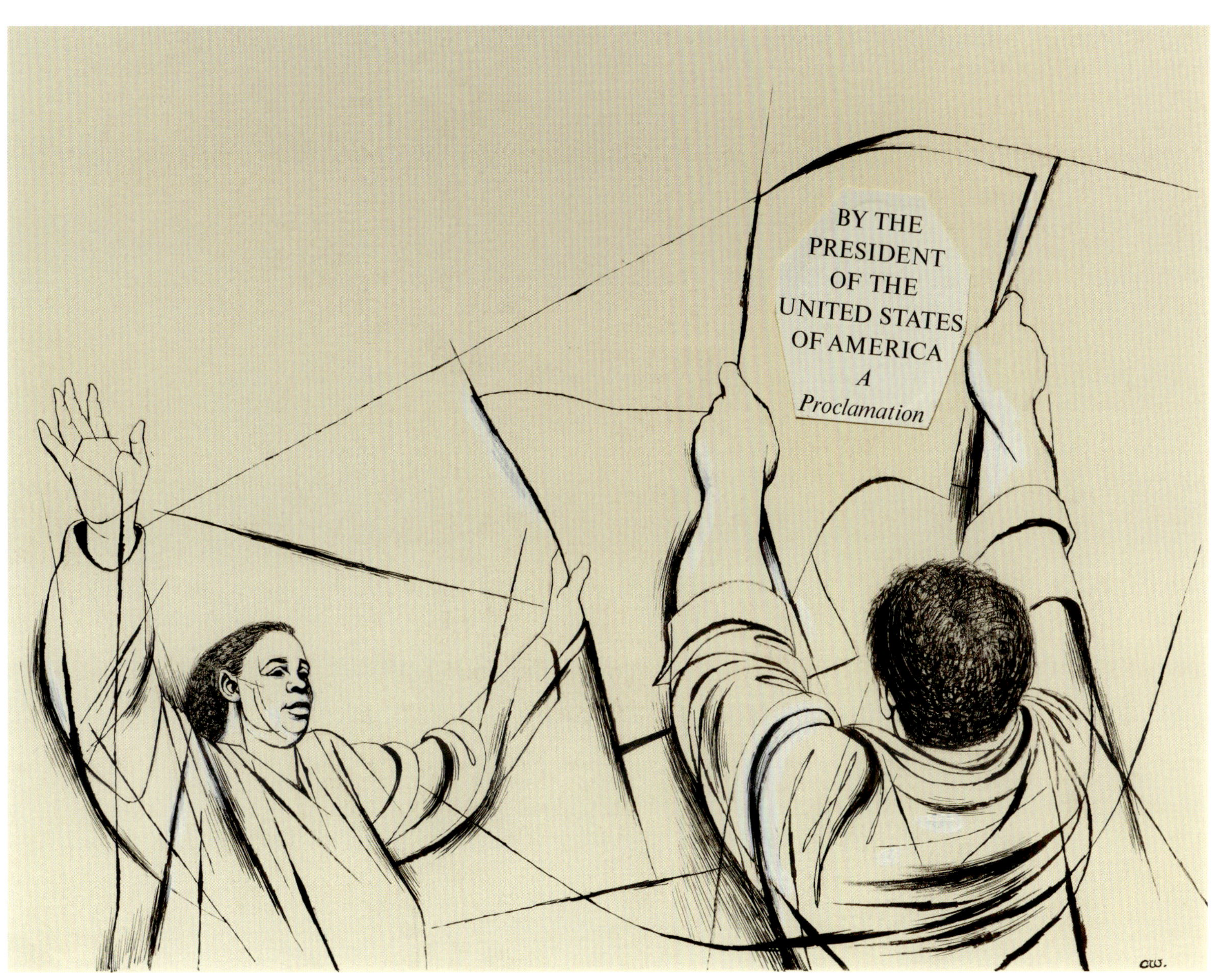
BY THE
PRESIDENT
OF THE
UNITED STATES
OF AMERICA
A
Proclamation
CW.

PLATE 18

Exodus II, 1966

Four color lithograph, printed by Gemini Ltd.
105.10 x 74.93 cm (41 3/8 x 29 1/2 in.)

This large-format lithograph was included in White's one-man show at Benjamin Horowitz's politically progressive Heritage Gallery in 1966. Interestingly, this is one of the few works from that show whose title the artist did not change; the majority of the works on the exhibition checklist being assigned new names by him (*J'Accuse* plus a sequencing number—see *J'Accuse #2* and *J'Accuse #6* [PLATES 15 and 19]) just prior to the opening. A partial explanation for this discrepancy may lie in the fact that this image was a lithograph, whereas the other works were executed in charcoal on paper (and, therefore, lent themselves more readily to be transformed into a cohesive "series"). Its visual language is also quite different, for this image is marked by a broad swath of ochre splattered with drab olive that not only creates an activated, yet abstract, background behind the cloaked figure but also actually envelops it. These same color overlays suggest, at first glance, that White's protagonist is a blond, light-eyed Caucasian. Such a choice would have been highly unusual for the artist, however. Indeed, closer inspection reveals that the subject's skin tone—visible on the presenting side of the face—is dark, and the nose more closely identified with that of White's other subjects, virtually all of whom were Black (Abraham Lincoln [PLATE 9] and the nineteenth-century white abolitionist John Brown being notable exceptions). The delicacy of White's protagonist's visible features suggests that this individual may be a woman, but with such limited visual data it is impossible to know for certain. What is clear is that the artist arrayed his subject in a pyramidal format, lending it potency and stability. This triangular shape is echoed and inverted in the amorphous background, an aesthetic call-and-response that endows the work with harmony and balance.

Fully wrapped in a cloak disassociated with the fashion of any era (which makes the work timeless, and its message endlessly resonant), the figure gazes off into the horizon at a point obscured from view. Though we cannot see what the figure sees, we can experience, through the figure's gaze, a shared sense of venturing forth or being inexorably drawn toward one's destiny. This feeling is reinforced by the work's title, a reference to the second book in the Bible, *Exodus*, which recounts the liberation of enslaved Israelites in fifteenth-century BCE Egypt. Spurred on by divine faith and led by Moses, the emancipated slaves eventually made their way to the Promised Land, Canaan. Clear parallels can be drawn between this Biblical account and the plight of enslaved African Americans, as well as to the figure of Moses, whom White referenced multiple times in his art (generally, in the guise of the Black emancipator Harriet Tubman [1822–1913], who was frequently referred to as "Black Moses"). Indeed, White created a lithograph that merges these two themes in a 1951 linocut entitled *Exodus*, which explains why the artist named this present work *Exodus II.*

Among White's early forays into color lithography, *Exodus II* was made in collaboration with master printer Kenneth Tyler at Gemini G.E.L., a Los Angeles–based artists' workshop and fine-art publishing housing that Tyler co-founded with Sidney Felsen and Stanley Grinstein the year this work was produced. Impressions of this work were widely exhibited throughout White's lifetime, in venues stretching from Europe and the USSR to Atlanta, Montgomery, Chattanooga, West Palm Beach, Little Rock, and Los Angeles. Printed on Rives Paper, the work is signed and numbered ("2/50," or the second print out of a limited run of fifty copies) by the artist, in addition to bearing Gemini G.E.L.'s distinctive chop mark.

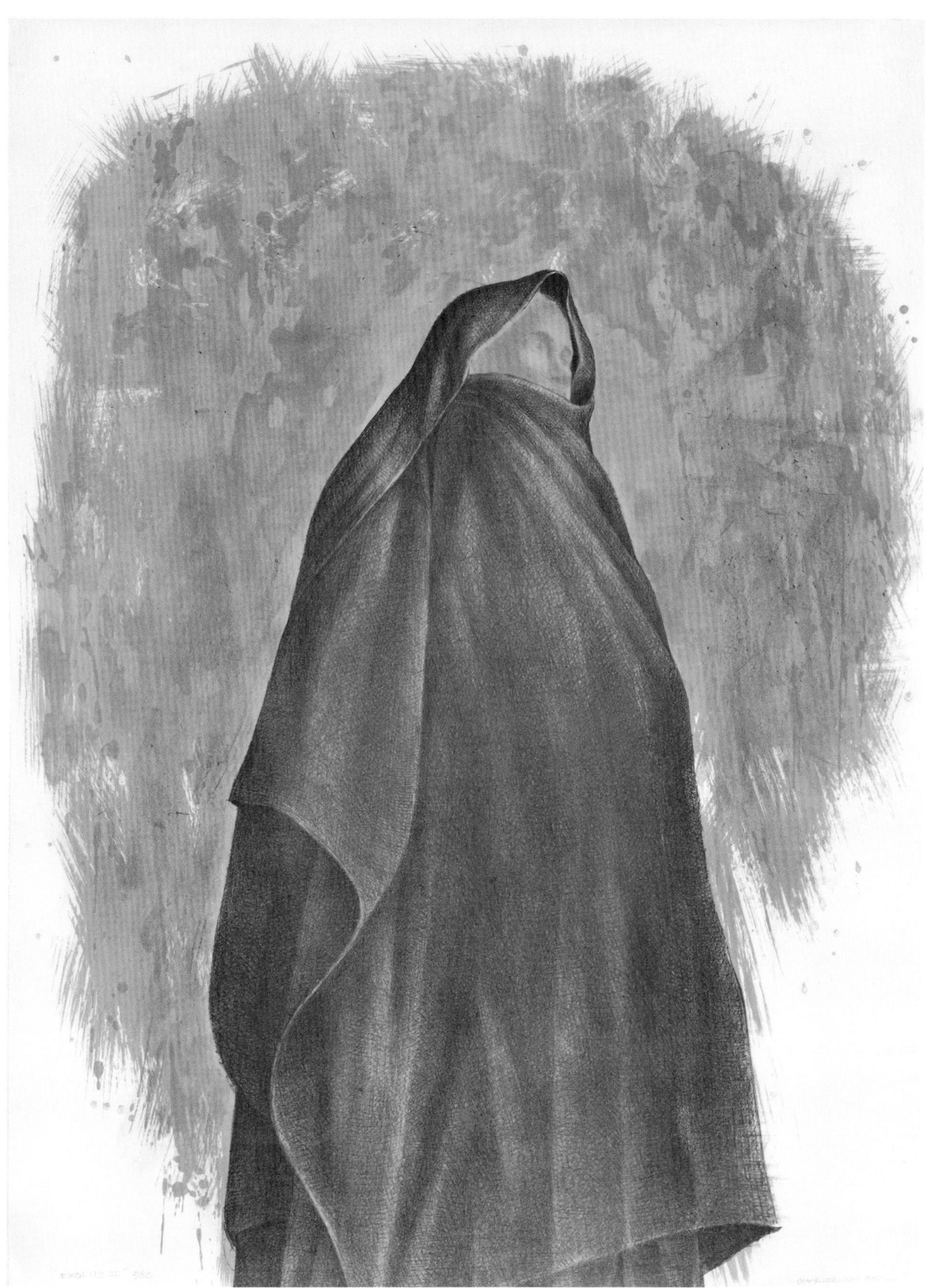

PLATE 19

J'Accuse #6, 1966

Charcoal on paper
93.98 x 119.38 cm (37 x 47 in.)

Like *J'Accuse #2* (PLATE 15), *J'Accuse #6* was included in White's 1966 solo show at the Los Angeles–based Heritage Gallery. Shortly before his solo show opened, the artist decided to change the titles of nearly every work on view (*Exodus II* [PLATE 18] being the notable exception), despite the fact that they were not intended to form a discrete series. His revised designations were arch references to France's 1894 Dreyfus Affair, in which a military officer of Jewish descent—Alfred Dreyfus—was improperly convicted of treason and sentenced to life imprisonment on Devil's Island. While White's objectives remain unclear, scholar Erica Moiah James has astutely observed that his dramatic renaming of these charcoal drawings represented

> a significant fracture in his political worldview centered on the representation of black people as universal signs of liberation—a perspective cultivated on the South Side of Chicago, crystallized as a member of the Artists' Union (AU) and the Works Progress Administration (WPA), globalized at the Taller de Gráfica Popular in Mexico, mobilized during the US long civil rights movement, and continuously challenged by shifting interpretations of American art in the 1930s, '40s, and '50s.[11]

White's focus in *J'Accuse #6* is a Black man, shown in a three-quarter view from the knees up. Behind him pulsing tones of black and grey—like the work's oval format—endow the image with a sense of animated vitality. His body, too, throbs with energy as he pivots away from us to shift his attention toward a brilliant point of light in the upper-left-hand margin. His arms are opened wide and his fingers are gently splayed as he closes his eyes, lifts his chin, and parts his lips. He is a man caught in mid-action, and that action is likely song and dance. Indeed, the man bears more than a passing likeness to White's lifelong friend and confidante, the entertainer and political activist Harry Belafonte (B. 1927). The artist deftly captures Belafonte's on-screen charisma as well as his easy appeal, which is heightened by his flowing, open-necked shirt and dark, form-fitting pants, a "look" that would have been familiar to the pop icon's many fans at that time. The work, though, is serious in nature, as is Belafonte's lifelong commitment to racial justice. A close friend of Dr. Martin Luther King Jr. (1929–1968), he has directly supported the Civil Rights Movement since the 1950s, and like White, leveraged his art and influence to fight for a more tolerant and just world.

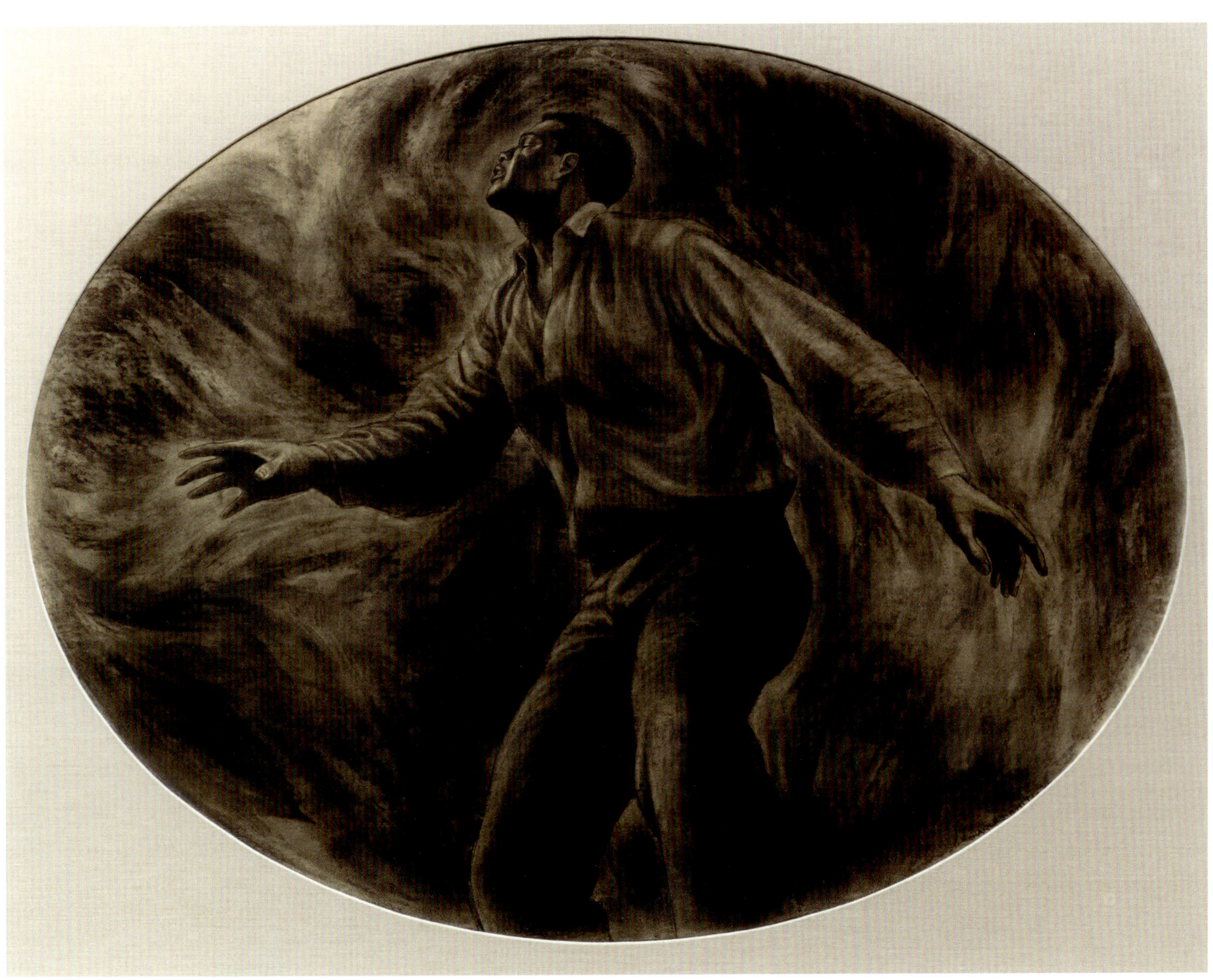

PLATE 20

Portrait (Head), 1967

Lithograph
27.31 x 18.42 cm (10 3/4 x 7 1/4 in.)

White began exhibiting at the Los Angeles–based Heritage Gallery in 1964. Founded by writer-turned-art dealer Benjamin Horowitz (1912–2004), this progressive gallery embraced the work of the Social Realists and did not shy away from a leftist agenda. It is not surprising, then, that Horowitz was one of White's most ardent champions and closest friends. Indeed, he was responsible for the publication of the artist's first monograph, *Charles White: Images of Dignity*, published by Ward Ritchie Press in 1967. Featuring a foreword by Henry Belafonte (B. 1927), an introduction by African American artist, art historian, and teacher James Porter (1905–1970), and a biographical essay by Horowitz himself, this important survey was printed in an edition of 250 numbered and signed copies, the first 125 of which contained autographed copies of *Portrait (Head).*

Created in 1967, this work is marked by a quiet poise and disarming tenderness. Though White's lithograph has, in the past, been referred to as a male head, the 2018 identification of the artist's source image makes clear that his subject is actually female. Specifically, the figure directly references Erica Anderson's 1955 photograph of an unknown woman, published in Eugene Exman's *The World of Albert Schweitzer*, a book that documents the Alsatian philosopher-physician's hospital in Gabon.[12] Beyond the physical beauty and allure of his subject's face, White may have seen in her a pointed message about the colonial, paternalistic, and racist aspects of the work of Schweitzer, whose writings leave no doubt that—though motivated by true humanitarianism and genuine piety—he viewed the African individuals for whom he was caring as vastly inferior. White alludes to this duality in the graphic density of his image, in which the alluring woman's downcast eyes and neutral expression create an insuperable barrier between us and her: We are allowed to gaze upon her but not to consume her or make her our own. By quoting just the woman's face and leaving out all other ancillary details shown in the source image—including her headscarf, beaded necklace, bared shoulders, and striped garment wrapped around her torso—White has heightened this sense of distancing, while simultaneously transforming his subject into a symbolic presence, unmoored from a specific time and place. Emerging from a dark net of hatching and cross-hatching marks and bathed in radiant light, she seems saintly, like a harbinger of hope in the face of despair. Clearly captivated by this anonymous woman's image (and all that she represented), White also incorporated her visage, with subtle changes, into both *Oh, Mary, Don't You Weep* (1956) and *J'Accuse #10 (Negro Woman)* (1966).

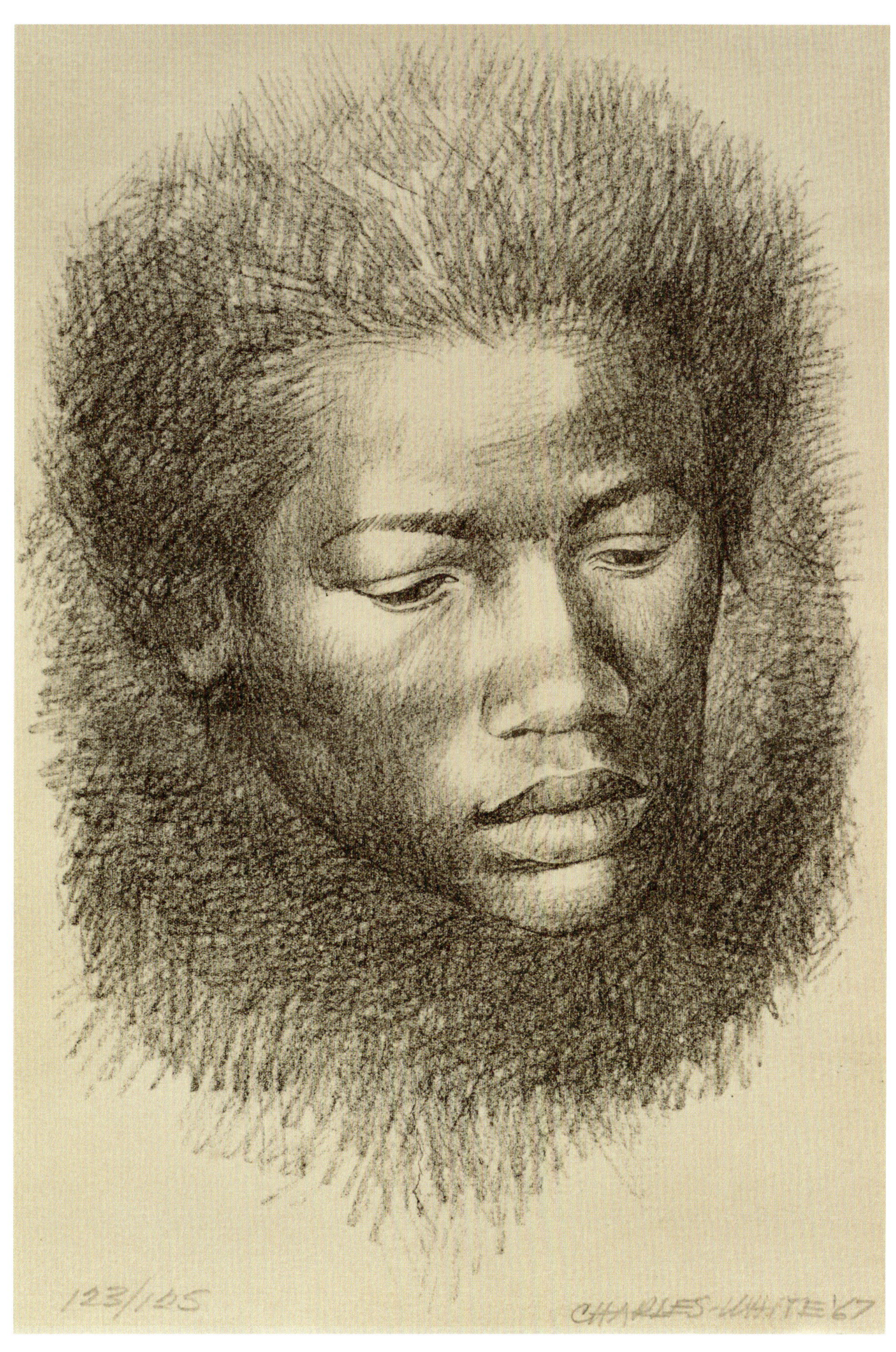
123/125
CHARLES WHITE '67

PLATE 21

Wanted Poster #5, 1969

Oil wash on paperboard
59.06 x 120.65 cm (23 1/4 x 47 1/2 in.)

Between 1969 and 1972 White created twenty-one thematically and aesthetically linked works whose powerful imagery was directly inspired by pre-Civil War "fugitive slave" posters and broadsheets advertising auctions of enslaved people. *Wanted Poster #5*, which was part of this series, features the beautifully rendered heads of three women of African American ancestry: "Ida," "Clotel," and "Edmonia." Ida, at left, is shown in near profile, her hair elegantly swept up and back and her eyes cast down in an expression of deep thought. The figure likely references renowned journalist, abolitionist, and anti-lynching activist Ida B. Wells (1862–1931), who favored a similar hairstyle and was known for her prodigious mind as well as her ardent commitment to the cause of Black advancement (she was one of the founders of the National Association for the Advancement of Colored People [NAACP]). Above her, White has stenciled "1619," the year that Angolans were first brought to Jamestown, Virginia, by Portuguese enslavers. Anchoring the center of White's composition is "Clotel," who looks out at us with defiant strength. Like the protagonist in Black playwright William Wells Brown's *Clotel; or, The President's Daughter: A Narrative of Slave Life in the United States*, White's eponymous figure is held captive by the political power and systemic racism of colonial America, referenced by the stars that encircle her. This imagery also echoes Brown's preface to his 1853 publication, in which he wrote, "On every foot of soil, over which Stars and Stripes wave, the negro is considered common property, on which any white man may lay his hand with perfect impunity. The entire white population of the United States, North and South, are bound by their oath to the Constitution, and their adhesion to the Fugitive Slave Law, to hunt down the runaway." Completing the trio is "Edmonia," who is shown in true profile and may pay homage to Edmonia Lewis (1844–1907), a gifted sculptor of African American and Native American descent. Stenciled above her is "19??," a pointed critique of the unequal treatment of Black individuals, which rhetorically asks when the injustices will end.

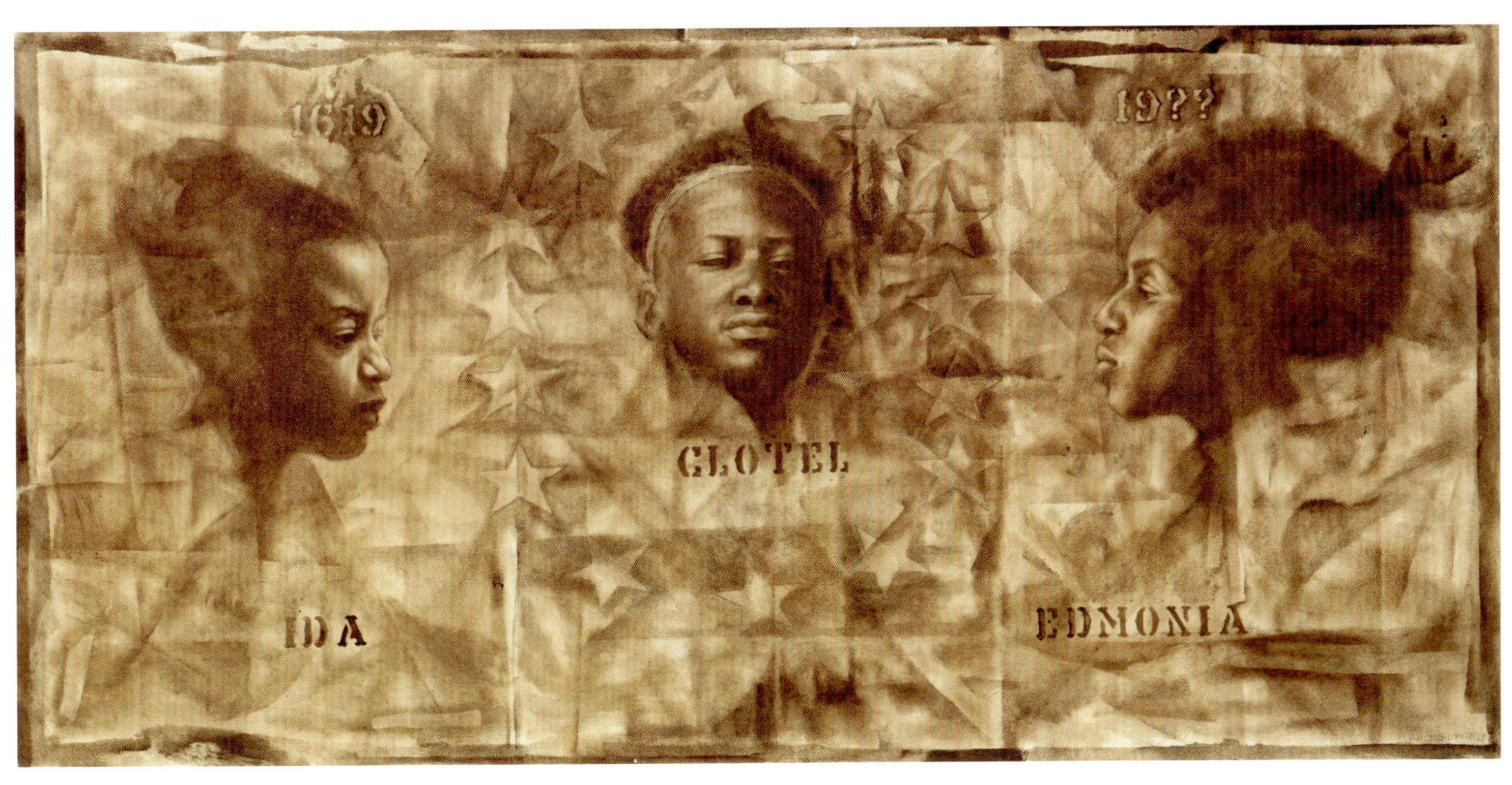
1619
19??
GLOTEL
IDA
EDMONIA

PLATE 22

Wanted Poster #14a, 1970

Lithograph
55.25 x 75.88 cm (21 3/4 x 29 7/8 in.)

Like White's *Wanted Poster #5* (PLATE 21), *Wanted Poster #14a* is part of a larger series of twenty-one images executed by the artist in oil wash on paperboard as well as lithography between 1969 and 1972. One of seven such lithographs, this piece was created in an edition of ten at Tamarind Lithography Workshop, a highly influential graphic studio established in Los Angeles in 1960 by artist and activist June Wayne (1918–2011). Despite Wayne's progressiveness, White was, at the time, the only African American at Tamarind, which funded his work there through a fellowship.

Pictorially and thematically linked to pre-Civil War broadsheets advertising "slave auctions" and published notices seeking the return of African American "fugitives," this lithograph showcases White's use of monochromatic sepia tones and all-over geometric patterning to evoke the faded, textured surfaces of aged documents and vintage photos. He employed these techniques to great effect in this work, which features an unnamed woman and child, each framed in a circular roundel and both endowed with expressions that, though distinct, telegraph the same sense of determined grit. Stenciled above the pre-pubescent boy is "1619," a reference to the year that Portuguese enslavers brought Africans from Angola to Jamestown, Virginia. "19??" appears at top right, book-ending the opposing date while also inviting the viewer to contemplate how and when racism might end. A bold "X" visually unites the two halves of the work, connecting the pair (who may be read as a mother and her son, but, more potently, may also be interpreted as representing all African Americans across time and space). White's graphic gesture also pointedly references the negation of Blacks by a homeland they did not choose, the effacement of enslaved people's identities by their enslavers, and the servitude of illiteracy, which continued to hold back people of color, many of whom were denied access to even the most basic of educational resources after the Civil War. Speaking in 1969, White explained that he had envisioned his *Wanted* series as highlighting parallels between contemporary FBI posters seeking Eldridge Cleaver (1935–1998) as well as other members of the Black Panthers and their historical antecedents. As curator Ilene Susan Fort notes, "The *Wanted Series* was White's most potent attack on the status quo."[13]

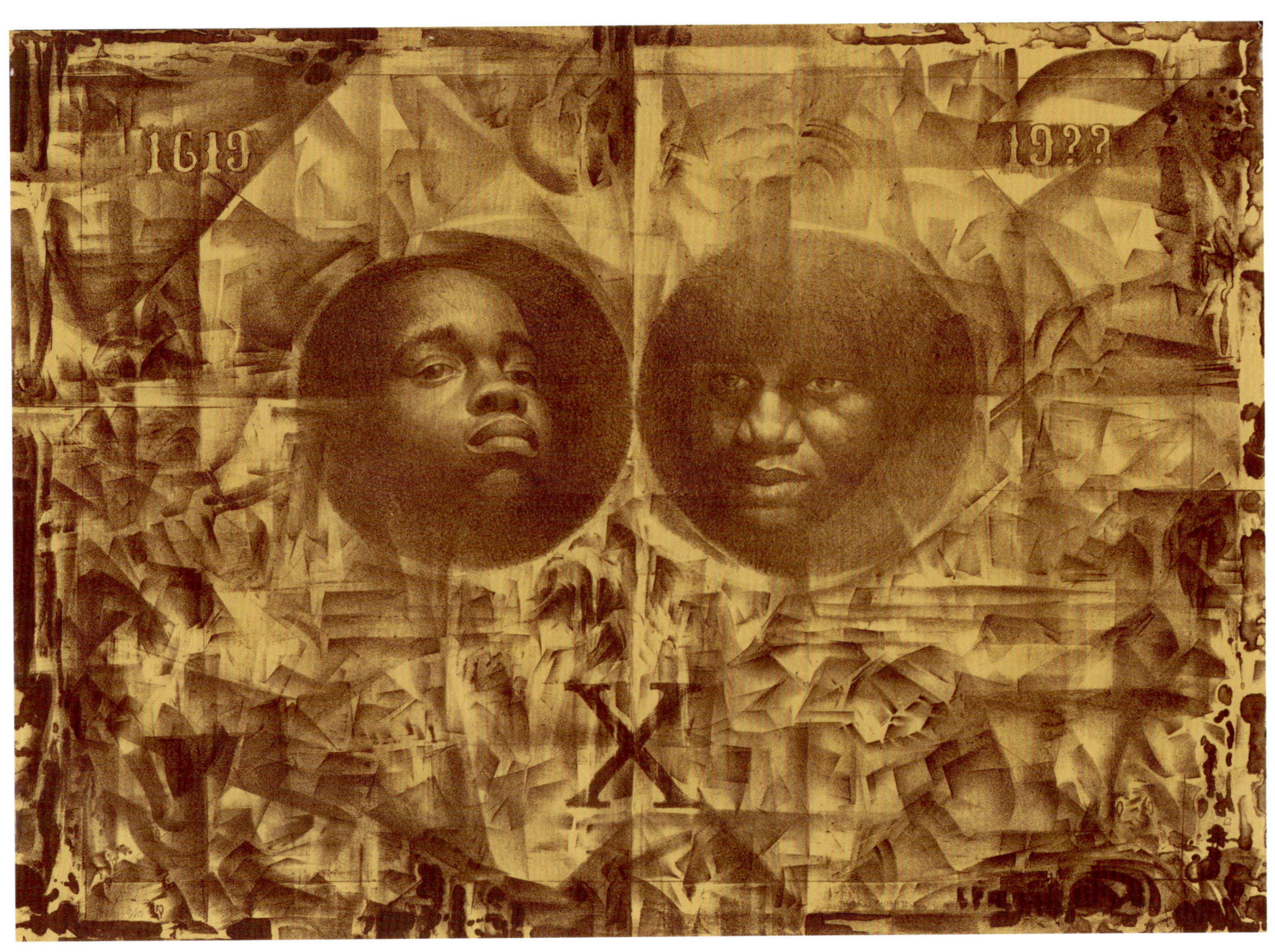
1619
19??
X

PLATE 23

Love Letter I, 1971

Lithograph
77.15 x 58.10 cm (30 3/8 x 22 7/8 in.)

Love Letter I was created by White in the last six years of his life as part of a limited series of three works bearing the same serialized name: *Love Letter I*, *Love Letter II*, and *Love Letter III* (PLATE 44). The focus in each of these images is a lone woman whom the artist transforms into a harbinger of powerfully complex messages. Here, White's protagonist dominates the upper register of the image field. She is presented frontally and engages our gaze directly with her own. The young woman's stern expression communicates both a seriousness of purpose and a steadfast determination. Her natural hair is arrayed in a soft afro, transforming her crown of curls into a secular halo that sets off the angular solidity of her features to great effect. A squared-off panel both conceals and reveals the woman's body, the curves and shapes of which are subtly suggested through White's faceted, neo-Cubist treatment of the area between her shoulders and mid-thigh region. Two roses hover in the center of the work, directly over her abdomen, a reference to the life-giving force within as well as to the strength, power, and dignity that White located in all women. Like other works created during the concluding decade of his career, *Love Letter I* includes a surprising pop of color—a pictorial gesture and aesthetic strategy that White increasingly embraced late in his career.

A supporter of activist causes throughout his life, White agreed to allow the National United Committee to Free Angela Davis and All Political Prisoners to use this image soon after it was created on pre-printed postcards addressed to Ronald Reagan (then governor of California). The postcards were part of a public defense campaign launched on behalf of Davis (B. 1944), a prominent educator as well as an active member of both the Black Panther and Communist parties, who had been arrested the previous October.

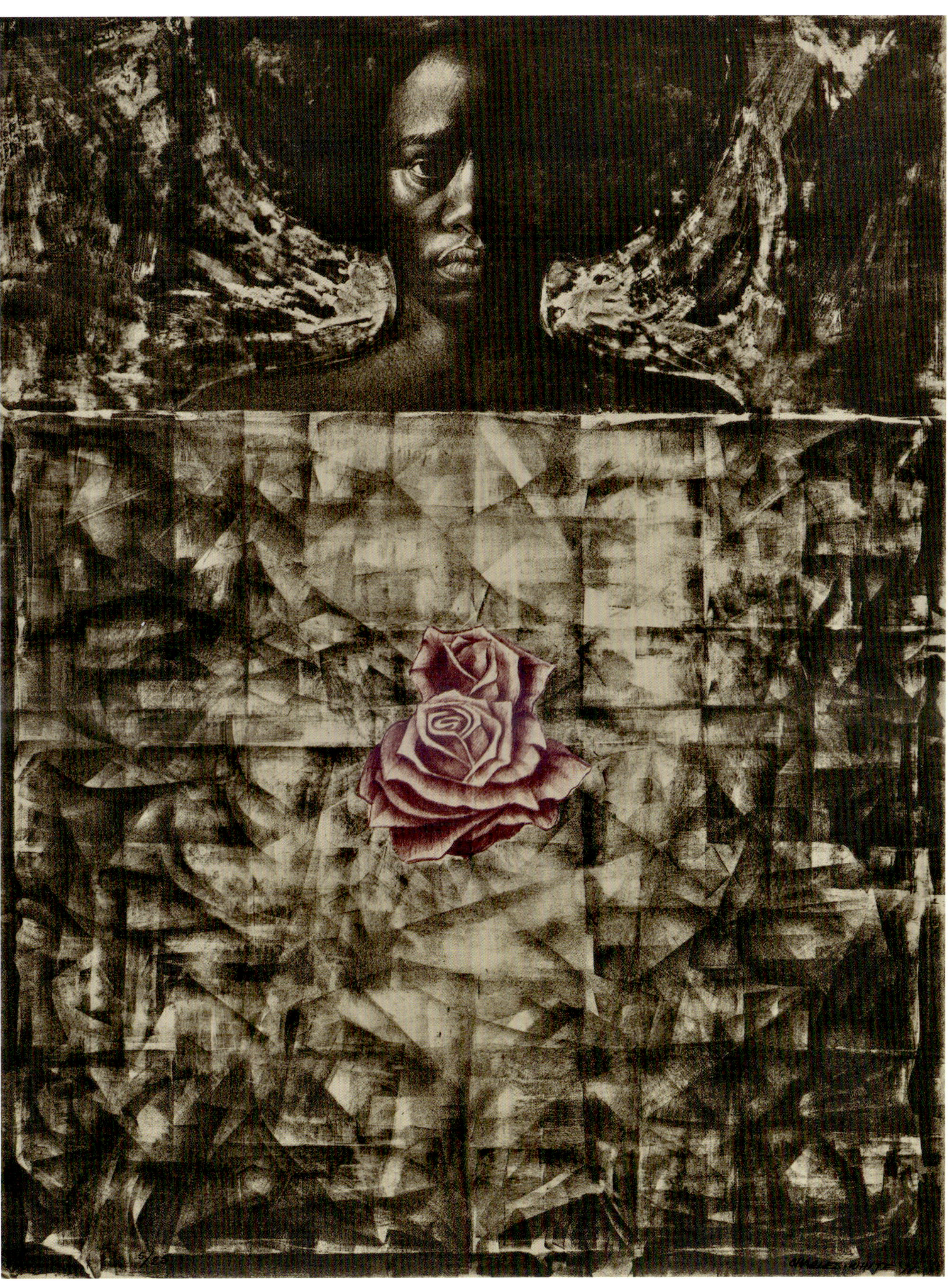

PLATE 24

Cat's Cradle, 1972

Etching
60.01 x 67.63 cm (23 5/8 x 26 5/8 in.)

Like *Missouri C* (PLATE 25), White executed this work just five years before his death, in the studio of his friend and Otis Art Institute colleague, printmaker Joseph Mugnaini (1912–1992). According to curator Mark Pascale, "[t]radition—artistic and otherwise—was important to White throughout his life. Not unexpectedly, he made his last prints in etching, a printmaking medium with a history dating back to the fifteenth century."[14] Pascale also observes that these works provided the artist with an opportunity to return to firm and controlled "mark making" after an extended period of time working with less decisive, more forgiving media.

White created multiple images of children—at rest, at play, or in the arms of their loving mothers—in a variety of media over the course of his career. While these works reflect the artist's persistent belief in the innocence of youth as well as his hope for a better tomorrow, they are no less sophisticated or challenging than the other images in his complex oeuvre. Here, for instance, a young Black boy, depicted in a shallow space and pushed close to the front of the picture plane, invites us into his world with a direct gaze and unflinching expression. Dressed only in shorts and seated on the ground with legs splayed before him, he leans against a pockmarked wall that creates an abstracted background. We have interrupted his game of Cat's Cradle, in which one creates a series of complex patterns in string by progressively shifting designs between outstretched or pinched fingers. Yet this image is no simple paean to the uncomplicated pleasures of youth. Rather, it is a deeply complex visual allegory. Consider, for instance, how the protagonist's feet are ensnared by two ropes that rise behind him and cross over his head, transforming the boy into a marionette whose agency—and by extension, his destiny—is controlled by an invisible puppeteer. The ropes may also be read as a reference to the gruesome legacy of lynching in America and further suggest that, despite the boy's innocence and youth, he is threatened by a dangerous snare. The very title of the work, too, is laden with meaning, as this was also the name of a widely read book published by Kurt Vonnegut (1922–2007) in 1963—a dystopic, apocalyptic satire that took on the Establishment and the status quo.

Despite the work's dark edge, White gives us cause for optimism. Just as he is controlled, so too does the boy exert his own will with the string he manipulates with his hands. And while the thin ropes rising behind him mark an "X" (possible references to the negation, disenfranchisement, and forced illiteracy suffered by African Americans) on the wall behind him, they also create a framing triangle (a powerful symbol in the history of Western Art), the apex of which rises toward the boy's head, seat of intelligence and control. White's young protagonist conveys sanguine poise in the face of unprovoked danger, thereby giving us a glimpse of the possible. Unlike White's earlier treatment of this same subject (a lithograph dating to 1965), the boy in this work seems to draw energy in toward his center rather than discharging it in an explosive gesture of release through his shoulders, arms, and hands. The net effect is one of concentrated calm and control.

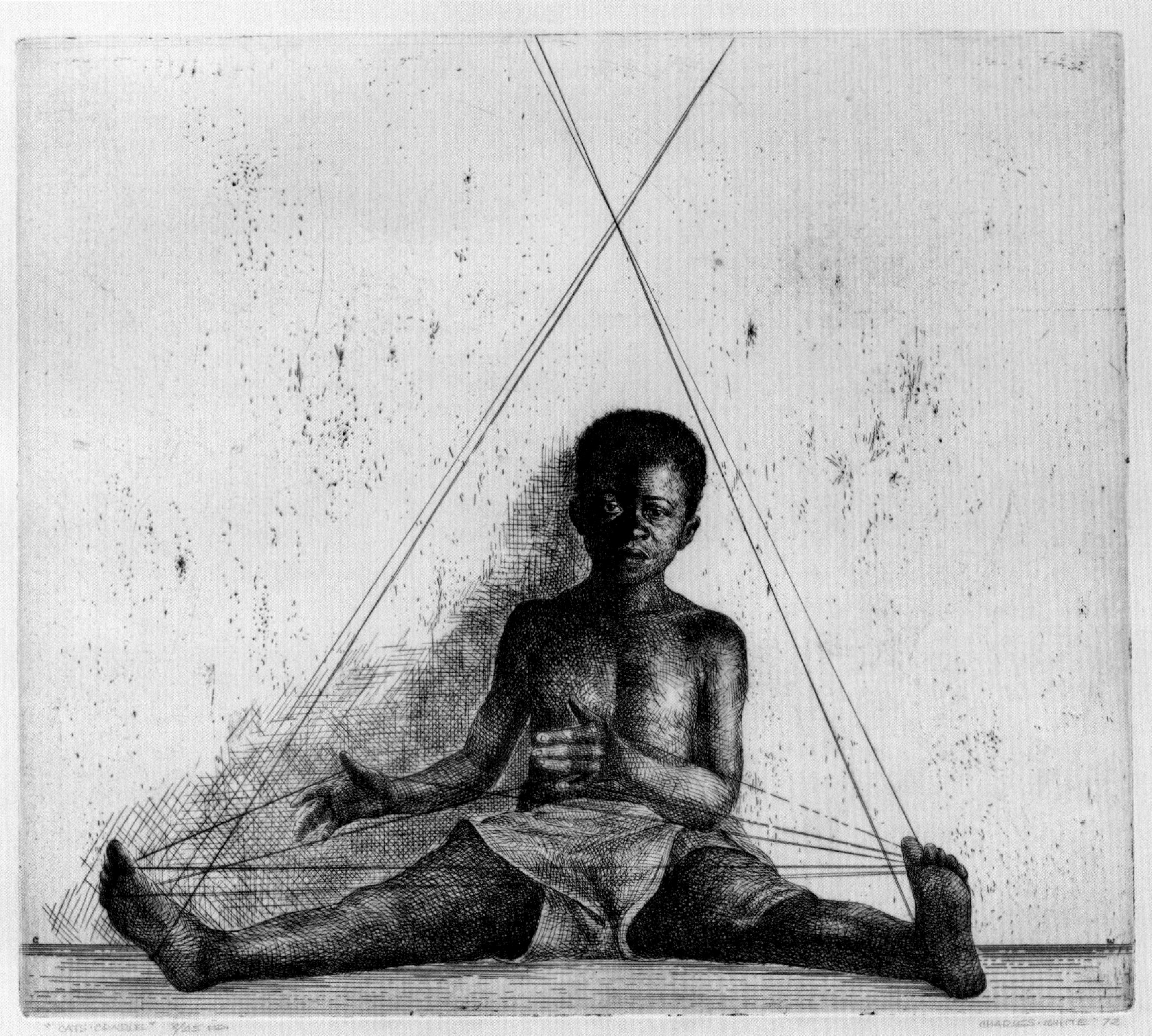
"CATS·CRADLE"
CHARLES·WHITE '72

PLATE 25

Missouri C, 1972

Etching
48.90 x 87.63 cm (19 1/4 x 34 1/2 in.)

Having suffered recurrent bouts of tuberculosis since 1944, White was advised by physicians to avoid painting out of concern that the associated fumes would aggravate his already vulnerable lungs. Health risks also kept the artist away from more noxious forms of printmaking, which involve corrosive acids used to "bite" into prepared metal plates and produces toxic gases. Despite his doctors' admonitions, White embraced etching anew in the late 1960s and 1970s, when he began creating decisive works with artist, illustrator, and Otis Art Institute colleague Joseph Mugnaini (1912–1992), who had mastered this challenging printmaking technique. Like *Cat's Cradle* (PLATE 24), *Missouri C* was executed in Mugnaini's studio in 1972. Also like the former, this work is marked by a graphic intensity that bears witness to White's remarkable skill as a draftsman.

Using a dense network of crosshatching (or closely placed, crossing lines), the artist created the illusion of three-dimensionality and perspectival depth. His subject is an African American woman, shown from the bust up in full profile. Her gaze is fixed on an unseen point on the horizon, and she is in a contemplative mood. Like the subjects of so many of White's works, this nameless woman is laden with symbolic meaning, including the artist's reverence for the dignity and strength of Black women as well as the fortitude, grit, and the hope a better tomorrow, referenced in the light that bathes this monumental figure's face and chest. Though we do not know the woman's identity, we do know White's source for her image: a photograph by Alwyn Scott Turner documenting passengers on a so-called Boblo Boat (steamboats that ferried people to Detroit's Boblo Island Amusement Park, which operated between 1898 and 1993) in *Photographs of the Detroit People* (1970), a copy of which White held in his personal library.[15]

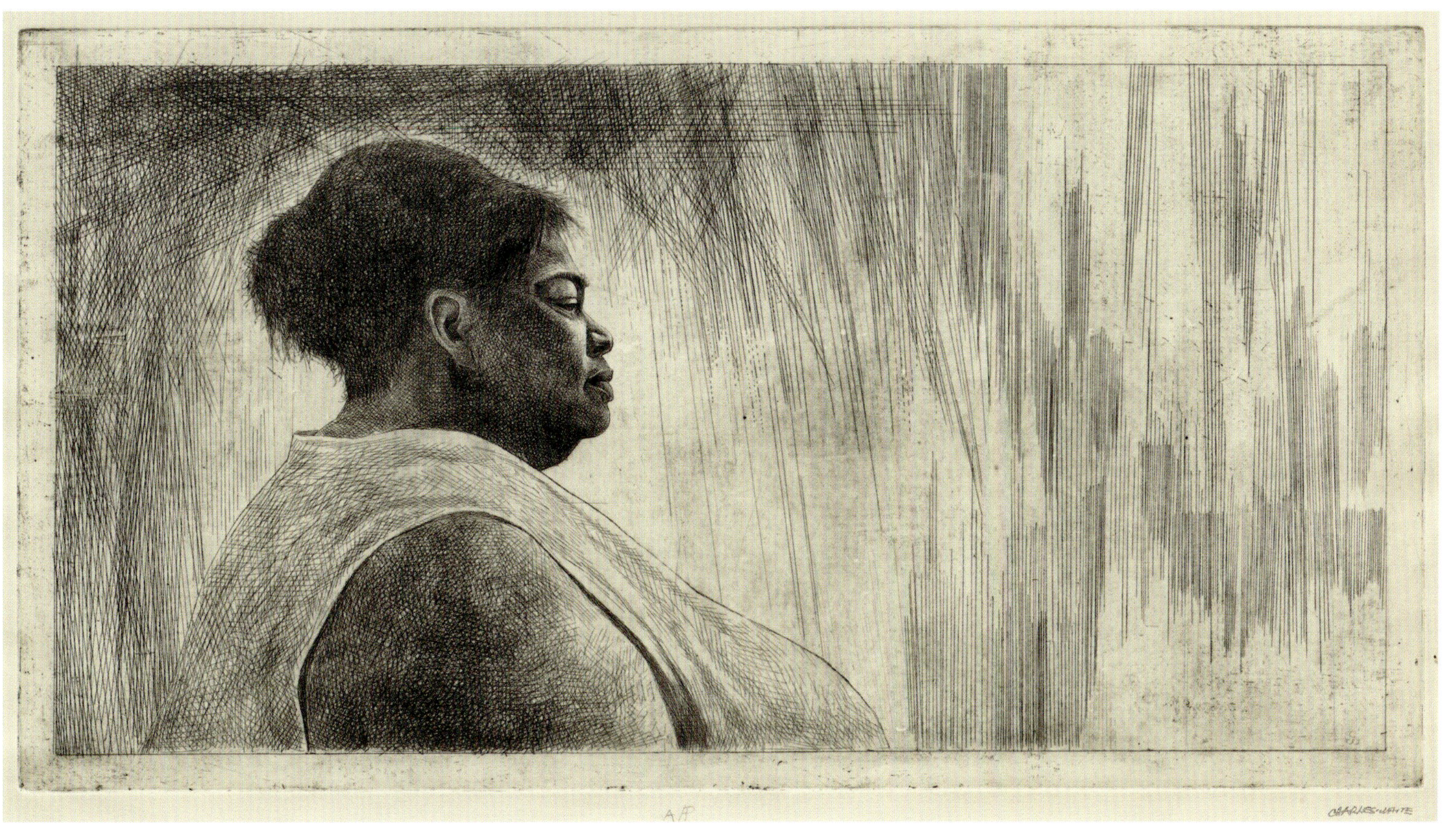

PLATE 26

Pope X, 1972

Etching
45.72 x 69.85 cm (18 x 27 1/2 in.)

As with White's earlier *Study for Pope X* (PLATE 12), this work invites us to consider what it would look like, and more significantly, what it would mean, if a Black man were elevated to the papacy, one of the most influential positions in the world. Interestingly, the artist chose to depict only the head of his subject in this image, suggesting that the figure has been decapitated. This visual innuendo, in turn, calls to mind not only Christian martyrs (in particular, John the Baptist, the first-century Christian saint whose head was presented to King Herod by his stepdaughter, Salome, on a salver), but more saliently, African Americans who sacrificed their lives in the name of Civil Rights and racial equality or had their lives taken from them simply because of the color of their skin. Depicted in profile, *Pope X*'s head is arranged at a thirty-degree angle, his heavy eyelids half closed. White's protagonist can be read as one who sacrificed his life for a higher cause, or alternatively, as a man immersed in prayer, lost in his thoughts, or perhaps gazing upon a celestial vision. What is evident is that our participation is not required to complete his meaning; his is a world unto itself, which the injustices of our mortal realm cannot penetrate or sully.

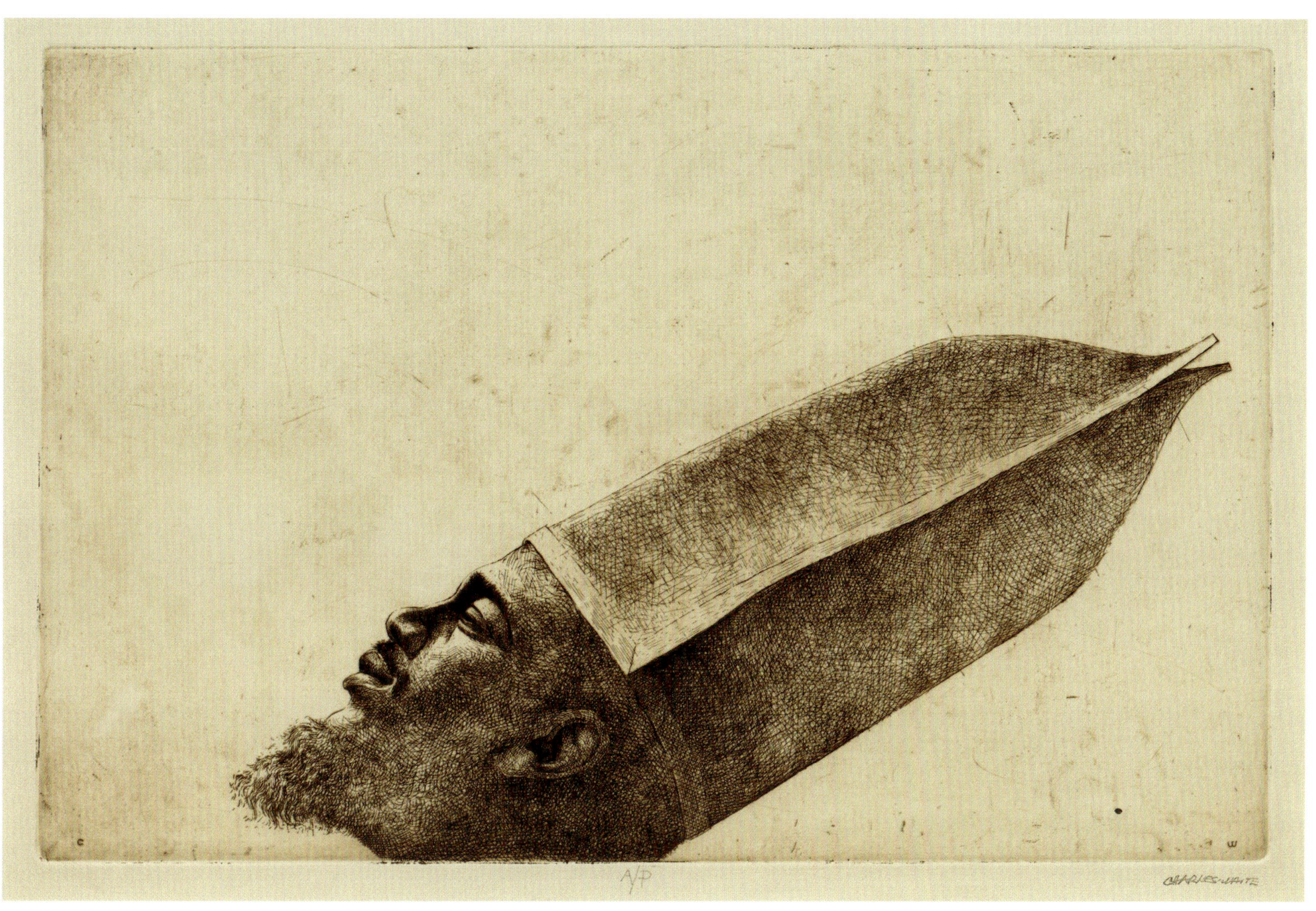
A/P
CHARLES-WHITE

PLATE 27

Vision, 1973

Etching on sterling silver plate
Image diameter: 19.69 cm (7 3/4 in.)

In 1969 White, in collaboration with the Los Angeles–based Heritage Gallery, published *I Have a Dream*, a portfolio of six lithographs including one entitled *Vision*. Reprinted on the overleaf of the portfolio cover was Langston Hughes's powerful poem "Harlem," which opens with the provocative question: "What happens to a dream deferred?" Among the answers this masterful writer, poet, and activist rhetorically invites us to ponder are "dry up," "fester," "stink," "crust and sugar over," "sag," or "simply explode." The works in *I Have a Dream* respond to these commanding lines in a manner that is itself poetic—an approach that characterizes much of White's oeuvre.

Four years after *Vision* was released as a lithograph, White issued a limited-edition version of this work etched onto sterling silver and bearing the same name. A dream-like image, *Vision* features the head and barely visible neck of a Black woman who lifts her chin and turns her gaze heavenward, toward a radiant glow in the upper left of the rounded image field. Though broad flames of light surround her, the effect is not menacing, but, rather, uplifting. The choice of support for this delicate image was perfect: Beyond the enhanced luminosity produced by the silver ground, the plate's spherical well was ideal for the original image, which had been conceived in a round format. His choice of shape, though unusual, was also laden with meaning, as the *tondo*, or circular image, was typically reserved for works celebrating marriage and childbirth—and, by extension, fecundity and maternal love—in Western European art. Like so many of the artist's other images of women, then, *Vision* not only speaks to the dreams of tomorrow but also to the critical role of courageous females (and mothers, in particular) in making those visions a reality.

Though visually consonant with White's *Nocturne* (an etching that also dates to 1969), this etching was clearly based on *Vision*. The marked similarities between the two works, however, may explain why the present piece is sometimes referred to as *Vision (Nocturne)*.

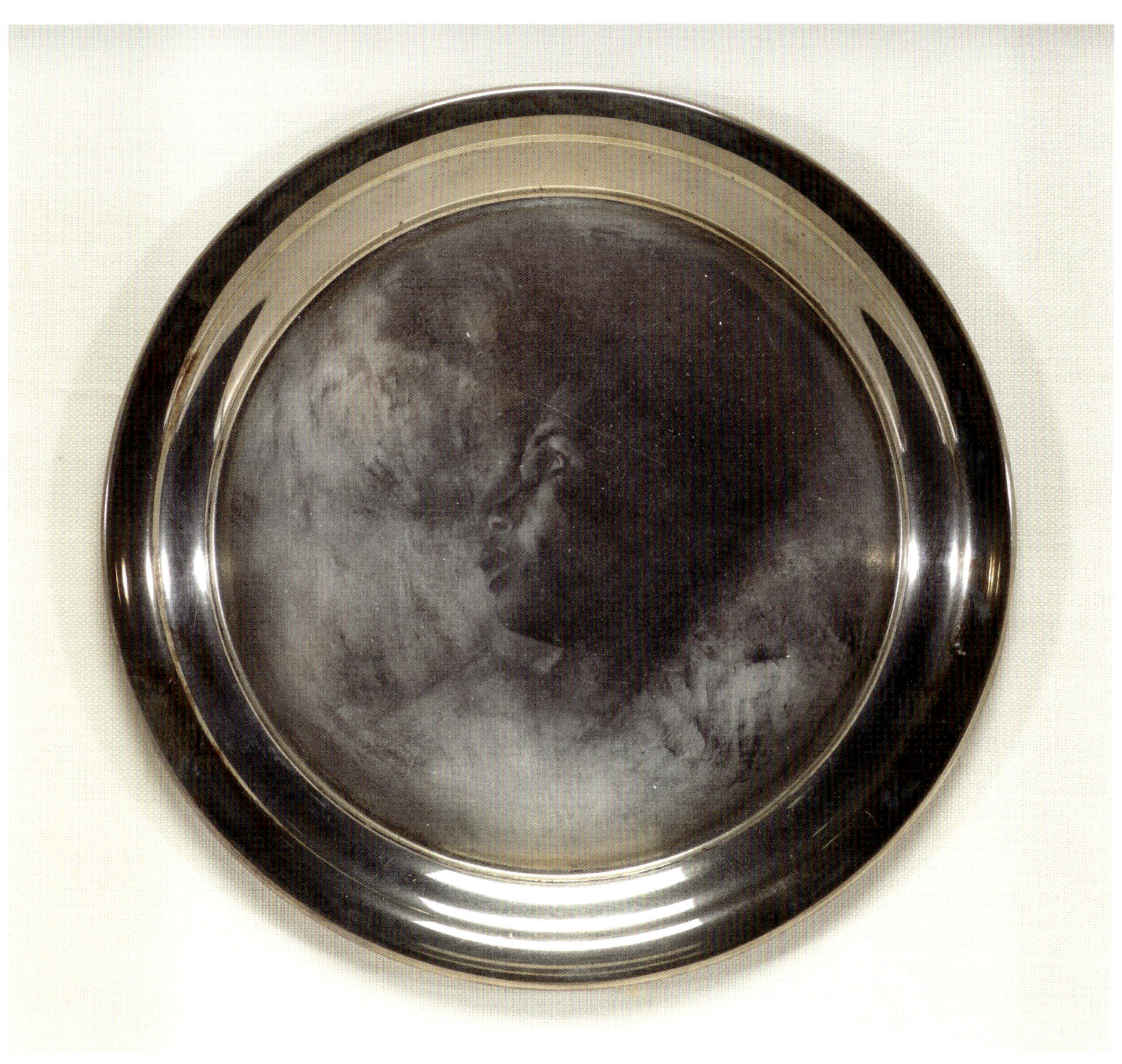

PLATE 28

Frederick Douglass, 1974

Etching
58.90 x 44.45 cm (23 3/16 x 17 1/2 in.)

Famed abolitionist and orator Frederick Douglass (1818–1895) was a subject to whom White returned multiple times over the course of his career, prominently featuring this towering historical figure in two of his murals (*Progress of the American Negro: Five Great American Negroes* [1939–40] and *The Contribution of the Negro to Democracy in America* [1943]) as well as in etchings such as this one. Presented in a roundel—a format used since Greco-Roman antiquity in Western culture to honor ancestors, heroes, or other illustrious figures—Douglass is turned slightly to the right. Crowned by his famously exuberant natural hair, he pierces us with his gaze. The sitter's stern set of mouth, like his furrowed brow, telegraph engaged concern, while Douglass's attire makes clear that he is an accomplished man of learning. Completed in 1974, this image resembles White's *System: Frederick Douglass* (PLATE 37), which White executed in oil wash on paperboard that same year. There are significant differences between the works, though, including his subject's deeper part and receding hairline in the latter. The works are also reversed. Even if allowances are made for the printing process (which creates mirror images), these images are distinct enough to belie the notion that either is a sketch for the other. They do, though, both reflect White's reverence for Douglass as well as his skill at not just capturing a likeness but also communicating important biographical details through meaningful visual cues.

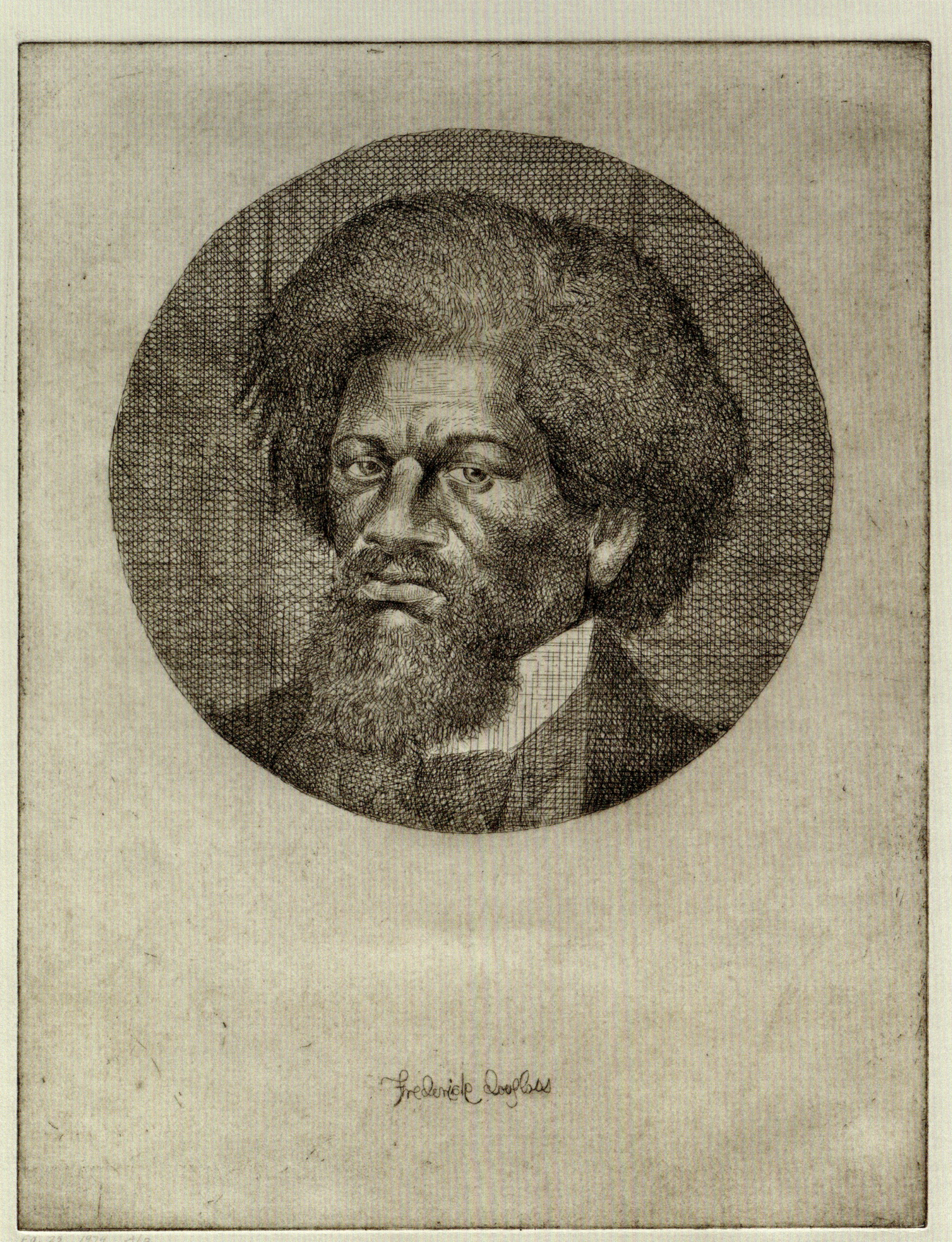
Frederick Douglass
CHARLES WHITE

PLATE 29

The First Generation (Arrival), 1974

Oil wash on paperboard
99.38 x 79.53 cm (39 1/8 x 31 5/16 in.)

First Generation is one of twelve oil wash on paperboard illustrations commissioned from White by the Johnson Publishing Company as illustrations for *The Shaping of Black America*. Released in 1975, this book was written by the prolific American historian, journalist, and longtime editor of *Ebony* magazine, Lerone Bennett Jr. (1928–2018), who had published earlier versions of the work's serialized chapters in *Ebony* between June 1969 and November 1974.

The First Generation opens Bennett's book, with a focus on what English colonist John Rolfe described as the "20 and odd" African people brought to North America. The author explains that these individuals were indentured servants whose status was then shifted to chattel enslavement: they were "the black gold that made capitalism possible in America."[16] White, referencing Rolfe via Bennett, commemorates the 1619 arrival of "20 INDENTURED BLACKS" in bold stencilling across the subject's midriff. Like the artist's other pieces associated with this project, *The First Generation (Arrival)* evokes faded notices and vintage broadsheets through its soft sepia notes, fictive creases and crinkles, and stenciled text, clear references to the posted bills and notices seeking fugitives who had escaped their enslavers.

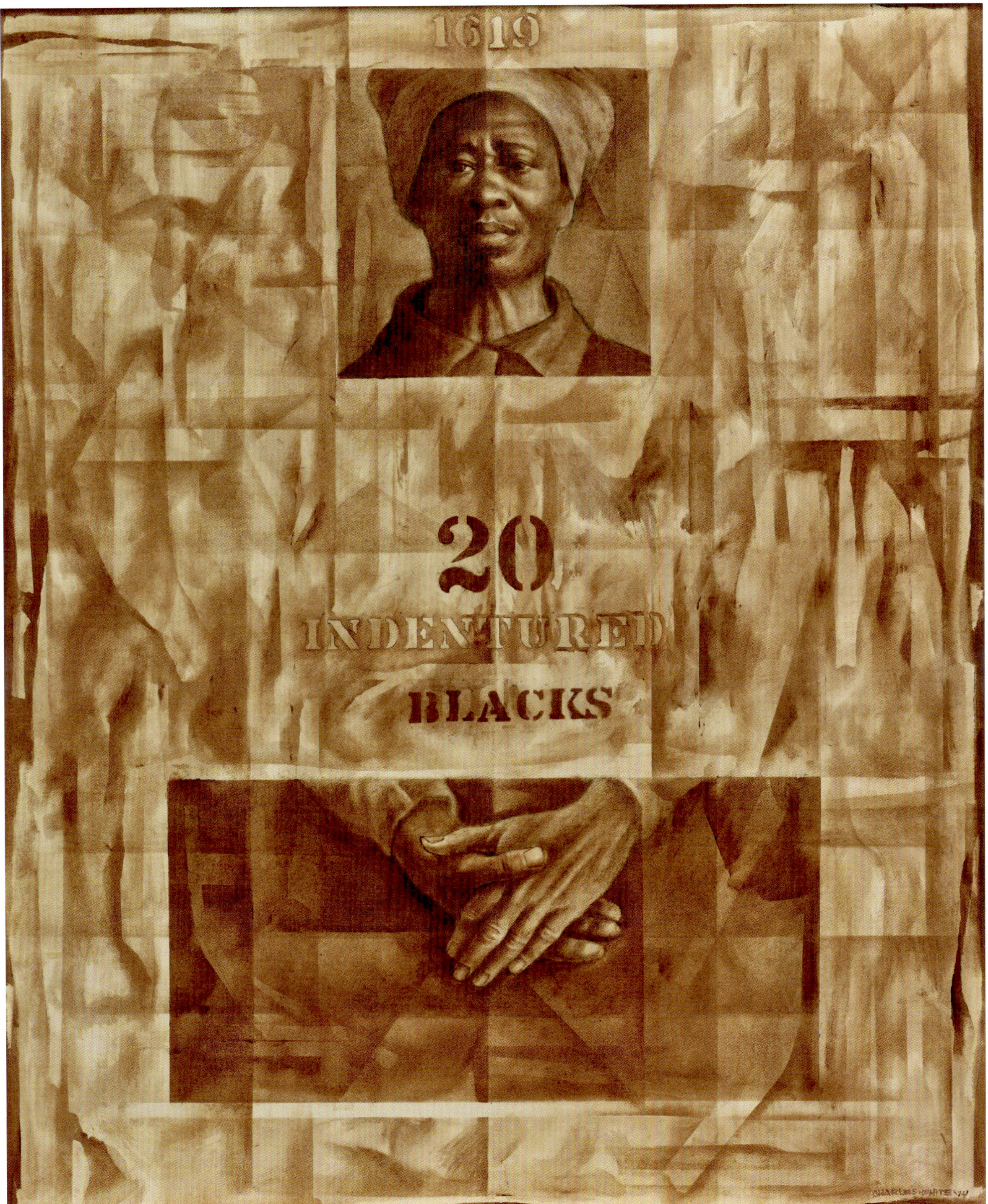
1619
20
INDENTURED
BLACKS

PLATE 30

White Servitude, 1974

Oil wash on paperboard
99.38 x 79.53 cm (39 1/8 x 31 5/16 in.)

Created by White under commission from the Johnson Publishing Company to open chapter two of Lerone Bennett Jr.'s *The Shaping of Black America* (1975), *White Servitude* features a lone female figure of ambiguous race. Dressed in a plain skirt and simple tunic with roughly shorn hair, she has large, expressive hands, at least one of which has an "X" prominently emblazoned on it. This letter potently references both the negation and invalidation of enslaved people by their enslavers as well as the mark used by illiterate individuals to sign their names. The latter allusion is particularly poignant since it was illegal for African Americans to learn to read and write in nearly every state between 1831 and the end of the Civil War, the result of legislation designed to keep the enslaved in a state of both physical and intellectual dependency by intentionally limiting their autonomy and self-sufficiency. Visible just behind the crown of the figure's head, a bold-faced inscription proclaims "SOLD." This powerfully concise word links White's image to pre-Civil War advertisements announcing the sale of enslaved human beings. So, too, does his use of sepia tones and geometric patterning throughout the composition, evocations of vintage handbills and old broadsheets advertising "slave auctions" or seeking the return of escaped "fugitives." Published in the November 1969 edition of *Ebony* magazine under the title "White Servitude in America," Bennett's writing explored the bondage of poor white Europeans in seventeenth-century America, a situation that, according to the author, would serve as a "the proving ground" for the enslavement of African Americans soon thereafter.

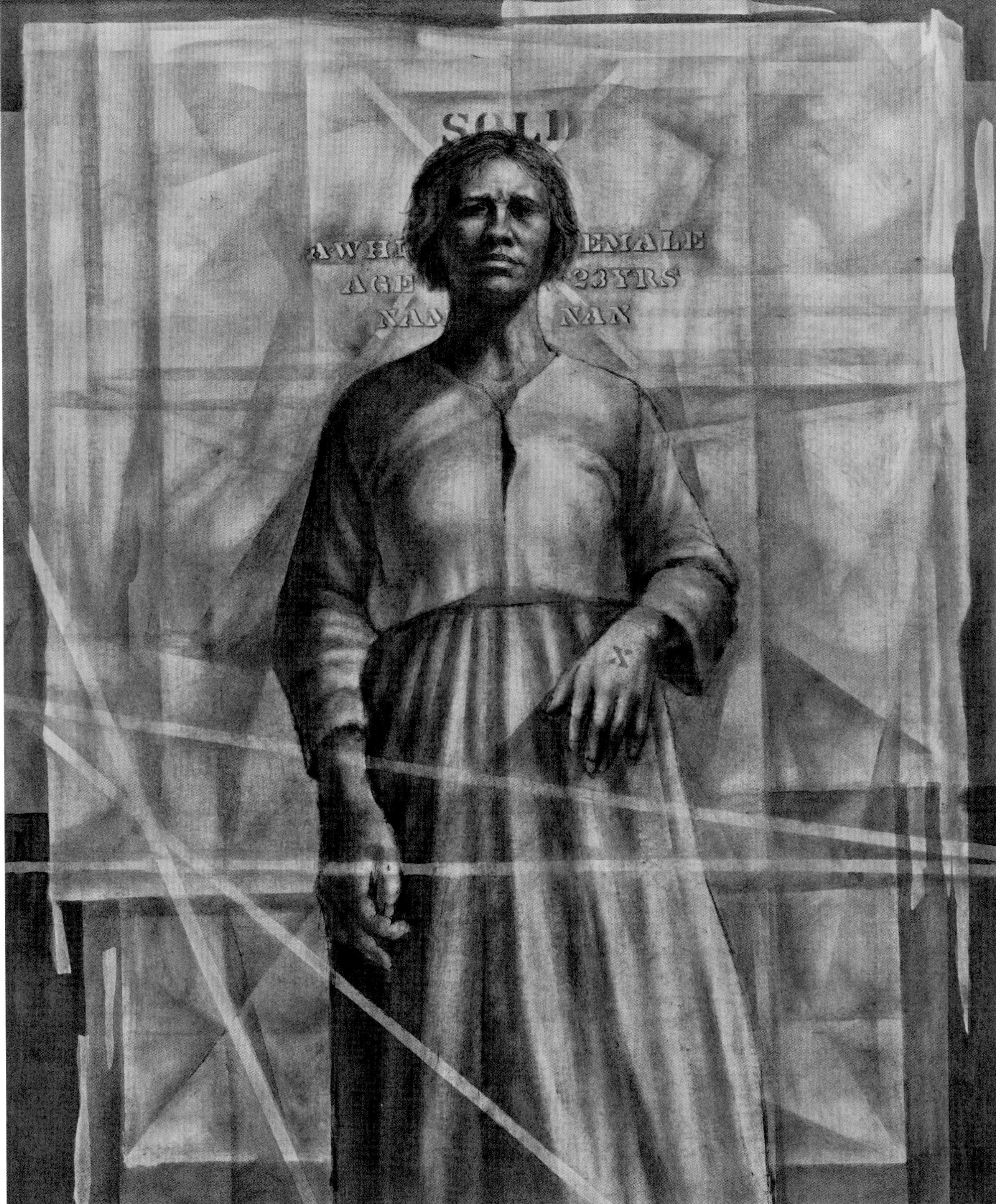
SOLD
A WHI
EMALE
AGE
23YRS
NAM
NAN

PLATE 31

The Road Not Taken, 1974

Oil wash on paperboard
99.38 x 79.69 cm (39 1/8 x 31 3/8 in.)

Opening the third chapter of Lerone Bennett Jr.'s *The Shaping of Black America* (1975), White's oil wash on paperboard image confronts the viewer with the fact that the enslavement of Africans and African Americans by European colonists and their descendants was neither preordained nor inevitable. Rather, "[t]he race problem in America was a deliberate invention of men who systematically separated blacks and whites in order to make money."[17] Here White literally embodies that choice: In the upper register, a figure of ambiguous race and gender (and therefore a stand-in for all oppressed peoples) stiffly faces us, staff in hand. The figure's posture is one of resignation, the expression one of sorrow. Their body partially obscures a word that emerges, miragelike, from the background: This is the metaphorical SOU[TH], where progress is halted and humanity is condemned to the same despondency that is imprinted on the protagonist's face. An active, energized figure—also androgynous and of unclear ancestry—occupies the lower half of the pictorial field, striding forward with purpose, chin lifted in defiant optimism, eyes on the horizon. This figure moves toward the NOR[TH], where, despite the fact that racist strictures are still in place, Black Americans have more opportunities for self-actualization, professional advancement, and personal fulfillment. Like the other works commissioned from White by the Johnson Publishing Company for Bennett's book, this image references crinkled and aged "slave auction" handbills and "fugitive slave" notices through its muted sepia palette and faceted, geometric patterning in the background.

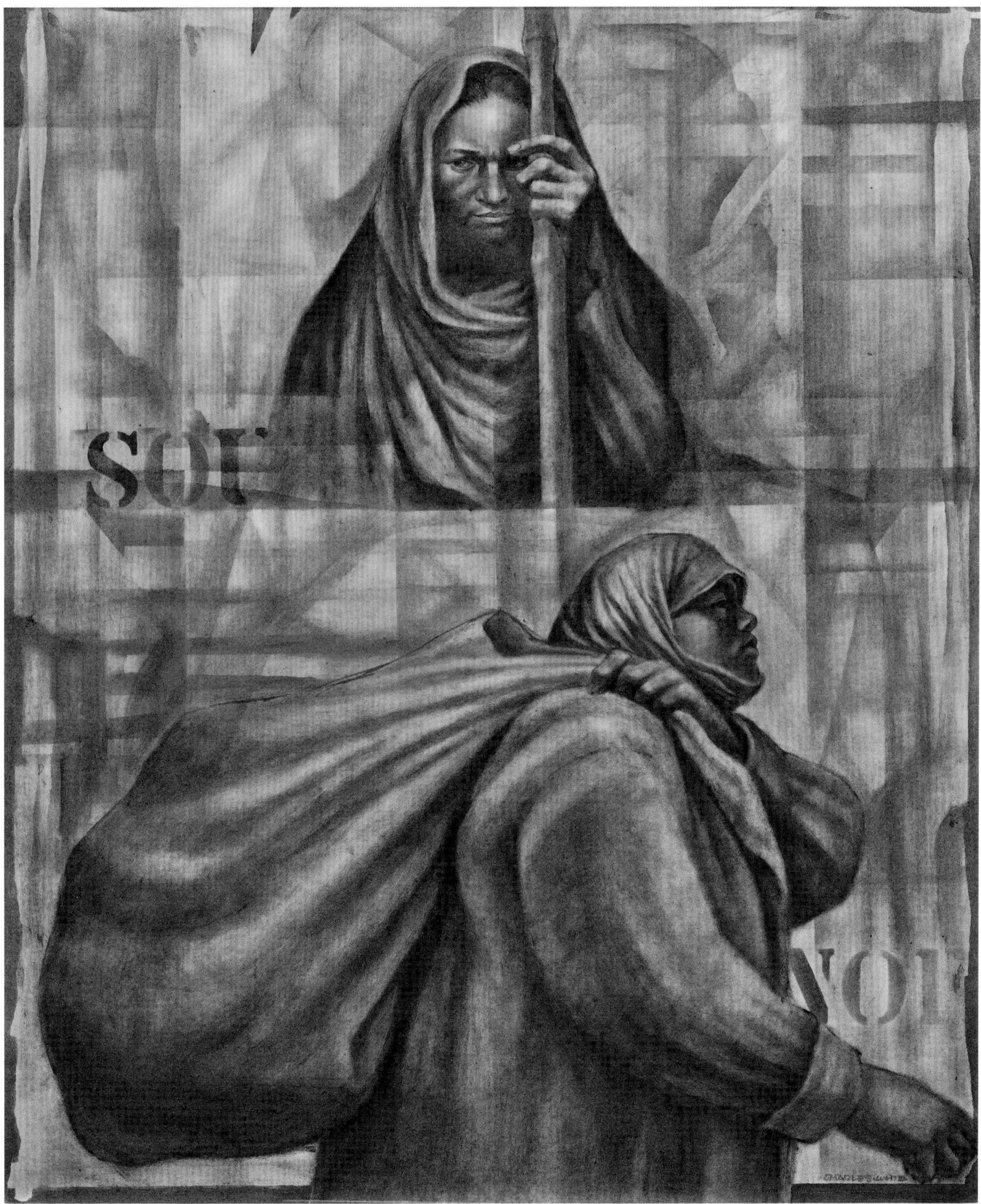
SOU
NOI

PLATE 32

Red and Black, 1974

Oil wash on paperboard
99.06 x 79.53 cm (39 x 31 5/16 in.)

Like the other chapter openers commissioned from White by the Johnson Publishing Company for Lerone Bennett Jr.'s *The Shaping of Black America* (1975), this monochromatic work is visually sparse but iconographically expansive. A group of three individuals arranged in a triangular formation occupy center stage. Though this trio is physically linked and quite literally overlap, each seems to occupy their own distinctive physical and psychological space. On the left, a woman of African heritage wears a cloak that obscures all but her face. She is turned at a forty-five-degree angle against the picture plane with an ambiguous expression that seems to toggle between wariness and hope. A man, also of apparent African descent, stands on the right, a full head lower than his female counterpart. Shown in profile, he, too, wears a wrap; his garment, however, reveals his body, rather than concealing it, by encircling his chest and far shoulder and emphasizing the top portion of his muscular arms. Like his feminine foil, the man's expression is indeterminate but clearly serious. An Indigenous American male, presented in attire meant to signal his indigeneity, marks the apex of this human triangle. Wearing a traditional breastplate, braids, and feathers, he engages us with a powerfully direct gaze.

Geometric forms behind the group function as a unifying backdrop while also conjuring such disparate sources as Britain's Union Jack, the flag of the Confederacy, and textiles from Africa as well as Indigenous America. A bullseye surmounts the group, encouraging the viewer to think about targets (as well as the targeted), infinity, perfection, and even Pop Art, as the motif had been rendered famous by Jasper Johns (B. 1930) just a decade earlier. Paralleling the chapter in Bennett's book for which this work was created, *Red and Black* references the exploitation and violence visited on people of color as well as the bonds of mutual support and volatile jealousies that simultaneously united and separated African Americans and Native Americans.

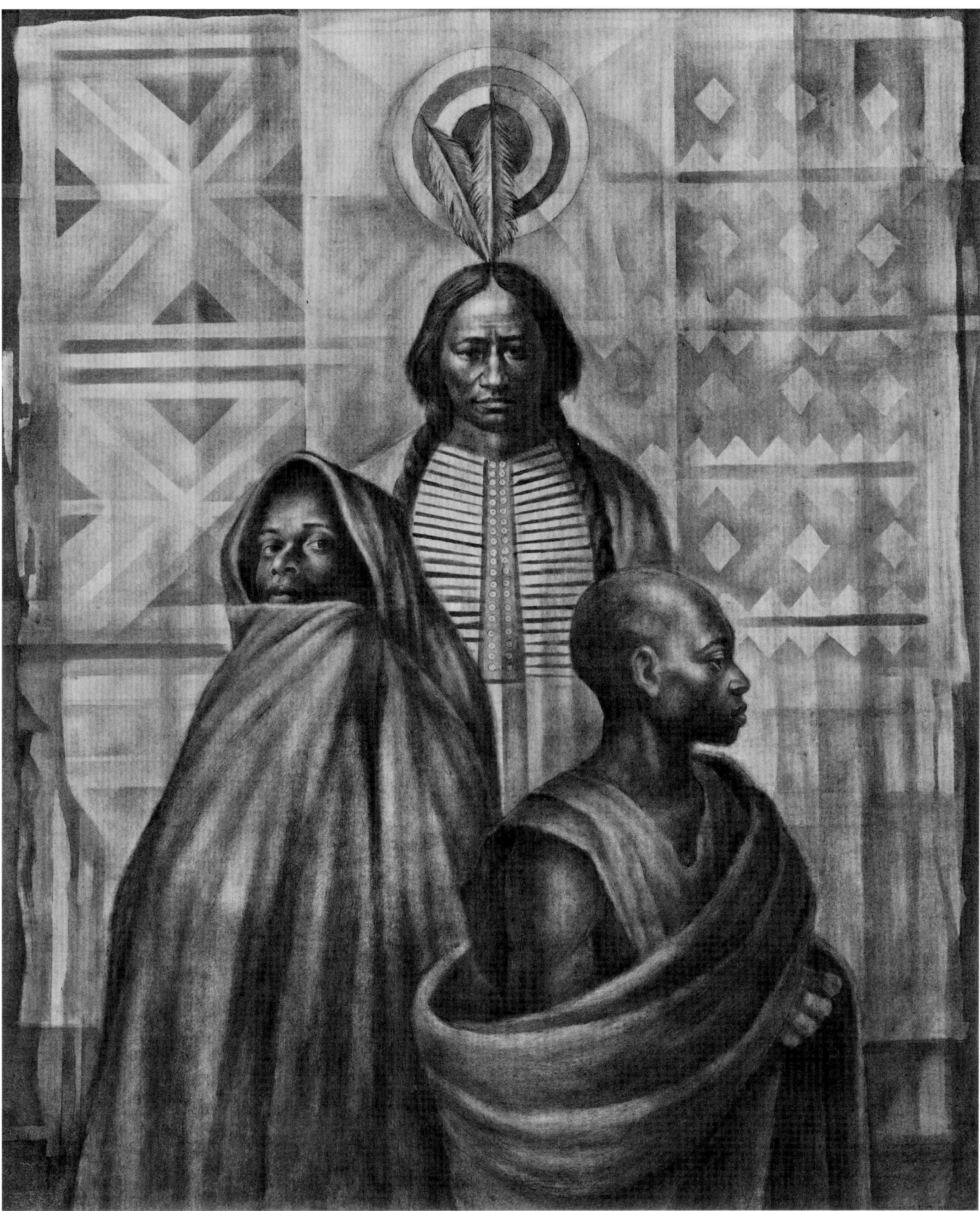

PLATE 33

***The Black Founding Fathers: Capt. Paul Cuffe*, 1974**
Oil wash on paperboard
64.14 x 42.86 cm (25 1/4 x 16 7/8 in.)

PLATE 34

***The Black Founding Fathers: Rev. Richard Allen*, 1974**
Oil wash on paperboard
64.14 x 42.86 cm (25 1/4 x 16 7/8 in.)

The Black Founding Fathers: Capt. Paul Cuffe and *Rev. Richard Allen* were both created to serve as a single opener for chapter five of Lerone Bennett Jr.'s *The Shaping of Black America* (1975). An influential abolitionist, philanthropist, and ship merchant, Cuffe (or Cuffee) (1759–1817) was, at the height of his career, one of the wealthiest African Americans of his generation. Born a free man on Cuttyhunk Island (Massachusetts), he was deeply devoted to the cause of Black emancipation and enfranchisement and directly engaged with the communities of freed slaves established by Great Britain in Sierra Leone. Unlike Cuffe, Allen (1760–1831) was born into enslavement. He paid $2,000 for his freedom in 1780, by which time he had already been directly involved with the Church for a number of years. Allen went on to found the Mother Bethel African Methodist Episcopal Church, which, under his leadership, merged with other African Methodist churches to form the African Methodist Episcopal (AME) Church, of which he was named bishop.

White depicts both men in roundels (a format associated with honor, pride, and dignity) placed in the upper half of the pictorial field with their names stenciled below. Cuffe is represented in near-profile while Allen is oriented frontally. Their elegant attire speaks to their respective successes and elevated stations in life, and both appear deep in contemplative thought. As such they are perfect exemplars, aptly illustrating the cultural, educational, and religious achievements of prominent eighteenth-century African Americans Bennett highlights in the related chapter of his text.

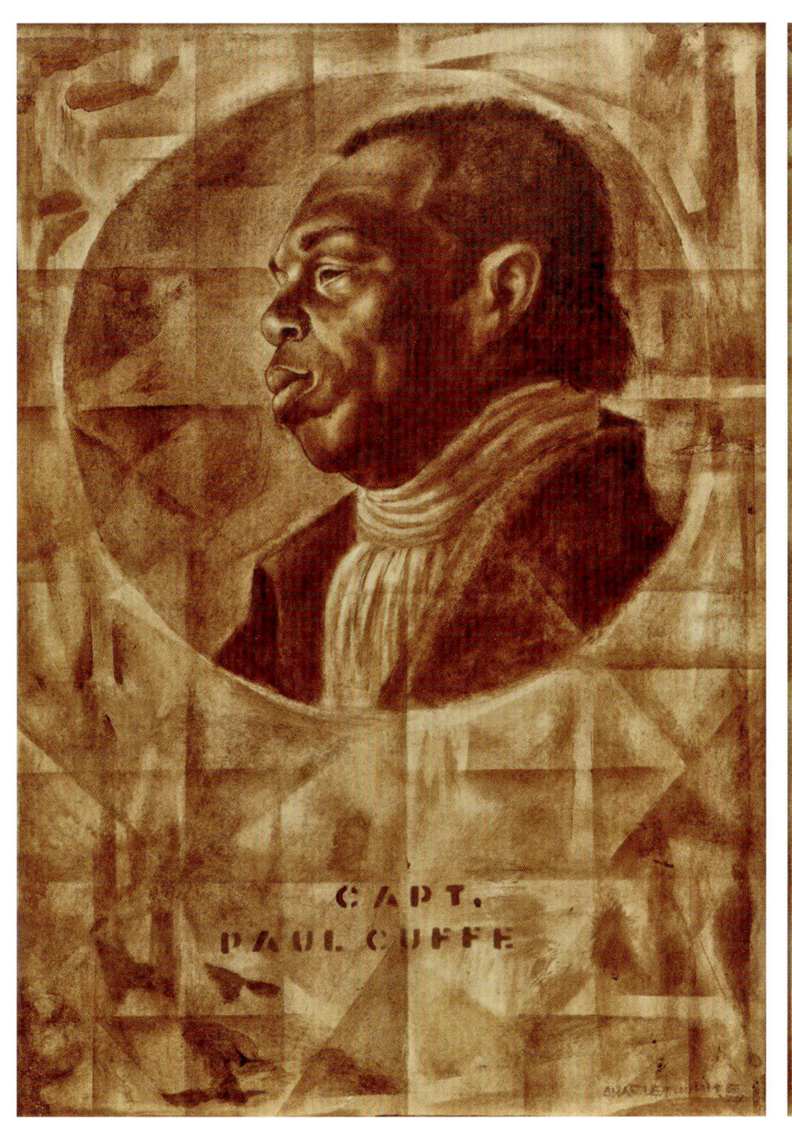
CAPT.
PAUL CUFFE

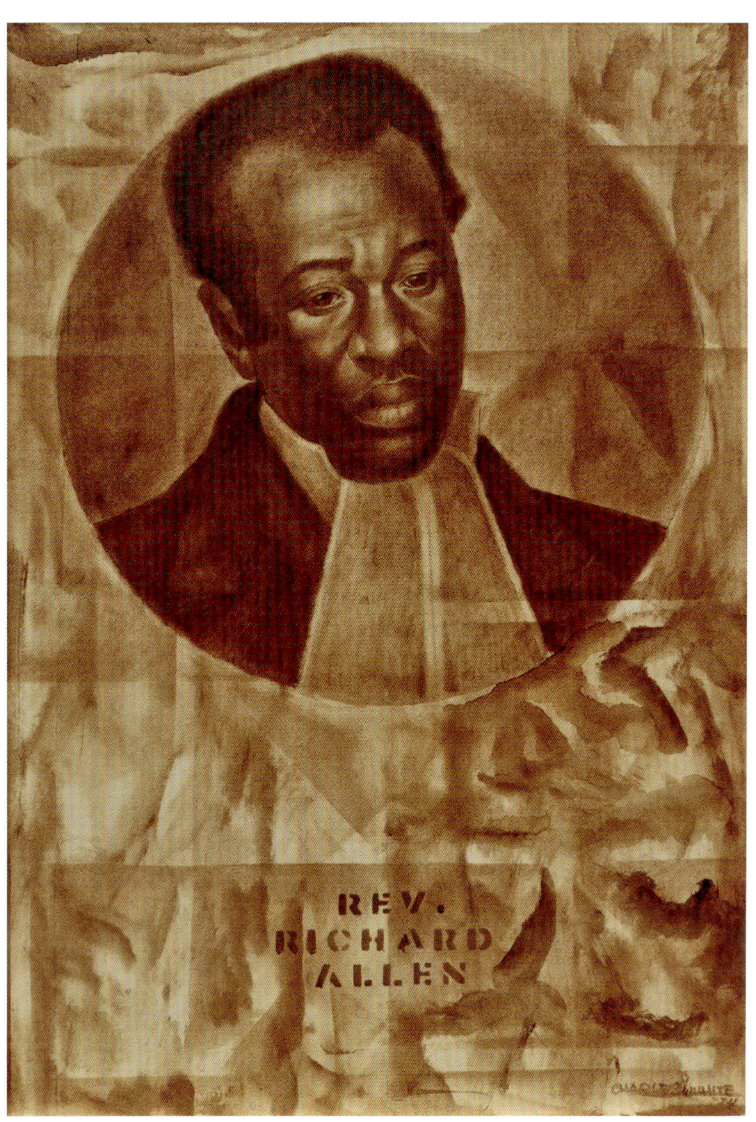
REV.
RICHARD
ALLEN

PLATE 35

The World of the Slave: Harriet Tubman, 1974

Oil wash on paperboard
64.45 x 42.86 cm (25 3/8 x 16 7/8 in.)

White created multiple images of the celebrated American abolitionist and Underground Railroad "conductor" Harriet Tubman (CA. 1822–1913) over the course of his prolific career. Some of these works were more allegorical in nature—casting her, for instance, as a modern-day Moses—while others, like this portrait bust, are more straightforward. Created as the opener for chapter six of Lerone Bennett Jr.'s *The Shaping of Black America*, this sepia-toned oil wash on paperboard image portrays a woman of concentrated strength and dignity. Her eyes are cast down, but not in an expression of sorrow or shame. Rather, this remarkable historical figure appears deep in thought, reflecting, perhaps, not only on the inhumanity of enslavement but also on strategies for leading her next group of individuals toward freedom. Alternatively, she may be contemplating the rich legacies that African Americans created in our country, in keeping with Bennett's writings. The author, in the chapter with which this image is directly associated, noted:

> Out of the world the slave made, out of his creative responses to a total attempt to destroy him and dehumanize him, came some of the deepest vibrations born this side of the seas. And these vibrations, expressed in folklore, song and dance, expressed in flights of the spirit and the soul, changed the culture and the social terrain of America. This is only another way of saying that the mark of the slave is deep in the flesh of every American. It is another way of saying that America is, in large part, what it is because of what it tried to do to the slave and what the slave did to what was done to him. It is another way of saying that the institution of slavery…is the key to the meaning of America.[18]

Wearing a distinctive headscarf and simple collared shirt layered under a darker garment, Tubman is presented in a roundel, a format associated—since the time of antiquity in Western culture—with dignitaries and venerated ancestors. The *tondo* —or round picture format—was also used in the European Renaissance for celebratory paintings proffered to new brides and mothers. In this instance, White may be alluding to a metaphorical birth (or, more accurately, rebirth): that of enslaved people, liberated by this extraordinary woman. Like the other images the artist created under commission for Bennett's book, the background here purposefully evokes vintage photos and aged papers while Tubman's stenciled name conjures up old "Wanted" posters used in the pursuit and intended recapture of "fugitives" who had escaped their enslavers.

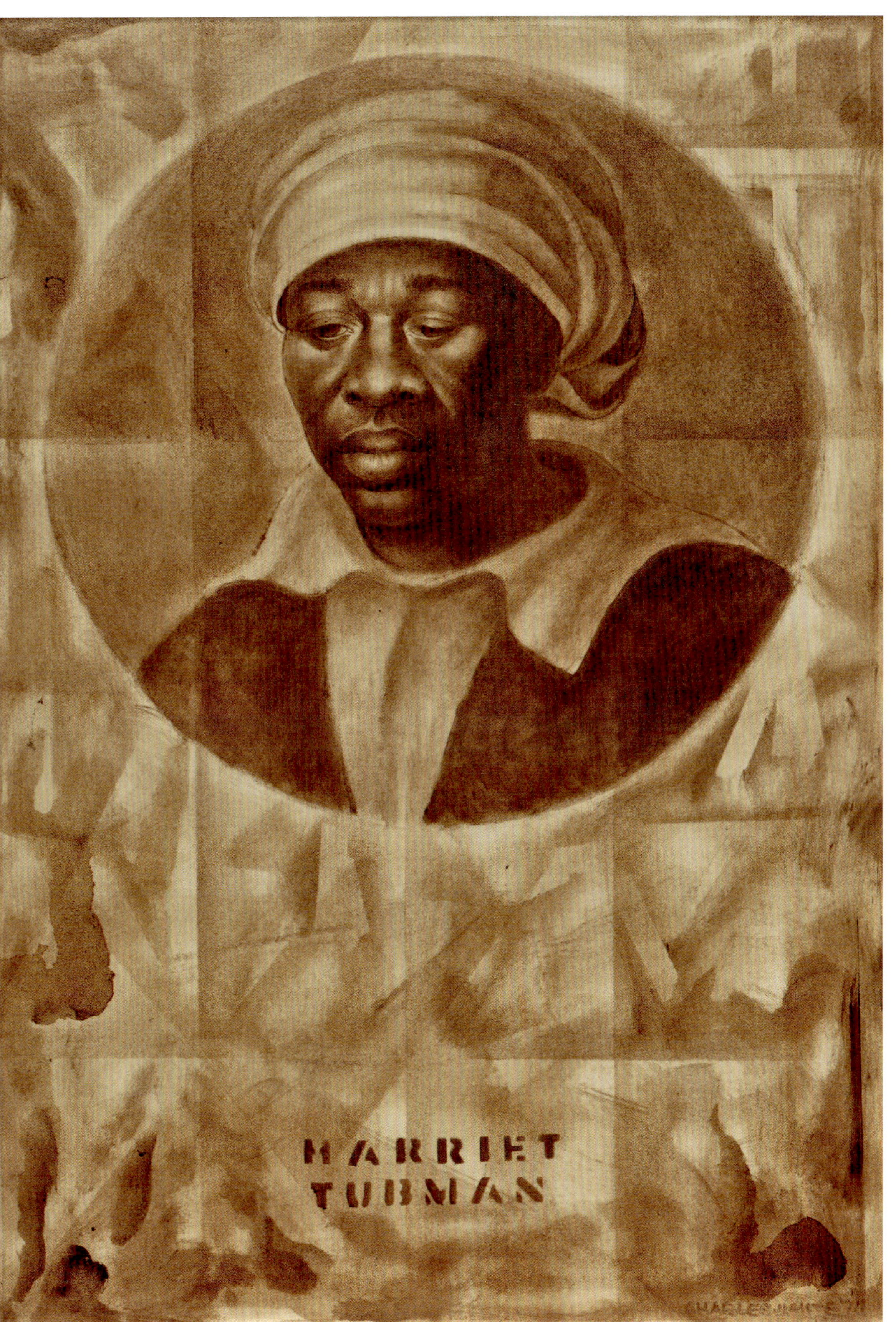
HARRIET
TUBMAN

PLATE 36

Jubilee, 1974

Oil wash on paperboard
99.22 x 79.06 cm (39 1/16 x 31 1/8 in.)

Used as both the opener for chapter seven of Lerone Bennett Jr.'s *The Shaping of Black America* (1975) as well as the book's cover image, *Jubilee* features a broadly grinning man with a toddler joyously hoisted on his shoulders. Like all the works in the series (created under commission from the Johnson Publishing Company), White executed this image in oil wash on paperboard, positioning his protagonists before an abstracted backdrop. Created in thin layers of oil, vigorously worked and reworked by the artist, the sepia ground is marked by radiating lines that conjure the fold marks in old paper, a reference to "Wanted" posters seeking "fugitive slaves" and flyers for "slave auctions." It also features a spangle of eight visible stars, an allusion, perhaps, to the "Stars & Bars," a colloquial name for the first flag of the Confederate States of America, which had seven stars and was flown between 1861 and 1863. The artist's oblique reference may be interpreted as an indictment of the South's steadfast championing of the institution of slavery in our nation—a stance that catalyzed the American Civil War, which White overtly references by stenciling "1865" above his subjects' heads.

White's protagonists are boldly frontal and clearly jubilant. But the man's posture, in particular, is complicated by layered meanings, not least, his posture of supreme vulnerability (the same pose assumed when law enforcement officials command one to "put your hands in the air"). These contradictions are addressed in Bennett's associated chapter, in which he discussed "the underside of the Jubilee." He writes:

> [I]f we are to assess the meaning of [federal emancipation]...then we must see it not only as a time of shouting and dancing, but also as a time of suffering and deprivation. We must see it...as a time of extravagant expectations and heartbreaking disappointments, a time when perhaps the greatest hope this world has known rose like dew from the unpromising soil of cataclysmic social upheaval that brought in its wake blood, tears, separation, smallpox, dysentery, cholera, hunger, and mass destitution.[19]

It is fascinating to note that White sketched an unfinished figure on the back of this image; a cloaked Black individual of ambiguous gender, who is reminiscent of the artist's earlier treatment of figures such as Harriet Tubman (ca. 1822–1913) and Sojourner Truth (ca. 1797–1883).

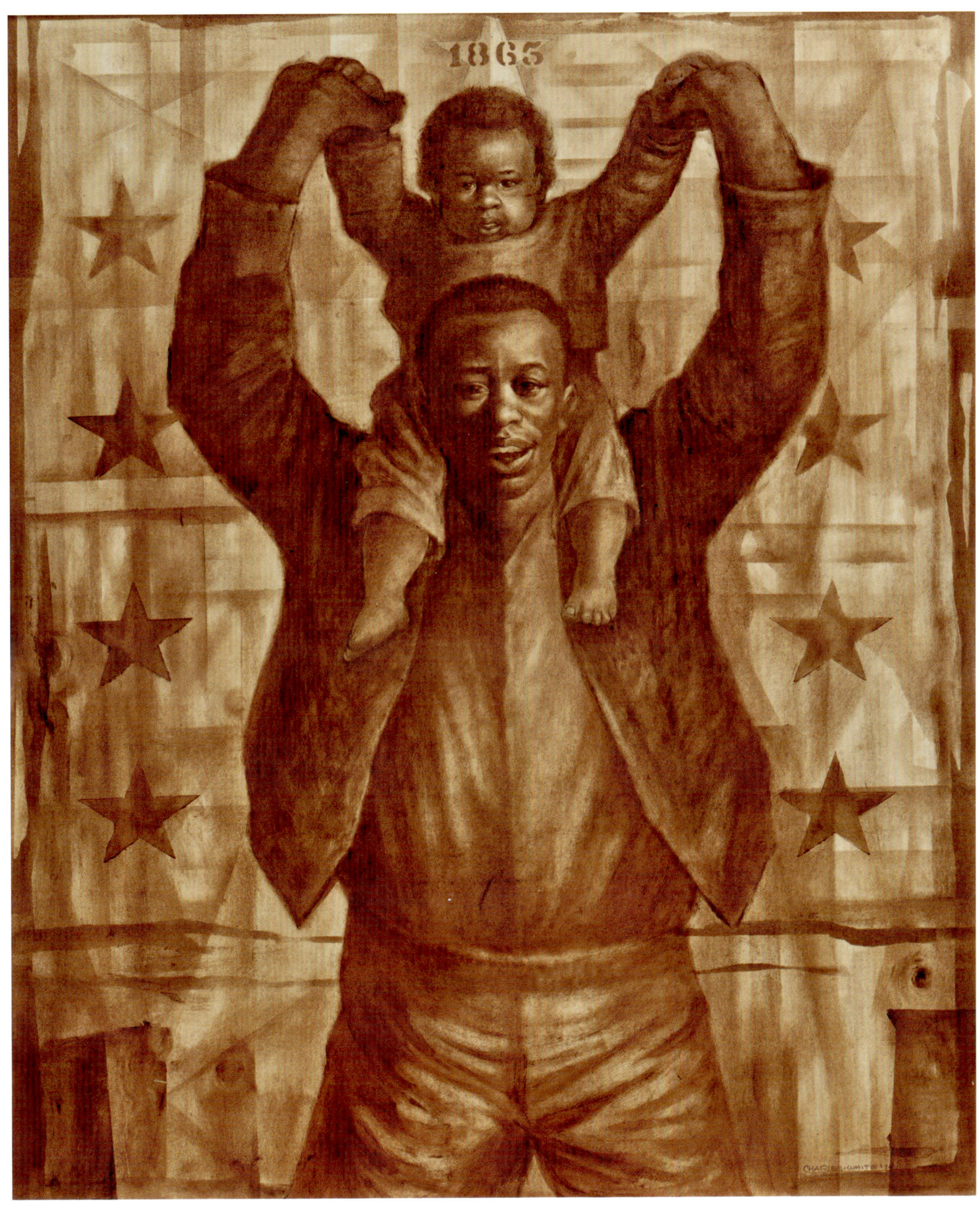
1865

PLATE 37

System: Frederick Douglass, 1974

Oil wash on paperboard
64.14 x 42.70 cm (25 1/4 x 16 13/16 in.)

Famed abolitionist and orator Frederick Douglass (1818–1895) was a subject to whom White returned multiple times. Prominently featured in the artist's early murals— *Progress of the American Negro: Five Great American Negroes* (1939–40) and *The Contribution of the Negro to Democracy in America* (1943)—Douglass also appears in a number of smaller, more intimate works such as White's 1973 etching of this immensely important figure in American history (PLATE 28) and this oil wash on paperboard work. Like *System: W.E.B. DuBois* (PLATE 38), this work was commissioned by the Johnson Publishing Company for Lerone Bennett Jr.'s *The Shaping of Black America* (1975). Thematically and aesthetically consonant, the two works open chapter eight of Bennett's work, which is devoted to exploring the "colonial system that perpetuated the political, economic, and cultural exploitation of non-Europeans..."[20] The round format used in these two portraits (like those of Harriet Tubman, Rev. Richard Allen, and Capt. Paul Cuffe [PLATES 35, 34, and 33, respectively]) lends them a dignified air and points to their elevated status.

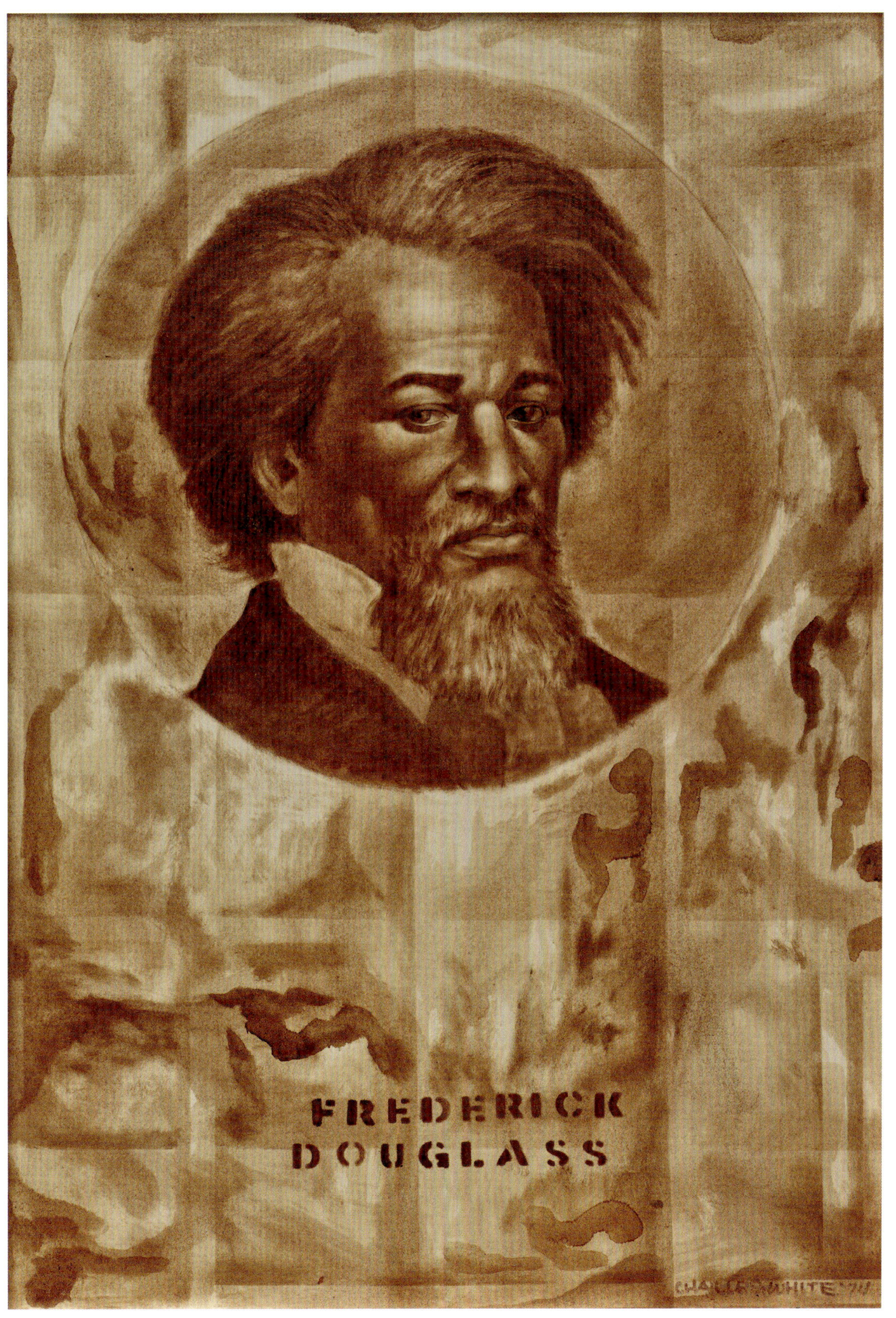
FREDERICK
DOUGLASS

PLATE 38

System: W.E.B. DuBois, 1974

Oil wash on paperboard
64.14 x 42.70 cm (25 1/4 x 16 13/16 in.)

System: W.E.B. DuBois is White's probing portrait of the renowned educator, sociologist, and activist Dr. W.E.B. DuBois (1868–1963). Framed within a roundel and inspired by a well-known Underwood & Underwood portrait of the sitter dating to ca. 1946, this oil wash on paperboard image reflects the artist's veneration of DuBois, whom he depicted multiple times in his mature oeuvre. White's fascination with this great man stretches back to his youth, when, while browsing the shelves of the Chicago Public Library, he stumbled upon Alain Locke's *The New Negro*, a 1925 anthology devoted to the flowering of African American culture during the Harlem Renaissance. White—whose teachers at his predominantly white high school not only did not teach the history of Black America but also shamed their curious young student for asking questions about his people—was stunned by what he read, including DuBois's "The Negro Mind Reaches Out," a searing critique of European colonialism. Locke's seminal text also introduced the fledgling artist to the work of Winold Reiss (1886–1953), whose powerful illustrations had a significant impact on White's emerging style. Decades later, he wrote: "[Locke's] book opened my eyes because I heard names, read of names, read of people that I had never heard of before."[21] Word and text are equally important in this work, which together with *System: Frederick Douglass* (PLATE 37), was commissioned by the Johnson Publishing Company to open the eighth chapter of Lerone Bennett Jr.'s *The Shaping of Black America* (1975).

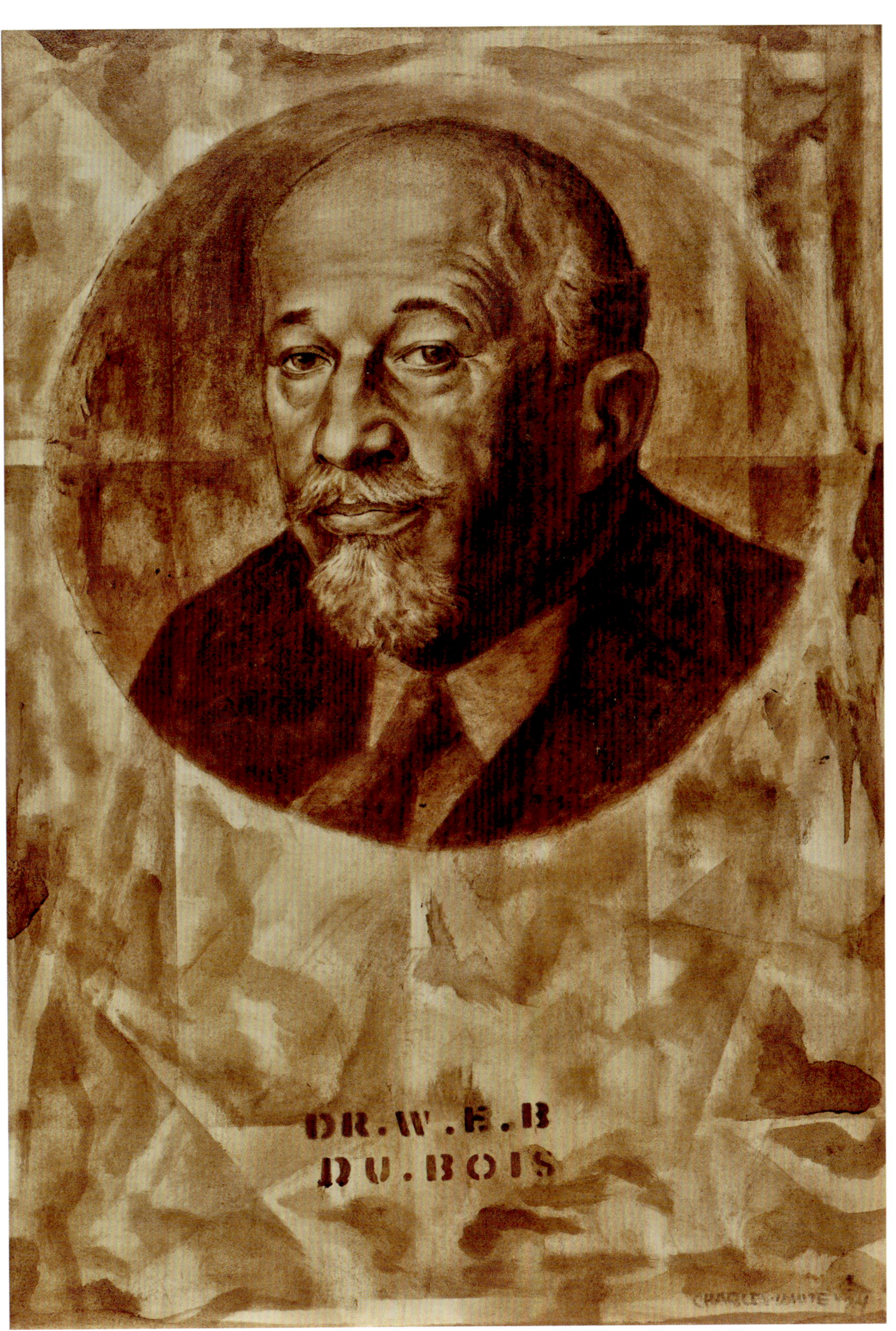
DR. W. E. B
DU. BOIS

PLATE 39

The Black Worker, 1974

Oil wash on paperboard
99.38 x 79.53 cm (39 1/8 x 31 5/16 in.)

Created by White to serve as the opener for chapter nine of Lerone Bennett Jr.'s *The Shaping of Black America* (1975), *The Black Worker* visually embodies "the arc of black labor from legal slavery to economic slavery," the focus of Bennett's associated writings.[22] A lone male figure stands firmly in the middle of the pictorial field, his arms crossed before him, powerful forearms pushing toward the front of the picture plane. Dressed in the utilitarian clothes of a manual laborer and wearing a cap in the style of a railroad engineer, the nameless man turns his head slightly to the left and trains his gaze on the distant horizon. Like a rising sun halted mid-ascent, a silhouetted head—shown in profile with its brain (the seat of emotion, intelligence, and agency) clearly visible—hovers behind him. Two arrows, right and left, dare us to overlook the importance of White's (and Bennett's) exploration of the severely constraining effects of systemic racism on professional opportunities for African Americans. Intentionally relegated to low-skill, low-wage jobs, Black people in the post-Civil War period were trapped in an endless cycle of racialized poverty and de facto servitude. The continuity of these systems of enslavement are referenced in White's insistent "X's," which speak not only to anonymity and illiteracy (those who were not able to read and write often signed their names with a simple "X") but also to the removal of the true identities of enslaved peoples, who were stripped of their given names and assigned new ones by their oppressors (sometimes the latter's own surname, sometimes just a simple "X" in place of a last name). *The Black Worker* also reveals the influence on White of American Regionalist painters, Social Realists, and Works Progress Administration photographers, who, collectively, celebrated farmers, factory workers, migrant workers, and others engaged in manual labor in America.

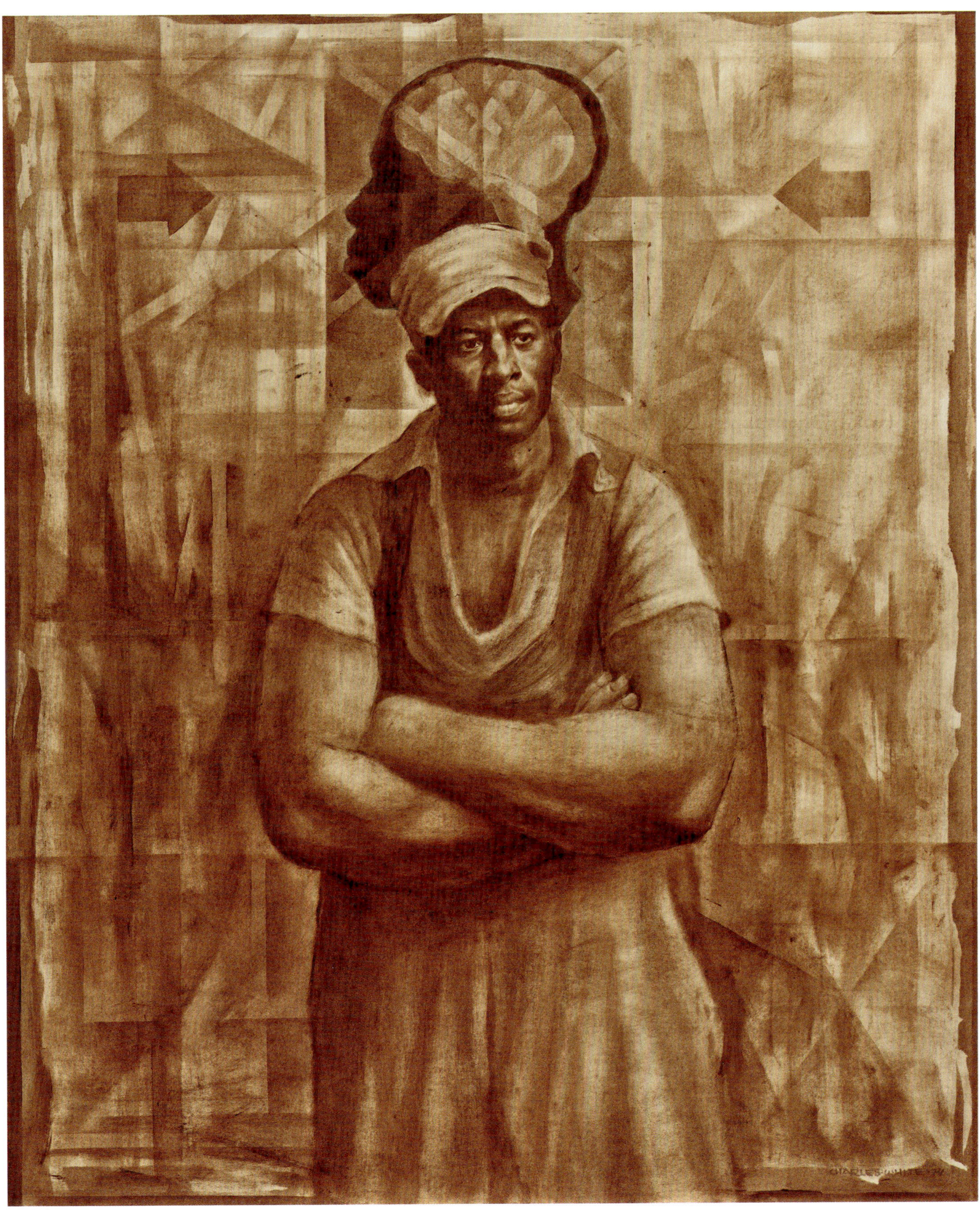

PLATE 40

Money, Merchants and Markets, 1974

Oil and collage on paperboard
99.22 x 79.69 cm (39 1/16 x 31 3/8 in.)

Money, Merchants and Markets was created by White under commission from the Johnson Publishing Company as the opener for the tenth and final chapter of Lerone Bennett Jr.'s *The Shaping of Black America* (1975). Like the text it was designed to complement, this image celebrates African Americans' business acumen, industry, and entrepreneurial spirit. A man, seated on a chair and deep in thought, anchors the pictorial field. Wearing a suit and brogues, he lifts the corner of an oversized sheet of paper from the floor as if to read or analyze it. Though neither text nor image is visible, the size and format of these pages are reminiscent of architectural blueprints or construction documents, a suggestion underscored by the three schematic diagrams pinned to the wall behind him. These sheets feature, in the center, a façade with the word "ATLANTA" emblazoned over it. It is flanked by abstracted, partially obscured images that carry the banners "SO. CAR[OLINA] and LOUI[SIANA]." The left and right edges of an American five-dollar bill (the currency on which President Abraham Lincoln's portrait bust appears) are visible on these cryptic sheets, which seem to simultaneously reference aerial maps, redistricting plans, military operational charts, and Industrial Age machinery. Though their meaning is not entirely clear, the pages are bound together not only by White's reference to Lincoln (whose 1865 Emancipation Proclamation marked a critical turning point in the history of enslavement in America) but also by a continuous dashed line, which metaphorically references the political dominion of these neighboring states and city in the Civil War from the Atlantic Ocean to the Gulf Coast.

White's protagonist raises his left hand—cupped, but with index finger extended—in a contemplative gesture. The artist's monochromatic sepia palette, like the faceting he used on the expanses of paper spread before and tacked behind the man, harken back to pre-Emancipation Proclamation "Wanted" posters seeking "fugitive slaves" and broadsheets advertising "slave auctions." The sheets that lie before this man, however, are blank, suggesting that he has stepped up and out of these nefarious notices from a bygone era to become the master of his own destiny. Like the history of African Americans after the Civil War, however, he is not entirely free. As Bennett explores in his writings, the story of educational progress, professional success, financial gains, and upward mobility for Black Americans has been hampered by the reality of two political economies, one Black and the other white. Bennett writes: "These...figures of growth, concentration, and continuing deprivation—cast a revealing light on the shape and structure of Black America in the third quarter of the twentieth century...[T]he figures and the forces behind the figures point to a critical watershed, whose streams run in one direction back to the Jamestown landing, in another forward to a shore shrouded in mist."[23]

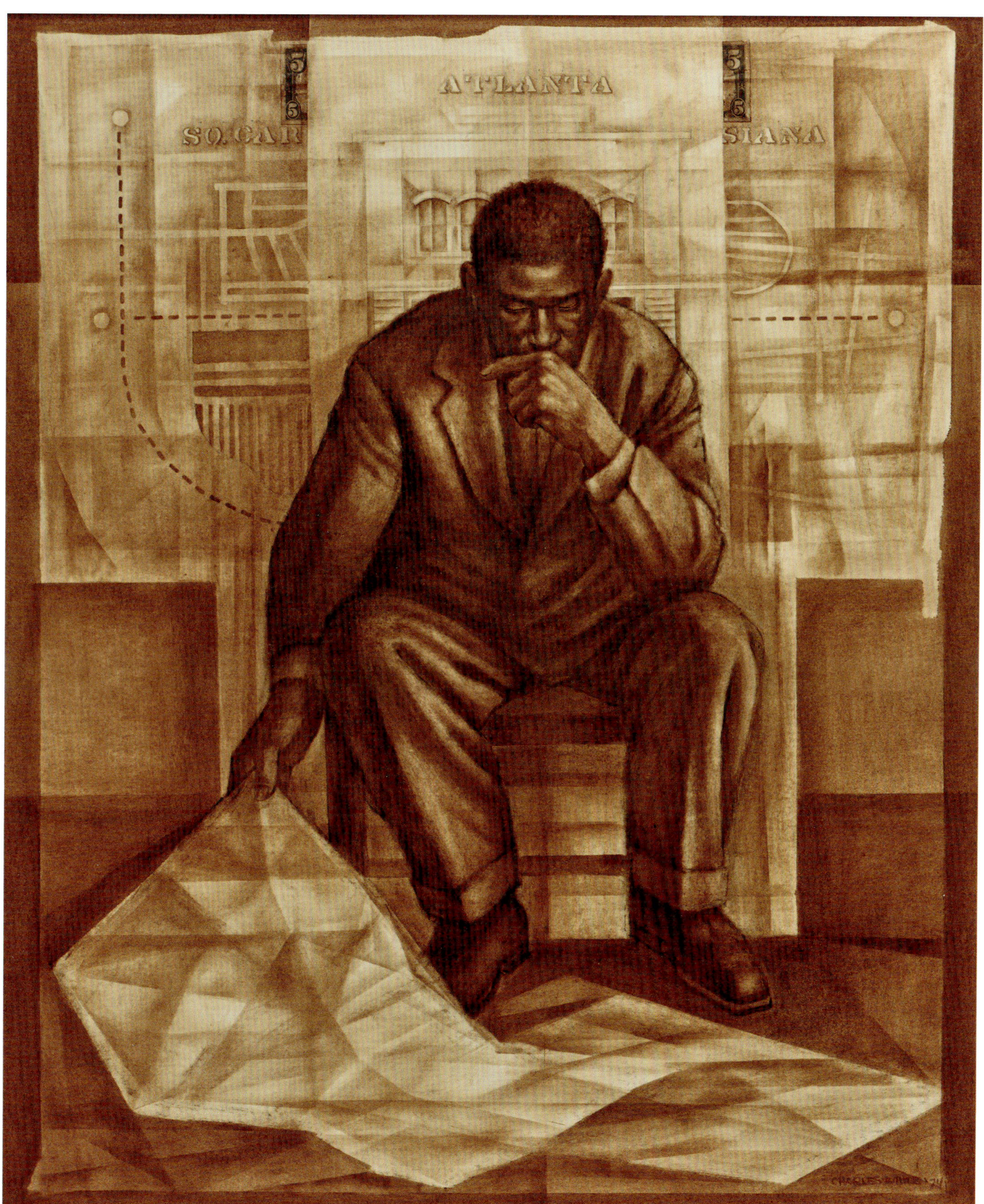
ATLANTA
SO. CAR
SIANA

PLATE 41

Study–Children's Games, 1975

Charcoal on heavy cream paper
80.01 x 120.65 cm (31 1/2 x 47 1/2 in.)

This meticulously crafted charcoal drawing is closely related to White's *Children's Games II* (1976), a work he completed the following year in oil wash on paper. Though the latter's background is much more complex, both visually and allegorically, the central figure—a solitary adolescent Black male—quotes this study almost exactly. In both works, the artist's subject engages us with pleading eyes and a direct, but non-confrontational, gaze. His body is activated and energized, with legs bent in anticipation of movement and arms outstretched to contain the looping arcs of rope he grasps in both hands. Far too long to be used for innocent childhood games—such as Cat's Cradle (the subject of a related work [PLATE 24]) or jump rope—and far too thin to be used for Tug-of-War, this is no ordinary tether. Rather, it is a menacing antagonist that may be read as a web of inevitability threatening to engulf the boy, or, more nefarious still, the murderous tool of lynching, an allusion heightened by the loops that fall from the child's left hand. In this reading, the rope's swooping forms, from which the boy seemingly tries to distance himself, become nooses and their overlapping pattern become repetitive figure eights (the symbol of infinity, and by extension, repeating, changeless cycles). A menacing shadow—far too broad to be his own—looms behind White's protagonist. Like the rope, the tenebrous shape threatens to consume him, heightening the work's chilling quality. Despite the somber overtones of this beautifully rendered image, White saw children as the future. This boy, then, is not only bearing witness to the bitter realities of systemic racism, he is an arch reminder of the possibilities of a better, more just tomorrow if only we make the right choices.

Study–Children's Games was first exhibited at the Los Angeles–based Heritage Gallery. It was also included in the September 1977 Invitational Drawing Show at the Fine Arts Gallery of San Diego, in addition to serving as the basis for a lithograph included in a limited-edition portfolio of six works, sponsored by White's close friend David A. Brown, through his Brown Pharmaceutical Co., Inc., in November 1977. Of this relationship, the artist's wife, Frances Barrett White, wrote:

> David...made possible several portfolio publications when there was extra money to be invested in these ventures. Charlie knew David and Amy in New York. Amy is the sister of Julie Belafonte and we also know her parents Clara and George. The Browns and their children have been close California friends. David has retired and is giving all his time to being a practicing artist. They live in New York now.[24]

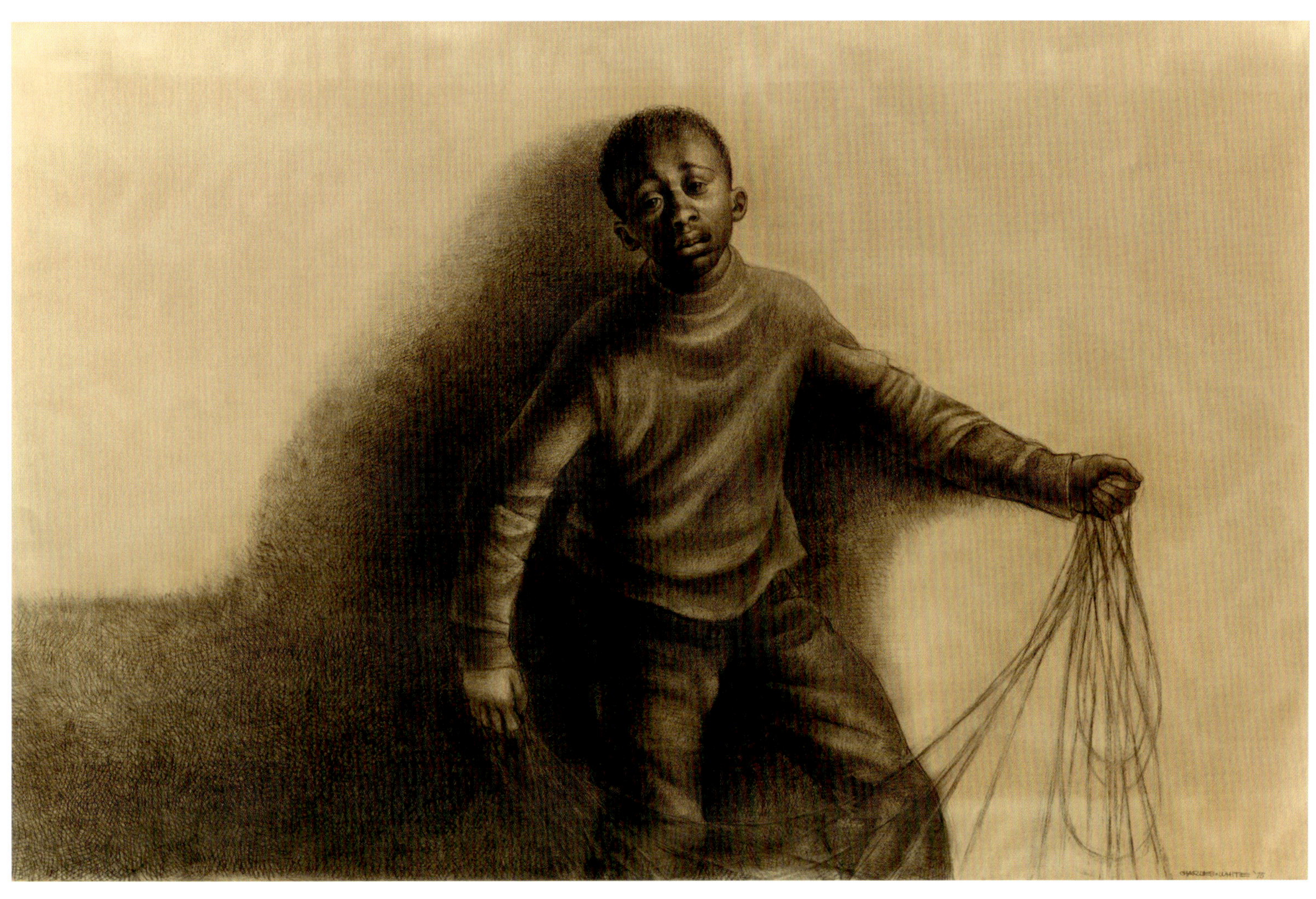

PLATE 42

I Have a Dream, 1976

Lithograph, from crayon on stone printed in brown/black ink
56.52 x 76.2 cm (22 1/4 x 30 in.)

I Have a Dream was commissioned by the Graphic Arts Council of the Los Angeles County Museum of Art for its groundbreaking 1976 exhibition, *Two Centuries of Black Art.* The lithograph alludes to the seminal speech delivered by Dr. Martin Luther King Jr. (1929–1968) from the steps of the Lincoln Memorial on AUGUST 28, 1963, during the March on Washington for Jobs and Freedom. King's seventeen-minute oration encapsulated the vibrant energy and passion of the Civil Rights movement. In his deeply moving address (which merits quoting at length), Dr. King proclaimed:

> I have a dream today. I have a dream that one day every valley shall be exalted, every hill and mountain shall be made low, the rough places will be made plain, and the crooked places will be made straight, and the glory of the Lord shall be revealed, and all flesh shall see it together. This is our hope. This is the faith that I go back to the South with. With this faith, we will be able to hew out of the mountain of despair a stone of hope. With this faith we will be able to transform the jangling discords of our nation into a beautiful symphony of brotherhood. With this faith we will be able to work together, to pray together, to struggle together, to go to jail together, to stand up for freedom together, knowing that we will be free one day.

White's work personifies Dr. King's vision of a more just future, built on a shared foundation of equity, dignity, and respect for all. It also directly references the strength and power White located in Black women as well as the hope for humanity he saw in children.

Firmly anchoring the work is a beautifully rendered half-length image of a woman. She is presented frontally with her head tilted back, chin raised, and eyes nearly closed in a reverent expression resembling prayer. Loose, flowing robes envelop her, creating a protective canopy for the woman and the sleeping child she cradles in a gesture that is simultaneously protective and supplicative.

This is a timeless image of maternity, harkening back to centuries of Western European paintings and sculptures depicting the infant Jesus in the arms of his mother the Virgin Mary (a trope commonly referred to as "Madonna and Child"). It also brings to mind depictions of the Madonna of Mercy, in which Mary stands above supplicants gathered under the protective folds of her cloak to find succor and salvation within. Further heightening the sense that we are in the presence of holy beings is the celestial light that bathes the pair. White deftly created this effect by leaving broad areas of the lithography stone on which this work was executed untouched so they would not absorb ink, and would instead read as luminous highlights when printed. White's mother figure bears a striking resemblance to the protagonist of his *Love Letter III* (PLATE 44), which he executed the following year. Indeed, the two women's features, expressions, postures, and cloaked heads and shoulders have only slight variations between them, suggesting that this iconography exerted a strong pull on White and on the shaping of his vision of female empowerment and maternal strength.

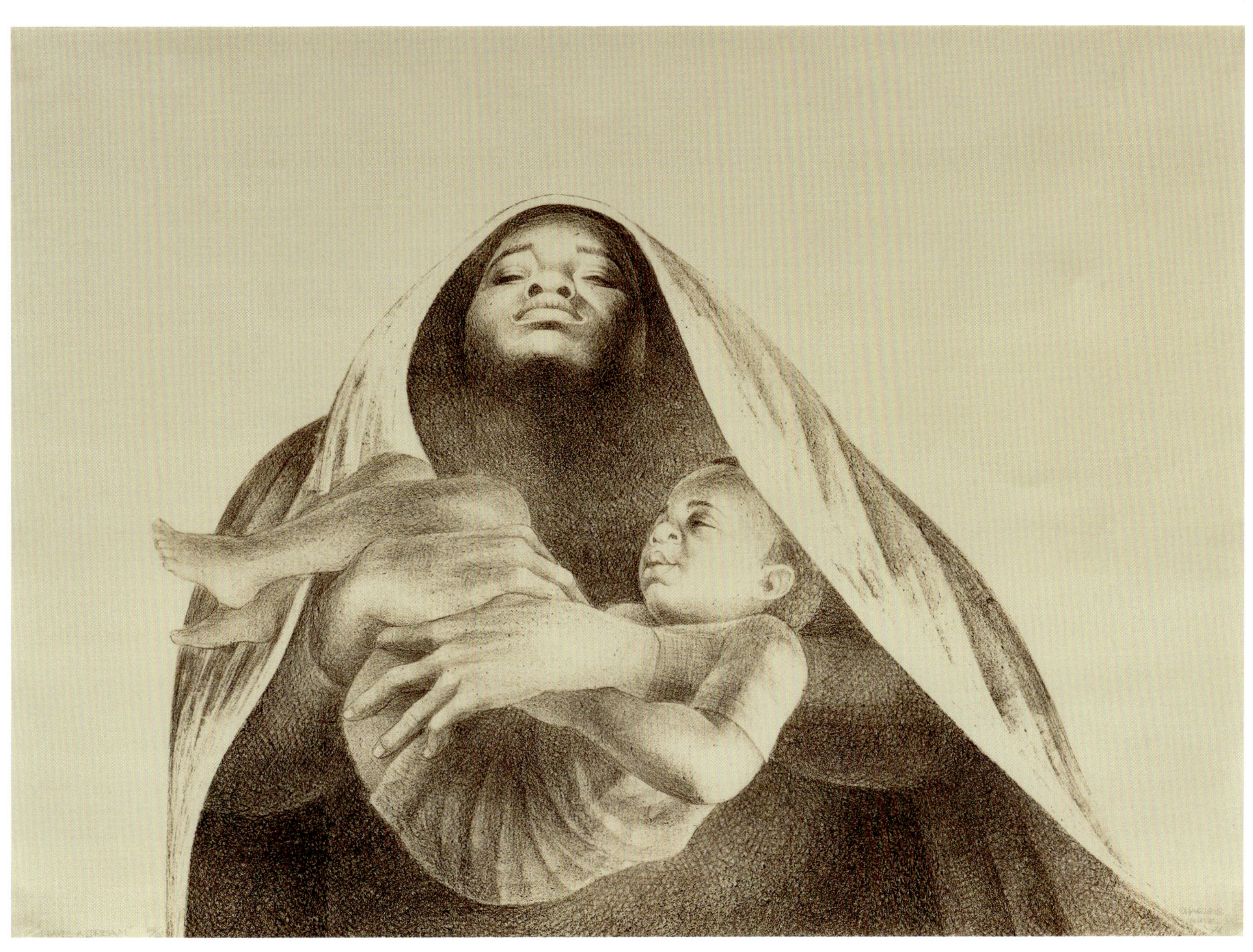

PLATE 43

Prophet I, 1976

Color lithograph
67.95 x 93.98 cm (26 3/4 x 37 in.)

By the mid-1970s, White had begun moving away from the monochromatic palette that characterized his earlier oeuvre and was embracing color with greater frequency. Created in 1976, *Prophet I* is emblematic in this regard. A single pink flower hovers above a gradiated cerulean background. The soft curves of this symbol of femininity and love stand in stark contrast to the crisp edges of the post and beam that intersect at right angles behind the work's lone figure: a solitary man, shown in profile. Like the architectural elements to his rear (whose disposition hints at a Christian cross), his head is a study in geometry. The man's bald pate is a perfectly rounded dome while his angular features are so crisp and clear as to appear chiseled from stone. His beard, on the other hand, is anything but staid: It bristles with a visceral energy that seems to pull the figure toward the disembodied blossom. Indeed, the man seems to rise up—out of his collared shirt and the lengths of white cloth that envelop him and toward the flower—as if by magnetic attraction. The ambiguous drapery in which he is cloaked is reminiscent of linen wrappings used in ancient burial rituals and conveys a sense of rebirth or redemption, as if the man has been raised, Lazarus-like, from the tomb. This sense of otherworldliness is heightened by the solemnity and stillness of the work, which seems to bear witness to a deeply personal, spiritually intense moment. *Prophet I* was used on the covers of both the Studio Museum in Harlem's *Images of Dignity: A Retrospective of the Works of Charles White* (1982) and Michael G. Cooke's *Afro-American Literature in the Twentieth Century: The Achievement of Intimacy* (1984).

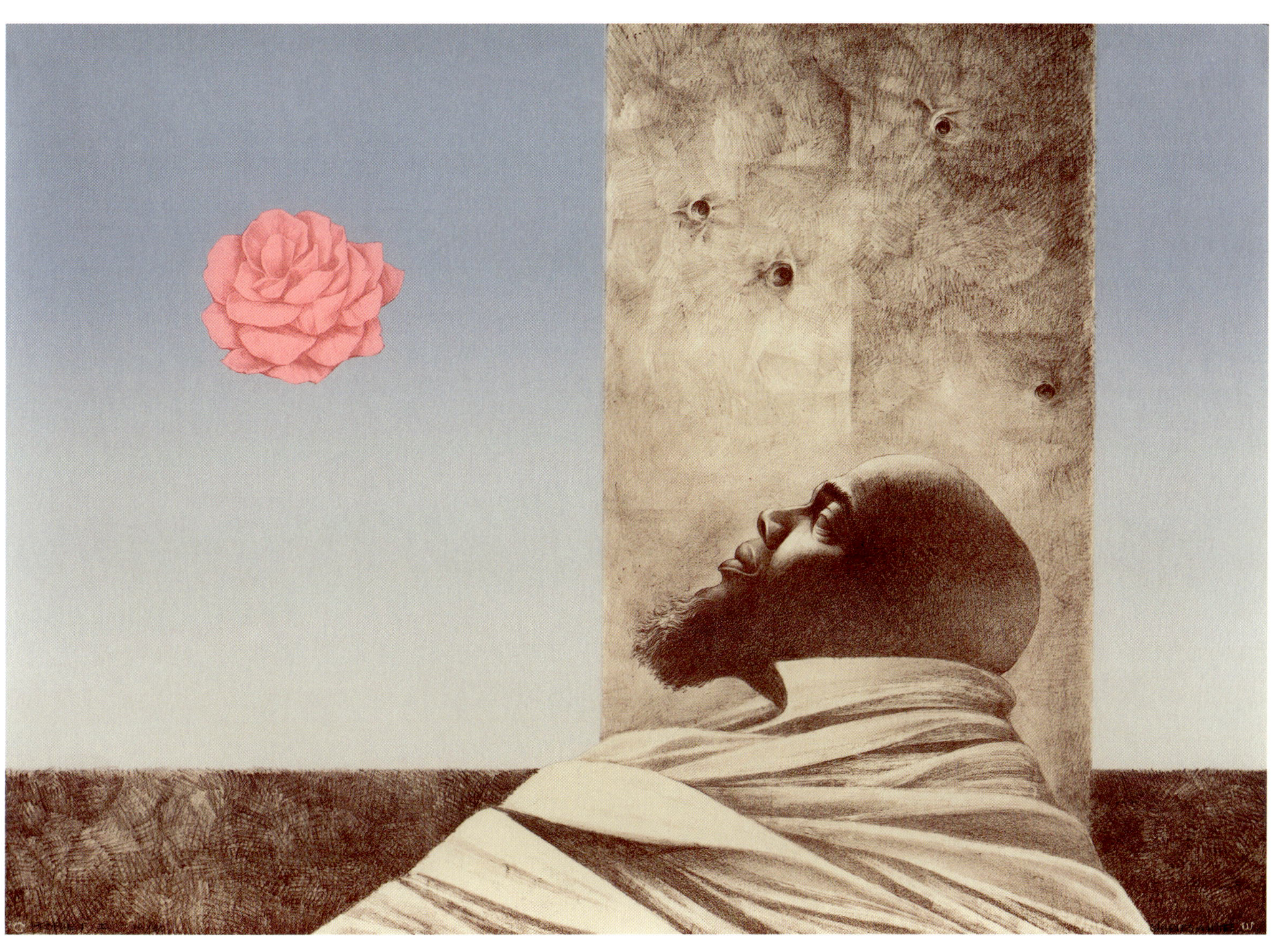

PLATE 44

Love Letter III, 1977

Lithograph
76.2 x 56.20 cm (30 x 22 1/8 in.)

For Charlie, the shell became a symbol. In one of his last color lithographs there was a strong, radiant head thrust upward—the head of a woman with a conch shell floating beneath [sic] her. I asked Charlie, "Why a shell?" He answered me, "It was one of man's earliest religious symbols. It represents woman." Hugging me, he told me, "This is my tribute to the wonderful woman in my life."
—Frances Barrett White[25]

The work described above by White's second wife, Frances Barrett White, in her memoir *Reaches of the Heart*, is *Love Letter III*. This color lithograph was the third and final work in a limited series bearing the same name. While *Love Letter I* (PLATE 23) and *Love Letter II* are associated with specific women (Civil Rights leaders and activists Angela Davis [B. 1944] and Fannie Lou Hamer [1917–1977], respectively), *Love Letter III* is a paean to women in general and to White's beloved wife in particular.

Executed just two years before the artist's death, the image is anchored by the cloaked head, neck, and shoulders of a woman who seems to rise from the lithograph's lower margin. So strong is her resemblance to the woman featured in White's *I Have a Dream* (PLATE 42), it is reasonable to assume that the artist used the same source image for both works (a creative strategy he was known to deploy, as *Portrait (Head)* [PLATE 20]) and *Missouri C* [PLATE 25] confirm). He may also have been inspired by the two sculptural renditions of women in states of spiritual transport created by the great Baroque artist and architect Gian Lorenzo Bernini (1598–1680): *Blessed Ludovica Albertoni* (1644) and *Ecstasy of Saint Teresa* (1647–52). Though the contexts and the intended messages of these works are vastly different, they share the same sensibility—one of feminine devotion to a higher cause.

The prominent shell that hovers above White's saintly figure is, as his wife tells us, a metaphor for both faith and femininity. Indeed, shells of various types have centuries-old, cross-cultural religious connotations in addition to being associated with women, beauty, and fecundity. The conch also had great personal significance for the artist, who traveled to Belize with his close friend Dr. Edmund W. Gordon in search of a deeper sense of identity a year or so before creating this work. White's son, Ian, spent the following Christmas with the Gordons in this Central American country (which had actively participated in the Caribbean slave trade), bringing home to his parents a very special souvenir: "a large, salmon-colored conch shell."[26] More than a call to action, then, White's *Love Letter III* is precisely that…a missive to Frances and the sorority of women.

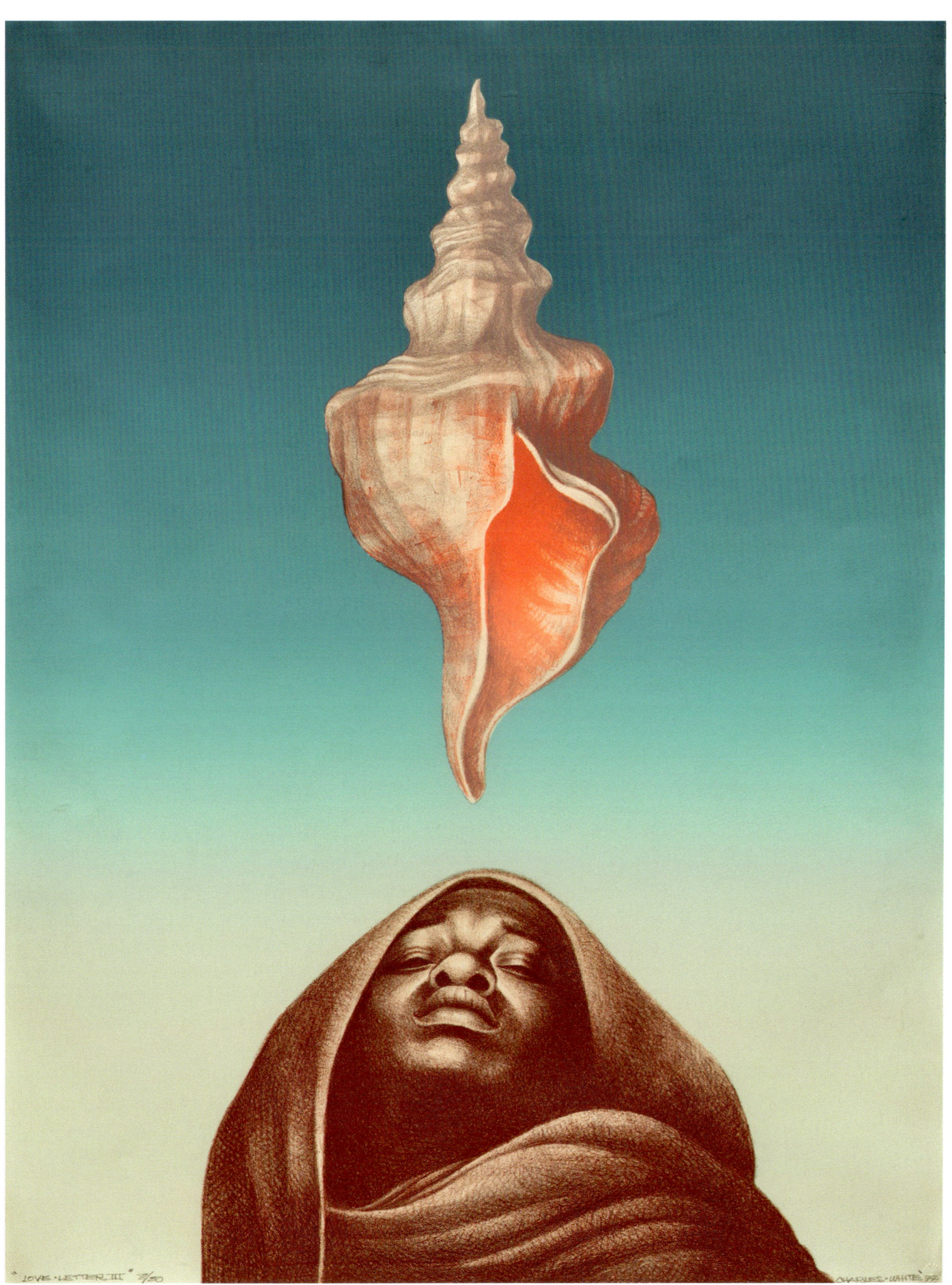
"LOVE·LETTER III"
CHARLES·WHITE

PLATE 45

Sound of Silence, 1978

Lithograph
66.04 x 88.58 cm (26 x 34 7/8 in.)

White produced multiple versions of this image in 1978, the year before he died. Toggling between a monochromatic and restrained but saturated color palette in his various editions, the artist seemed to be channeling a certain restlessness in these works, as if he sensed Death's approach. This disquiet also marks his manipulation of the image's protagonist, a young Black man, who in one version is rendered only as negative space, the shell he holds presented with phantom hands pressing in upon it.

The title of this series assuredly references Paul Simon and Art Garfunkel's eponymous hit song, formally released on their second studio album twelve years earlier. The pop duo described the message of their song, which Simon is said to have written in response to the assassination of President John F. Kennedy (1917–1963), as an invocation to us all not just to hear, but to actually listen to one another. This entreaty would have resonated with White, who devoted his life and his art to promoting racial justice, equity, and agency on behalf of himself and his fellow African Americans. Like Simon & Garfunkel's song, this lithograph may also have a scriptural overlay, in particular Psalm 88 of the Bible. Written "[f]or the director of music" and intended to accompany Israelites on their way to worship, this concise text is a powerful mediation on both human mortality and God's omnipotence. The somber psalm concludes, "the darkness is my closest friend," an apt bridge to Simon & Garfunkel's song (which opens with the line, "Hello darkness, my old friend") and a clause that aligns well with the mood of *Sound of Silence.*

Presented frontally and anchoring the center of the pictorial field, a young man engages us with a direct, unflinching gaze. His expression is doleful and his gesture ambiguous, for he stands in a posture that is simultaneously open and closed. The positioning of the figure's arms, in particular, feels unnatural to the point of suggesting that someone else, unseen but present, is hoisting his arms behind his back. A mysterious shell hovers above the young man's thorax, heightening the work's slightly mystical qualities while also conjuring a panoply of richly symbolic associations, from Christian faith to feminine beauty. And though White had incorporated shells into other works dating from this period, including *Love Letter III* (PLATE 44), he emphasizes the darkness of the chamber's opening in this image as well as in the related, polychromed *Sound of Silence II* (PLATE 46), endowing the shell's interior with a tomb-like, murky stillness. It is also in this cavity that if we listen, really listen, we will "hear" the ocean. "The words of the prophets" are "whispered in the sounds of silence," Simon & Garfunkel—and White—tell us.

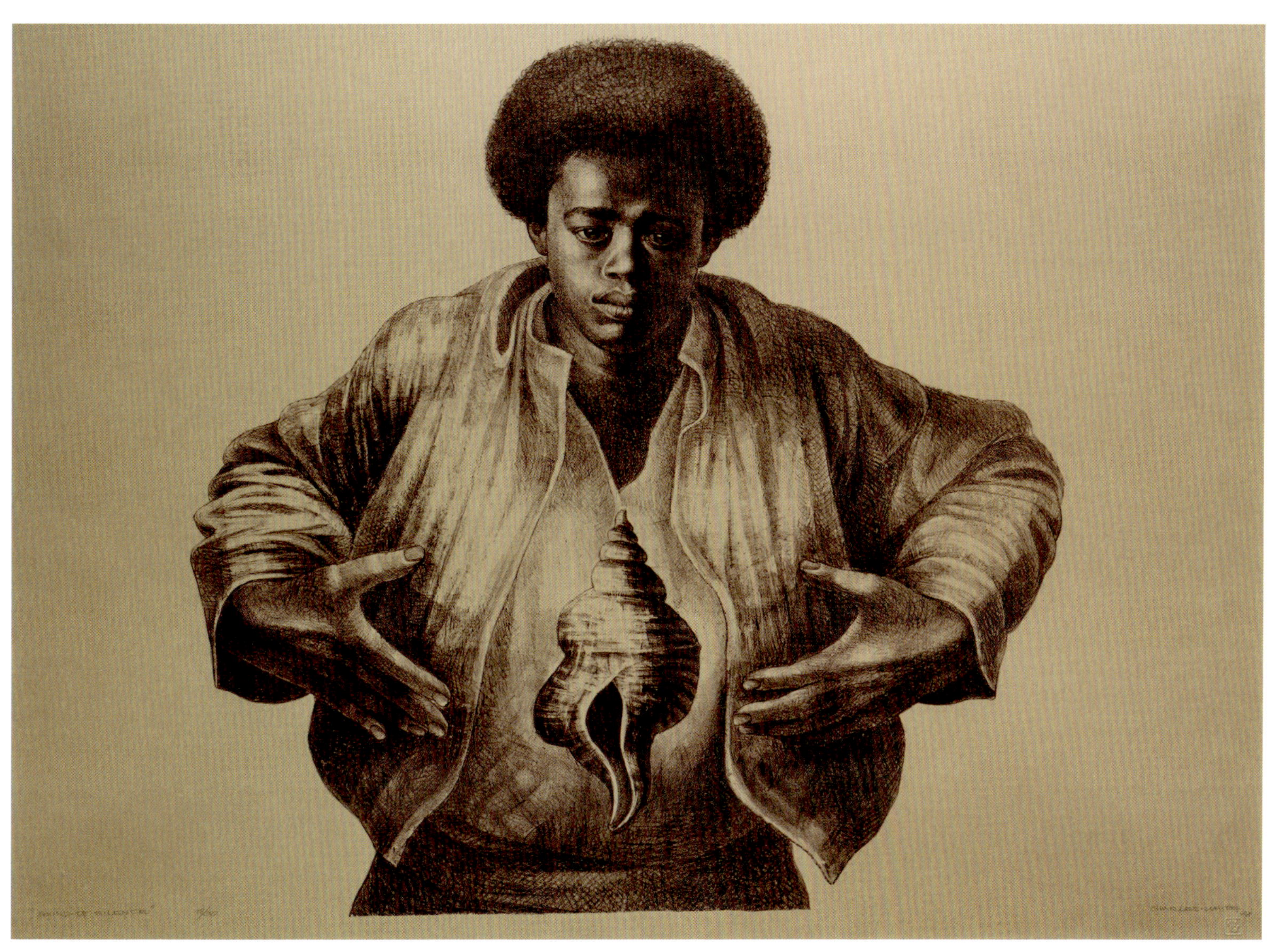

PLATE 46

Sound of Silence II, 1978

Lithograph
63.5 x 89.54 cm (25 x 35 1/4 in.)

Completed the year before White's death, this work, like the contemporaneous *Sound of Silence* (PLATE 45) is richly symbolic. The artist's subject is a young Black male whose carefully coiffed afro resembles a halo, a symbol that is associated in Christianity with martyrdom or sainthood. He gazes solemnly at us with luminous, piercing eyes, while slowly pulling his bent elbows up and back. This unusual gesture causes his jacket to fall open, revealing a brilliantly white shirt beneath. A mysterious shell emerges from between the two halves of his jacket and seems to both emanate from and float above him. The figure's large, prominent hands appear forceful yet delicate as his fingertips just brush his outer garment. This sense of strength in vulnerability is enhanced by White's inclusion of the shell. A typically feminine motif with significant religious connotations, it creates a physical barrier between us and the young man while also providing a portal into his chest, and by extension, his inner self.

Beyond referencing the pop duo Simon & Garfunkel's hit song of this same name (which had been a runaway hit in 1966) as well as possibly alluding to themes of fecundity, maternity, mortality, and Christian salvation, White may have been thinking about *Nkisi Nkondi* (or power) figures when he created this series of images. Produced by the Kongo peoples of the Democratic Republic of the Congo for ritual use, these sculpted wooden figures often take the form of a slightly abstracted standing male figure. With hands placed on hips and clusters of nails and other sharp objects embedded in the figure's various body parts, they serve as spiritual containers after *nganga* (or healers) place medicinal herbs and other sacred substances in them (thereby endowing the figures with healing or restorative powers).

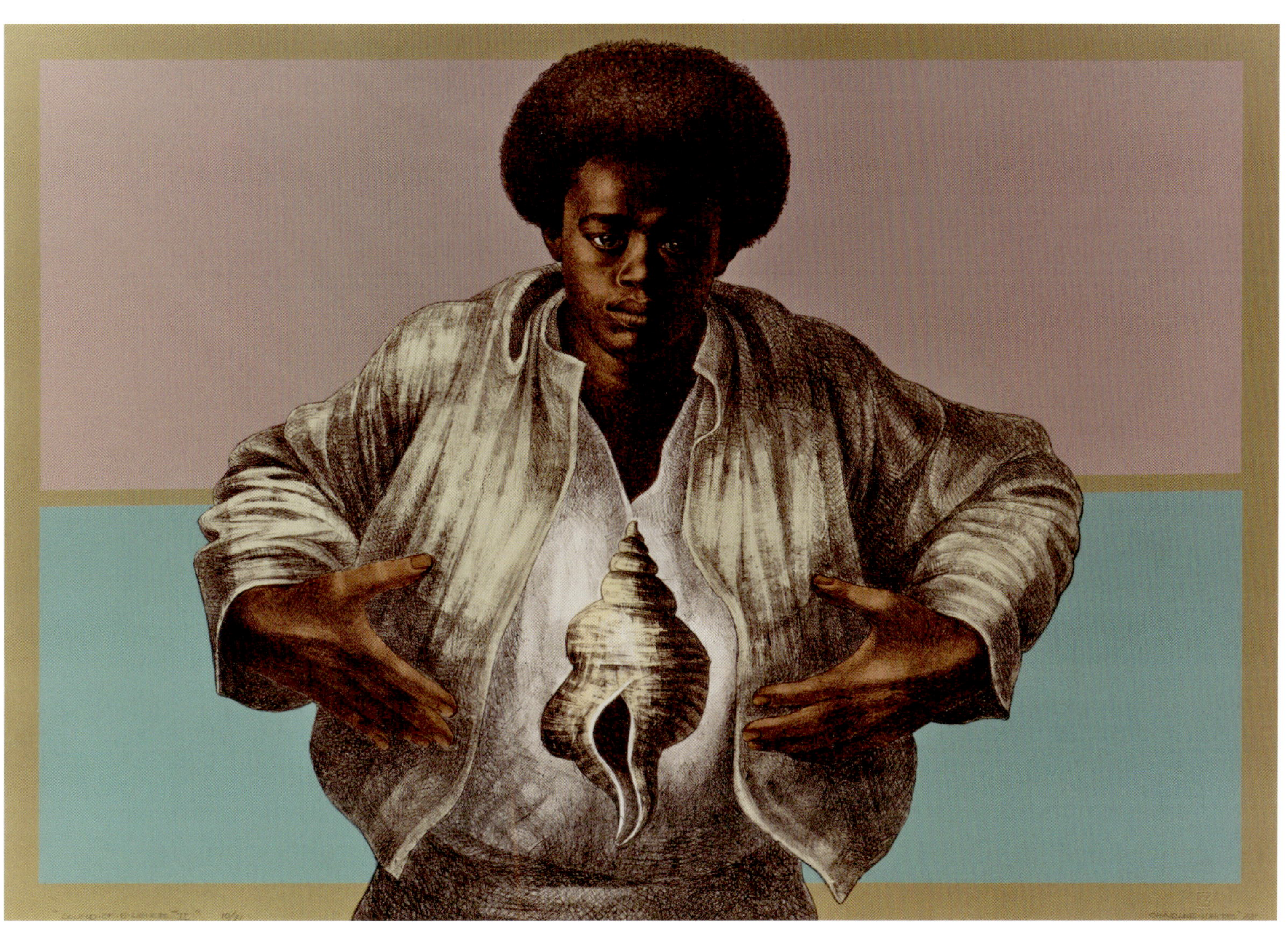

NOTES

DIRECTOR'S FOREWORD

1. W. Herbert Brewster, "Move on Up a Little Higher," 1946. © Warner Chappell Music, Inc.
2. Benjamin Horowitz, "Images of Dignity," in *Images of Dignity* (Los Angeles: The Ward Ritchie Press, 1967), 23.
3. John Oliver Killens, "Charles White: The People's Artist," *The Georgia Review* 40, no. 2 (Summer 1986): 453.
4. Harry Belafonte, in conversation with Esther Adler, Museum of Modern Art, audio interview and transcript, 2018, https://www.moma.org/audio/playlist/54/797.
5. Harry Belafonte in conversation with Esther Adler.
6. Guthrie P. Ramay, *Race Music: Black Cultures from Bebop to Hip-Hop* (Berkeley: University of California Press, 2003), 52.

COLLECTOR'S NOTE

1. Charles White, quoted in Jeffrey Elliot, "Charles White: Portrait of an Artist," *Negro History Bulletin* 41, no. 3 (May–June 1978): 828.

CHARLES WHITE: A LIFE, EXTRAORDINARY

1. Art Seidenbaum, "The Racial Picture in Black and White," *Los Angeles Times*, February 3, 1964, quoted in Kellie Jones, *South of Pico: African American Artists in Los Angeles in the 1960s and 1980s* (Durham and London: Duke University Press, 2017), 33 and 286n35.
2. Reflecting on his early forays in artmaking, White noted: "I was an emotional painter. I was a romanticist. Now this isn't to say that I was a person who was so in love with everybody that I wasn't capable of a little hate. I was capable of a lot of hate, and I'm capable of a lot of hate now…However, I can't paint hate. I couldn't paint hate then. I can't paint hate now. I can't use this medium through which if there's any possibility for me to feel some kind of universality with people, A ONENESS WITH MAN [emphasis his], and to believe in my man, to believe in myself and to believe in my fellow man, I can't use this medium to paint something that's negative, that's against man. I can't do this." Charles W. White Papers, 1933–1987, bulk 1960s–1970s. Series 1: Biographical Material, circa 1934–1987 (Box 1, Folder 9: Interview Transcripts, circa 1965). Archives of American Art, Smithsonian Institution, https://ids.si.edu/ids/deliveryService/?id=AAA-AAA_whitchar_3199258&max=1300.
3. White's great-grandmother was enslaved in her native Trinidad by an Englishman—"Yellowbee" or "Yellerby"—who brought her to Mississippi, where he "fathered her ten children." Andrea D. Barnwell, *Charles White* (San Francisco: Pomegranate, 2002), 14; and Frances Barrett White with Anne Scott, *Reaches of the Heart: A Loving Look at the Artist Charles White* (New York: Barricade Books, 1994), 154. See also John Murphy and Ashley James, comps., "Chronology," in Sarah Kelly Oehler and Esther Adler, eds., *Charles White: A Retrospective* (New Haven and London: Yale University Press, 2018), 192–209.
4. Barnwell, *Charles White*, 12.
5. Economic historian William Collins noted: "Between 1910 and 1970, several million Black Americans migrated from the South in what became known as 'the Great Migration.' This resulted in a large-scale redistribution of the Black population—nearly 90 percent of Black Americans lived in the South in 1910, but by 1970, less than half did. Over the same 60-year period, the Black share of residents in New York, Philadelphia, Chicago, Detroit, and Los Angeles, some of the main destinations for Black migrants, increased from approximately 3 percent to 26 percent." William J. Collins, "The Great Migration of Black Americans from the US South: A Guide and Interpretation," *Explorations in Economic History* 80 (April 2021), https://doi-org.access.library.miami.edu/10.1016/j.eeh.2020.101382.
6. These discriminatory efforts included "Black laws" that required African Americans to produce proof of their emancipation before taking up residence in that state, as well as "Black codes" denying these same individuals civil rights. See Janet L. Abu-Lughod, *Race, Space, and Riots in Chicago, New York, and Los Angeles* (Oxford: Oxford University Press, 2007).
7. White recalled: "I used to see my mother when I'd go to work with her. I used to always wonder why did she have to scrub floors in these peoples [sic] houses and then come home and scrub our floor. And it used to disturb me. I used to be a little ashamed to see my mother do this. I used to be embarrassed by it. I used to be embarrassed because some of the other kids around my neighborhood…had parents who were doing something that may not be quite as menial, but which seemed to be a little more dignified. Waiting tables seemed to be a little more dignified than my mother scrubbing floors. But somehow what used to get through to me…was the fact that this woman had dignity…dignity." White Papers (Box 1, Folder 9), https://ids.si.edu/ids/deliveryService/?id=AAA-AAA_whitchar_3199255&max=1300 and https://ids.si.edu/ids/deliveryService/?id=AAA-AAA_whitchar_3199256&max=1300.
8. Charles White, "Path of a Negro Artist," *Masses & Mainstream* (April 1955): 33. According to White, Charles Sr. earned his living as "a railroad worker and a construction worker." White Papers (Box 1, Folder 9), https://ids.si.edu/ids/deliveryService/?id=AAA-AAA_whitchar_3199285&max=1300. See also Benjamin Horowitz, "Images of Dignity" in *Images of Dignity* (Los Angeles: The Ward Ritchie Press, 1967), 7; Breanne Robertson, "Pan-Americanism, Patriotism, and Race Pride in Charles White's Hampton Mural," *American Art* 30, no. 1 (Spring 2016): 64; and Barnwell, *Charles White*, 13.
9. White and his mother sat at the rear of an unfamiliar church during his father's memorial service while another woman and her offspring sat up front, grieving. As an adult, the artist alluded to the confusion this arrangement caused him, a state of bewilderment compounded by his mother's unwillingness to discuss their unorthodox family situation. Barrett White, *Reaches of the Heart*, 31; and Barnwell, *Charles White*, 14.
10. Barnwell, *Charles White*, 14; and Horowitz, "Images of Dignity," 7–8.
11. White, "Path of a Negro Artist," 33.
12. White, "Path of a Negro Artist," 33.
13. White, "Path of a Negro Artist," 33–34.
14. Writing in 1955, White noted: "I like music, and I think that music has had a deep and helpful influence on my painting." White, "Path of a Negro Artist," 34. Indeed, the painter engaged directly with music—and musicians (including Harry Belafonte and Paul Robeson)—throughout his career. Of theater, he shared: "I was avidly interested not only in painting, but in literature and drama. The drama group in the school allowed me to paint the scenery, and design the sets and costumes. But I also wanted to act, and this was forbidden to a Negro." White, "Path of a Negro Artist," 35. Faced with blatantly discriminatory strictures at his high school (Englewood)—which, according to the artist, was more than seventy percent white—White focused his energies on the Negro People's Theatre, with which he also became involved as a teenager. Horowitz, "Images of Dignity," 14. See also Oral History Interview with Charles W. White, Smithsonian Archives of American Art (March 9, 1965), 5, https://www.aaa.si.edu/download_pdf_transcript/ajax?record_id=edanmdm-AAADCD_oh_213975; and White, "Path of a Negro Artist," 34–35. His interest in the stage remained with him throughout his life. As Kellie Jones writes: "Having once considered an acting career, White had close relationships with actors, musicians, as well as writers and enjoyed visiting movie and TV sets whenever friends such as [Sidney] Poitier, Ivan Dixon, and others were in the cast." Jones, *South of Pico*, 26.
15. George Inness (1825–1894) and Winslow Homer (1836–1910) numbered among his particular favorites. Oral History, 3.
16. "My [step-father] was a night watchman, and he worked at some mail order house, and so he used to get all kinds of magazines. And I used to spend endless hours just making copies of the cartoons and everything." White Papers (Box 1, Folder 9), https://ids.si.edu/ids/deliveryService/?id=AAA-AAA_whitchar_3199250&max=1300. An avid reader, Gary also brought home discarded periodicals from her places of employment. Barrett White, *Reaches of the Heart*, 29.
17. Horowitz, "Images of Dignity," 9. The 1932 inauguration of the George Cleveland Hall branch of the Chicago Public Library under the visionary leadership of Vivian Harsh—just blocks from White's childhood home—deeply influenced his learning, intellectual growth, and ideological development. Sarah Kelly Oehler, "Yesterday, Today, Tomorrow: Charles White's Murals and History as Art," in Oehler and Adler, *Charles White*, 25–26. This facility, which opened when White was fourteen, was "a crucial institution for Chicago's South Side Black community [that] during its first five years of operation, [loaned] an annual average of two hundred thousand books." Erik S. Gellman, "Chicago's Native Son: Charles White and the Laboring of the Black Renaissance," in Darlene Clark Hine and John McCluskey, eds., *The Black Chicago Renaissance* (Chicago: University of Illinois Press, 2012), 229. Indeed, it was at the library that White discovered Alain Locke's *The New Negro*, a revolutionary book that completely transformed the fledgling artist's future by "[opening] his eyes" to the richness of Black culture. Oral History, 5. See also Ashley James, comp., "Selected Inventory of Charles White's Library," in Oehler and Adler, *Charles White*, 210–17.

18. White Papers (Box 1, Folder 9), https://ids.si.edu/ids/deliveryService/?id=AAA-AAA_whitchar_3199287&max=1300; https://ids.si.edu/ids/deliveryService/?id=AAA-AAA_whitchar_3199288&max=1300; and https://ids.si.edu/ids/deliveryService/?id=AAA-AAA_whitchar_3199289&max=1300. Recognizing the limits of informal instruction, members of the Art Crafts Guild pooled their funds, enabling one of their number to take weekly lessons at the Art Institute and then share that learning with the broader group. Horowitz, "Images of Dignity," 10. Having joined the group when he was only fifteen, White was among the youngest guild participants, and as such, never selected to fulfill this role. White, "Path of a Negro Artist," 37; and Esther Adler, "Charles White, Artist and Teacher," in Oehler and Adler, *Charles White*, 142.

19. White Papers (Box 1, Folder 9), https://ids.si.edu/ids/deliveryService/?id=AAA-AAA_whitchar_3199297&max=1300; and White Papers (Box 1, Folder 50), https://ids.si.edu/ids/deliveryService/?id=AAA-AAA_whitchar_3199171&max=1300. See also Oral History, 6.

20. Horowitz, "Images of Dignity," 11.

21. White, who had worked odd jobs since he was nine "to earn money to help out in the house," was no stranger to labor and toil. White, "Path of a Negro Artist," 34. In the words of his Los Angeles gallerist and close friend, Benjamin Horowitz: "Too often the luxury of creation had to be deferred while [White] delivered packages, ran errands, cleaned and swept, shined shoes or performed other odd chores to add his earnings–usually about 75 cents—to the family purse." Horowitz, "Images of Dignity," 8.

22. Horowitz, "Images of Dignity," 12; Adler, "Charles White, Artist and Teacher," 142; and Oral History, 6–7.

23. Adler, "Charles White, Artist and Teacher," 142.

24. Oehler, "Yesterday, Today, Tomorrow," 24 and 36n14.

25. Other titles for *Techniques Used in the Service of Struggle* include *Struggle for Liberation; Chaotic Stage of the Negro, Past and Present; Revolt of the Negro during Slavery;* and *Chaos of Negro Life*. Oehler, "Yesterday, Today, Tomorrow," 30 and 37n44. See also Mark Pascale, "'Graphic Interpreter of the Black People': Charles White as Draftsman and Printmaker," in Oehler and Adler, *Charles White,* 41; and Mary Helen Washington, *The Other Blacklist: The African American Literary and Cultural Left of the 1950s* (New York: Columbia University Press, 2014), 82. In addition to these works, White executed *The History of the Negro Press* in 1940 under commission from Claude Barnet on behalf the Associated Negro Press, which Barnet helmed. Oehler, "Yesterday, Today, Tomorrow," 24.

26. Barrett White, *Reaches of the Heart*, 37.

27. Rosenwald funding stemmed from "a private grant program that supported Black artists and writers between 1920 and 1948." Robertson, "Pan-Americanism, Patriotism, and Race Pride," 58. Alain Locke wrote a letter in support of White's first Rosenwald Foundation proposal. Robertson, "Pan-Americanism, Patriotism, and Race Pride," 62. See also Daniel Schulman and Peter Max Ascoli, eds., *A Force for Change: African American Art and the Julius Rosenwald Fund* (Chicago: Spertus Museum and Northwestern University Press, 2009).

28. Barnwell, *Charles White*, 30.

29. Jones, *South of Pico*, 38. "The idealist [sic] who would found Wo-Chi-Ca wanted their children to experience 'The World of the Future' today, through shared living with those of different racial and ethnic backgrounds. They especially wanted to welcome negro children to their new camp. Labor-based, co-educational, affordable, interracial—for a children's camp in 1934, a revolutionary concept." June Levine, Gene Gordon, and Ronnie Gilbert, *Tales of Wo-Chi-Ca: Blacks, Whites and Reds at Camp* (San Rafael, Calif.: Avon Springs Press, 2002), 3. See also https://judyhodges.wordpress.com/2015/10/07/wo-chi-ca/; and https://patch.com/new-jersey/longvalley/multiracial-camp-called-our-community-home-was-helpedc5aefc908f. Wo-Chi-Ca's impact on White's life cannot be understated since it was there that he met the woman who would become his second wife, Frances Barrett.

30. Jones, *South of Pico*, 39 and 290n56. White referred to the experience as "one of the deeply shaking and educative experiences of my life." White, "Path of a Negro Artist," 39. Unfortunately this "culture" also included racist violence: White was forcibly expelled from a New Orleans restaurant and beaten on the street in addition to having a streetcar conductor draw a gun on him in Hampton, Va. Jones, *South of Pico*, 39. White also lived the trauma of racist violence through the experiences of his family, including two uncles and three cousins who were lynched. White Papers (Box 1, Folder 9), https://ids.si.edu/ids/deliveryService/?id=AAA-AAA_whitchar_3199271&max=1300.

31. See Adler, "Charles White, Artist and Teacher," 145; Washington, *The Other Blacklist*, 85; and Jones, *South of Pico*, 38.

32. Oehler, "Yesterday, Today, Tomorrow," 33.

33. Horowitz, "Images of Dignity," 19.

34. Oral History, 8–9. White's ongoing health issues made drawing a more practical creative vehicle for him than painting. But he also expressed a preference for the medium, noting: "I guess in my work, I've always had a stronger leaning toward the graphics, and I've found that my own talents were best suited sometimes for the black and white medium rather than color. And I have never felt that color itself was absolutely necessary for an artist to be an artist. In other words, we could say that [Kathë Kollwitz (1867–1945)] never did a painting that I know of... And she is a great artist. And if Goya never painted, he would still have been a great artist. So I've always felt this way about black and white." White Papers (Box 1, Folder 9), https://ids.si.edu/ids/deliveryService/?id=AAA-AAA_whitchar_3199269&max=1300; and https://ids.si.edu/ids/deliveryService/?id=AAA-AAA_whitchar_3199270&max=1300.

35. White Papers (Box 1, Folder 6: Catlett, Elizabeth, 1940s), https://ids.si.edu/ids/deliveryService/?id=AAA-AAA_whitchar_3199235&max=1300. Adler, "Charles White, Artist and Teacher," 146. See also Oehler, "Yesterday, Today, Tomorrow,"33; and Pascale, "Graphic Interpreter of the Black People," 42.

36. White and Catlett lived with Siqueiros and his wife for a time. Horowitz recounted: "Siqueiros lived in a large house guarded by a tremendous, groaning iron gate. White and his wife were invited to stay and use the top floor—a penthouse surrounded by a balcony. From this balcony, they could look down on Siqueiros' studio, which was partially roofed in glass. White spent long hours on the balcony watching Siqueiros at work below, with Mrs. Siqueiros reading Spanish poetry to him. Siqueiros needed her there in order to work, and she would not close her book until Siqueiros put his brushes away." Horowitz, "Images of Dignity," 19–20.

37. Jones, *South of Pico*, 39. Of this experience, White later stated: "I learned how to do better what I wanted to express. The people I wanted particularly to impress were indeed the masses of the black population; but they came not even in hundreds to my exhibition, and I had to find ways and means to reach them because my ambitions and topics were connected with them and should be made accessible to them..." Academy of Arts: GDR, "The Impact of His Art Crossed the Borders of North America," quoted in *Freedomways* 20, no. 3 (1980): 185 (no citation given).

38. Adler, "Charles White, Artist and Teacher," 146.

39. For more on Catlett's time in Mexico, see Melanie Anne Herzog, *Elizabeth Catlett: An American Artist in Mexico* (Seattle: University of Washington Press, 2000).

40. Barnwell, *Charles White*, 47; and Barrett White, *Reaches of the Heart*, 49. The Whites later moved to 148th Street and Riverside Drive. Barrett White, *Reaches of the Heart*, 66.

41. Adler notes: "Organized in 1947 with support from a broad interracial coalition of major figures that included poet Langston Hughes, writer Dorothy Parker, and entertainers Harry Belafonte and Paul Robeson, among many others, the CNA was 'dedicated to the integration of Negro artists into all forms of American culture on a dignified basis of merit and equality.'" Adler, "Charles White, Artist and Teacher," 147 and 156–57n36, quoting a circular letter from CNA, June 17, 1949, W.E.B. Dubois Papers, MS 12, Special Collections and University Archives, University of Massachusetts Amherst Libraries, https://credo.library.umass.edu/view/pageturn/mums312-b128-i052/#page/1/mode/1up. See also Jones, *South of Pico*, 44; and Barrett White, 55–57.

42. Washington, *The Other Blacklist*, 94.

43. White, "Path of a Negro Artist," 41. White's work was particularly well-received in the German Democratic Republic, which he visited in 1951, 1974, and 1978. In their posthumous encomium, the GDR's Academy of Arts acknowledged the early success White's works had achieved in Paris and Prague (both late 1940s) and, later, in solo shows in Budapest, Warsaw, Oslo, Moscow, and Leningrad (1960s). The academy went on to laud the artist's multiple visits to the GDR, noting of his final stay: "It was a great experience to see the complete blending of this man's personality with his artistic accomplishments, revealing that the source of his power was his great love of human beings." Academy of Arts: GDR, "The Impact of His Art Crossed the Borders of North America," 186.

44. White, "Path of a Negro Artist," 42

45. Barrett White, *Reaches of the Heart*, 61–62.

46. The Whitney acquired White's *Preacher* in 1952. Horowitz, "Images of Dignity," 25.

47. White was subpoenaed to appear before the House Un-American Activities Committee. After being postponed without explanation, the subpoena was ultimately dropped. Nevertheless, the FBI continued to monitor White's activities (as it had done since his return from the USSR), maintaining a full dossier on his engagement with leftist organizations since at least the late 1940s. See Washington, *The Other Blacklist*, 95–96; and Barnwell, *Charles White*, 41–42.

48. Despite these physical setbacks, White continued to garner accolades and awards, including a John Hay Whitney Opportunity Fellowship (April 1955) and solo shows at Hunter College and New York University. Barrett White, *Reaches of the Heart*, 81.

49. Barrett White, "He Could Make Change in Harmony with the Demands of Life," *Freedomways* 20, no. 3 (1980): 172. See, generally, Ilene Susan Fort, "Charles White's Art and Activism in Southern California," in Oehler and Adler, *Charles White*, 123–39.

50. Fort, "Charles White's Art and Activism," 123, quoting a letter from White to Margaret Burroughs (April 9, 1957), Charles White Archives.

51. See, generally, Gene Slater, *Freedom to Discriminate: How Realtors Conspired to Segregate Housing and Divide America* (Berkeley: Heydey Publishing, 2021).

52. Barrett White, *Reaches of the Heart*, 117; and Barrett White, "He Could Make Change in Harmony with the Demands of Life," 172.

53. Barrett White, *Reaches of the Heart*, 92, 100–103, 112–115, and 134–35.

54. See https://www.lacma.org/art/exhibition/life-model-charles-white-and-his-students. Of teaching, White said in an interview: "[I]t's such a beautiful relationship, one in which both teacher and student grow as a result of the mutual contact. I'm not too happy about my own peer group. They're too self-satisfied. They're not willing to take risks. They're not questioning. Youth has a tendency to do those things. There are no sacred cows to them. I like the fact that they're willing to challenge the accepted ideas." Jeffrey Elliott, "Charles White: Portrait of an Artist," *Negro History Bulletin* 41, no. 3 (May–June 1978): 826. For White's legacy as a teacher, see Adler, "Charles White, Artist and Teacher," 141–55.

55. Harry Belafonte, "Foreword," in *Images of Dignity*, 1–2.

56. White was only the third Black artist (after Henry Ossawa Tanner [1859–1937, NA 1927] and Hughie Lee-Smith [1915–1999, NA 1967]) to be thus honored. Barrett White, "He Could Make Change in Harmony with the Demands of Life," 173–74. See also, https://nationalacademy.emuseum.com/internal/media/logodispatcher/Complete%20List%20of%20NAs_1826_2021.pdf, https://nationalacademy.emuseum.com/objects/2119/henry-ossawa-tanner; and https://nationalacademy.emuseum.com/people/1277/hughie-leesmith.

57. It was White who recommended Driskell to LACMA's deputy director, Rexford Stead. Fort, "Charles White's Art and Activism," 136.

58. Benjamin Horowitz, "On the Road with Charlie White," *Freedomways* 20, 169, and Barrett White, "He Could Make Change in Harmony with the Demands of Life," 173.

59. Barrett White, "He Could Make Change in Harmony with the Demands of Life," 174.

60. Barrett White, "He Could Make Change in Harmony with the Demands of Life," 174. See also Academy of Arts: GDR, 184–86.

61. C. Gerald Fraser, "Charles W. White is Dead at 61; Artist with Work in 49 Museums," *New York Times*, October 6, 1979.

62. Gellman, "Chicago's Native Son," 228.

63. In an interview dating to the mid-1960s, White offered: "So you know what's behind my pictures, this so-called love that I talk about, this beautiful thing, this love affair with people, this universality, this universal symbol that I talk about that I'm trying to create here to have meaning to all people regardless of color, what's behind it? It's because I can feel identity with Watts, oddly enough I can see myself with Watts, I can still see Mississippi, no matter where I am. I'm part of that... All artists should pick out something to say something about. I use Watts as a symbol because it's the closest thing to us, the freshest thing in our minds. But there are other kinds of things to talk about. But this is...the foundation for what I do." White Papers (Box 1, Folder 9), https://ids.si.edu/ids/deliveryService/?id=AAA-AAA_whitchar_3199261&max=1300; and https://ids.si.edu/ids/deliveryService/?id=AAA-AAA_whitchar_3199262&max=1300.

64. It bears emphasizing that White's tactics were in a very real sense constrained by the realities of twentieth-century America. "Like most African American artists throughout the twentieth century, he shied away from debilitating caricature and abject violence. The great effort for African Americans even to be able to be recognized as artists meant that this space was in some ways sacred. It could be a place for protest, yes, but most of all it was reserved for reflections on beauty that were often otherwise misrecognized or unseen." Jones, *South of Pico*, 32. Though beyond the scope of this essay, White's embrace of leftist values equally bears careful consideration when considering his oeuvre. Art historian Breanne Robertson notes: "A pronounced leftist consciousness distinguished Chicago's black cultural milieu of the late 1930s and 1940s from the earlier movement in Harlem. These artists and intellectuals professed the desire to create a more just society and embraced the Communist Party's Popular Front politics as a means to do so." Robertson, "Pan-Americanism, Patriotism, and Race Pride," 55. See also Washington, *The Other Blacklist*, 69–122; and John P. Murphy, "Charles White: The Art and Politics of Humanism, 1947–1956," *American Communist History* 17 nos. 3–4 (2018): 282–300.

MEXICO WAS A MILESTONE–CHARLES WHITE'S *NEGRO: U.S.A.* PRINTS

1. Charles White, quoted in John Pittman, "He was an Implacable Critic of His Own Creations," *Freedomways* 20, no. 3 (January 3, 1980): 191.

2. The revolutionary tenor of the Mexican Muralists' work, and their incorporation of an aesthetics drawn from Cubism, Italian Renaissance mural techniques, Social Realism, and Surrealism, gained increasing global influence during the 1920s through the 1940s. For an overview of Rivera's visibility and impact, in particular, in the United States during the Depression era, see Francis V. O'Connor, "The Influence of Diego Rivera on the Art of the U.S. During the 1930s and After," in *Diego Rivera: A Retrospective* (New York: Founders Society; Detroit Institute of Arts; Norton, 1986), 157–83; and James Oles, *Diego Rivera's America* (Berkeley: University of California Press and San Francisco Museum of Modern Art, 2022).

3. It was not until 1981 that the subject of the former image was correctly identified as Rivera. A 2015 Swann Galleries auction house catalogue for the Conté crayon and pencil work, in a sale entitled "Ascension: A Century of African-American Art" (Sale 2378), notes, "Curiously, despite a strong resemblance, an identification of Rivera was never made with this drawing," drawn from Lucinda Gedeon's text referencing the image identified as D10, in Lucinda Heyel Gedeon, "Introduction to the Work of Charles W. White with a Catalogue Raisonné" (master's thesis, University of California Los Angeles, 1981), 348.

4. Taller artists worked with trade unions, student organizations, and others, producing collaborative prints that addressed social and political concerns.

5. See Lizzetta Collins et al., *In the Spirit of Resistance, African-American Modernists and the Mexican Muralist School*, exh. cat. (New York: American Federation of the Arts, 1996); and Alison Cameron, "Buenos Vecinos: African American Printmaking and the Taller de Gráfica Popular," *Print Quarterly* 16, no. 4 (Dec. 1999): 353–67 for examinations of the relationship between African American artists and the Taller.

6. Closely related to the Social Realists, the American Regionalists' works underscored the beauty of the American landscape and celebrated the resilience of farmers and other hard-working Americans. For White's interest in American Regionalism, see Lizzette LeFalle-Collins and Shifra M. Goldman, *In the Spirit of Resistance: African American Modernists and the Mexican Muralist School* (New York: The American Federation of the Arts, 1996), 56; and Andrea D. Barnwell, *Charles White, The David C. Driskell Series of African American Art* (Petaluma, Ca.: Pomegranate, 2002), 26.

7. For additional details re: the Guild, see "Chicago's Native Son: Charles White and the Laboring of the Black Renaissance"; and Murry N. DePillars, "Chicago's African American Visual Arts Renaissance," in Darlene Clark Hine, John McCluskey Jr., and Marshanda A. Smith, eds., *The Black Chicago Renaissance* (Urbana, Chicago, and Springfield: University of Illinois Press, 2012).

8. This critical period in White's development is surveyed in Richard Courage, "Charles White and the Black Chicago Renaissance," *International Review of African American Art* (Hampton, Va.: Hampton University, 2012); and in Sarah Kelly Oehler and Esther Adler, *Charles White: A Retrospective* (New Haven and London: Yale University Press, 2018).

9. See George Mavigliano and Richard Lawson, *The Federal Art Project in Illinois, 1935–1943* (Carbondale, Ill.: Southern Illinois University Press, 1990). For a discussion of the African American artists working with the WPA, see *Alone in a Crowd: Prints of the 1930s–40s by African American Artists* (New York: American Federation of the Arts, 1993; 2nd revised ed), 7; and Gina Costa, *Para la Gente: Art, Politics and Cultural Identity of the Taller de Gráfica Popular*, exh. cat. (Notre Dame, Ind.: Snite Museum of Art, University of Notre Dame, 2009), 18.

10. The federal FSA program, first known as The Resettlement Administration, was initially aimed at assisting struggling, impoverished farmers and sharecroppers, then became known for its extensive and increasingly influential photography program, led by Roy Styker. For detailed considerations of the New Deal and FSA photographers, see Beverly Brannan and Gilles Mora, *FSA: The American Vision* (New York: Harry N. Abrams, 2006); and Cara A. Finnegan, *Picturing Poverty: Print Culture and FSA Photographs* (Washington, D.C.: Smithsonian Institution Books, 2003).

11. Yet, it must be noted that White continued his stylistic experimentations throughout his career, drawing sustenance from a broad range of artists and artistic movements.

12. The portfolio includes a striking print by Harlem Renaissance Modernist Jacob Lawrence (1917–2000), *Underground Railroad: Fording a Stream*. Here, Lawrence's vision of an escape to freedom is a stark, triangular configuration of mask-like, Cubist figures, executed in simplified lines. These abstracted figures, semi-submerged in an expanse of water, form a rhythmic, boat-like unit, hovering above and within the waves of water, isolated in a sea of white space.

13. For additional details regarding the Port Chicago disaster, see Regina T. Akers, "The Port Chicago Mutiny," in Christopher M. Bell, Bruce A. Elleman, eds., *Naval Mutinies of the Twentieth Century: An International Perspective, Cass Series: Naval Policy and History* (London: Routledge, 2003).

14. Later, through the efforts of Thurgood Marshall, who would be named to the U.S. Supreme Court, their sentences were reduced, and most of the men were released in January 1946. In 1948, President Harry Truman issued an Executive Order that desegregated the military, a direct result of the controversy over the mutiny convictions. In 1999, President Bill Clinton granted a pardon to Freddie Meeks, one of the few remaining living sailors.

15. For additional details regarding Keller and his circle of leftist artists, writers, and intellectuals, see Andrew Hemingway, *Artists on the Left: American Artists and the Communist Movement 1926–1956* (New Haven and London: Yale University Press, 2002); and Ellen G. Landau, *Artists for Victory*, exh. cat. (Washington, D.C.: Library of Congress), 1983.

16. See Alison Cameron, "Buenos Vecinos: African American Printmaking and the Taller de Gráfica Popular," *Print Quarterly* 16, no.4 (December 1999): 353–67.

17. See Stacy I. Morgan, *Rethinking Social Realism: African American Art and Literature, 1930–1953* (Athens, Ga.: University of Georgia Press, 2004) for a comprehensive survey of Black Social Realist artists and writers, as well as Hemingway, *Artists on the Left: American Artists and the Communist Movement 1926–1956* for the impact of Communist ideas on American artists' work.

18. Melanie Anne Herzog, *Elizabeth Catlett: An American Artist in Mexico* (Seattle and London: The University of Washington Press, 2000), 26. As Herzog writes in Herzog, 46, "In 1945, Catlett had assisted several artists, including White, who was then her husband, in writing successful proposals for submission to the Julius Rosenwald Foundation. Catlett received her first Rosenwald fellowship that year." Barnwell, in *Charles White*, 38–39, also notes that "The decision was beneficial for White as well," providing him with an opportunity to work with the Mexican Muralists and to refine his printmaking skills.

19. The National Negro Congress was established at Howard University in 1936, and it was focused on labor and civil right and on strategies for engendering economic, political, and social progress for African Americans.

20. Charles White, oral history interview with Betty Hoag, Archives of American Art, Smithsonian Institution, March 9, 1965. https://www.aaa.si.edu/collections/interviews/oral-history-interview-charles-w-white-11484.

21. Erica Moiah James, "Charles White's *J'Accuse* and the Limits of Universal Blackness," *Archives of American Art Journal* 55 no.2: 15.

22. For additional surveys of Catlett's work, see Lucinda Gedeon, Michael Brenson, and Lowery Stokes Sims, *Elizabeth Catlett Sculpture*; Melanie Anne Herzog, *Elizabeth Catlett: An American Artist in Mexico* (Seattle and London: The University of Washington Press, 2000); and Mora J. Beauchamp-Byrd, ed., *Struggle and Serenity: The Visionary Art of Elizabeth Catlett* (New York: Franklin H. Williams Caribbean Cultural Center, African Diaspora Institute), 1996.

23. In a February 17, 1996, interview in New York City with the author, Catlett noted that her first encounter with traditional African art was at a Howard University Gallery exhibition organized by Professor James Herring. Through studio art courses with James Porter and James Lesesne Wells, Catlett was introduced to the Mexican Muralists. Herzog, *Elizabeth Catlett*, 16.

24. In her 1945 "Plan of Work" for the fellowship, Catlett wrote, "Negro women in America have long suffered under the double handicap of race and sex. Because of subtle American propaganda in the movies, radio, and stage, they have come to be generally regarded as good cooks, housemaids and nurses and little else. At this time when we are fighting an all-out war against tyranny and oppression it is extremely important that the picture of Negro women as participants in this fight, throughout the history of America, be sharply drawn." Elizabeth Catlett, "Plan of Work" for Rosenwald fellowship, 1945, Rosenwald Collection, Box 400, Folder 7, John Hope and Aurelia E. Franklin Library Special Collections, Fisk University.

25. Elizabeth Catlett, "Plan of Work" for Rosenwald fellowship.

26. Herzog, *Elizabeth Catlett*, 65.

27. For further discussion of Catlett's involvement with the Taller, see LeFalle-Collins et al., *In the Spirit of Resistance: African American Modernists and the Mexican Muralist School*; Herzog, *Elizabeth Catlett*; and Cameron, "Buenos Vecinos: African American Printmaking and the Taller de Gráfica Popular."

28. At the Taller, Catlett met Mexican artist Francisco Mora and later married him in 1947.

29. Melanie Herzog has written that Marvel Cook, a friend of Catlett's, "remembers that when Catlett and White lived in Harlem," from 1944 to 1946, while Catlett worked at The Carver School, "people would compliment White on work that was actually Catlett's." Herzog, *Elizabeth Catlett*, 44.

THE MISEDUCATION OF CHARLES WHITE

This essay relies heavily on the bibliography compiled by Ashley James of the books and periodicals that Charles White had in possession at the time of his death and remain housed in the Charles White Archives. James's work is a testament to the "think rooms" that Black women's labors have engendered. The author also thanks C. Ian White for his generous insights and consultation. Ashley James, "Selected Inventory of Charles White's Library," in Sarah Kelly Oehler and Esther Adler, eds., Charles White: A Retrospective *(New Haven and London: Yale University Press, 2018), 210–217.*

1. Esther Adler, *Charles White: Black Pope* (New York: The Museum of Modern Art, 2017), 24. Adler credits artist Kerry James Marshall for first discovering the source image.

2. For an extensive mediation on complex transformations of White's political world view see Erica Moaih James, "Charles White's *J'Accuse* and the Limits of Universal Blackness," *Archives of American Art Journal* 55, no. 2 (Fall 2016), 4–25.

3. Frances Barrett White, *Reaches of the Heart: A Loving Look at the Artist Charles White* (New York: Barricade Books, 1994), 115.

4. See Toni Morrison, "The Site of Memory," in *Inventing the Truth*, William Zinsser, ed. (New York: Houghton Mifflin, 1995), 83–102.

5. Walter Benjamin, "Unpacking My Library: A Talk about Book Collecting," in Hannah Arendt, ed., *Illuminations: Essays and Reflections* (1968; repr., New York: Schocken Books, 2007), 60.

6. Christina Sharpe, *In the Wake: On Blackness and Being* (Durham, N.C.: Duke University Press, 2016).

7. Charles White, "Path of a Negro Artist," *Truth and Beauty: Charles White and His Circle* (New York: Michael Rosenfeld Gallery, 2018), 8.

8. White, "Path of a Negro Artist," 8.

9. White, "Path of a Negro Artist," 8.

10. Sarah Jane Cervenak, *Wandering: Philosophical*

Performances of Racial and Sexual Freedom (Durham: Duke University Press, 2014), 66, 161. See also W. E. B. Du Bois, *Black Reconstruction in America 1860–1880* (1935, repr.; New York: The Free Press, 1998).

11. David C. Driskell, "Foreword," Andrea D. Barnwell, *Charles White* (San Francisco: Pomegranate, 2002), v.

12. "The histories from which we were taught [his teachers] would say, were written by competent people, and whatever they did not mention was simply no important enough to mention." White, "Path of a Negro Artist," 8.

13. James, "Selected Inventory of Charles White's Library," 210–217.

14. Benjamin, "Unpacking My Library," 60.

15. Benjamin, "Unpacking My Library," 60.

16. David C. Driskell, "Foreword," Barnwell, *Charles White*, v; and Saidiya Hartman, "The Dead Book Revisited," *History of the Present* 6, no. 2 (Fall 2016): 210.

17. Charles White quoted in Joseph E. Young, *Three Graphic Artists: Charles White, David Hammons, and Timothy Washington* (Los Angeles: Los Angeles County Museum of Art, 1971), 5.

18. Kellie Jones, *South of Pico: African American Artist in Los Angeles in the 1960s and 1970s* (Durham: Duke University Press, 2017), 46.

19. See "Excerpts from an Interview with Drs. Edmund W. Gordon and Edmund T. 'Ted' Gordon," in Veronica Roberts ed., *Charles White: the Gordon gift to the University of Texas* (Austin, Texas: Blanton Museum of Art, 2019).

20. Ilene Susan Fort, "Charles White's Art and Activism in Southern California," in Oehler and Adler, *Charles White,* 132.

21. Jones, *South of Pico*, 46.

22. Jones, *South of Pico*, 46.

23. Alain Locke, "The Legacy of the African Arts," in Locke, ed., *The New Negro: An Interpretation* (1925, repr.; New York: Touchstone, 1997). In his autobiographical essay "Path of A Negro Artist," White describes how discovering The New Negro "opened up new vistas" when he was young. See White, "Path of A Negro Artist," 8.

24. J. R. Johnson (C.L.R. James), "Freeport and Columbia Murders," *Labor Action* 10, no. 10 (March 11, 1946): 3, https://www.marxists.org/archive/james-clr/works/1946/03/tenth1.html.

25. C. L. R. James, "The Revolutionary Answer to the Negro Problem in the United States," in *C. L. R. James on the 'Negro Question'*, ed. Scott McLemee (Jackson: University Press of Mississippi, 1996), 139.

26. Harry Belafonte, "Foreword," *Images of Dignity* (Los Angeles: The Ward Ritchie Press, 1967).

27. Mark Pascale, "'Graphic Interpreter of the Black People': Charles White as Draftsman and Printmaker," in Oehler and Adler, *Charles White*, 46.

28. Ashley James, "Selected Inventory of Charles White's Library," 214.

29. Alwyn Scott Turner, *Photographs of the Detroit People* (U.S.: Alwyn Scott Turner, 1970), n.p.

30. A. D. Coleman, "The Torch-Bearer of Eroticism?" *New York Times*, November 22, 1970.

31. Coleman, "The Torch-Bearer of Eroticism?"

32. Young, *Three Graphic Artists*, 5.

33. This reference to embodiment becomes even more significant when one considers how White decided to use the dry-point technique to avoid the chemical process associated with traditional etching due to the bouts with tuberculosis that weakened his lungs.

34. C. Ian White, interview with the author, May 20, 2022.

35. Barnwell, *Charles White*, 14.

36. Patrick Livingston, *Summer Dreams: The Story of Bob-Lo Island* (Detroit: Wayne State University Press, 2008), 87.

PLATES

The author thanks Mora J. Beachamp-Byrd for her pointed observations related to the works in Charles White: A Little Higher.

1. Kellie Jones, "Charles White, Feminist at MidCentury," in Sarah Kelly Oehler and Esther Adler, eds., *Charles White: A Retrospective* (New Haven and London: Yale University Press, 2018), 73–74, quoting Stacy I. Morgan, *Rethinking Social Realism: African American Art and Literature, 1930–1953* (Athens: University of Georgia Press, 2004), 54.

2. James A. Porter, "The Art of Charles White," in *Images of Dignity: The Drawings of Charles White* (Los Angeles: The Ward Ritchie Press, 1967), 5, quoting *Los Angeles Times*, Art Seidenbaum interview with Charles White (no citation given).

3. Charles White, "Path of a Negro Artist," *Masses & Mainstream* (April 1955): 33–34.

4. Frances Barrett White with Anne Scott, *Reaches of the Heart: A Loving Look at the Artist Charles White* (New York: Barricade Books, 1994), 106 (no citation given).

5. Andrea D. Barnwell, *Charles White* (San Francisco: Pomegranate, 2002), 80.

6. Barnwell, *Charles White*, 80.

7. Erica Moiah James, "*J'Accuse* and the Limits of Universal Blackness," *Archives of American Art Journal* 55, no. 2 (Fall 2016): 18.

8. Ilene Susan Fort, "Charles White's Art and Activism in Southern California," in Oehler and Adler, *Charles White*, 130.

9. Joanna Brooks, *American Lazarus: Religion and the Rise of African American and Native American Literatures* (Cambridge, Mass.: MIT Press, 2003), 3.

10. Philip Sterling and Rayford Logan, *Four Took Freedom: The Lives of Harriet Tubman, Frederick Douglass, Robert Smalls and Blanche K. Bruce* (Garden City, N.Y.: Doubleday & Co., 1967), 53.

11. James, "*J'Accuse* and the Limits of Universal Blackness," 5.

12. White had a copy of this publication in his personal library. Ashley James, comp., "Selected Inventory of Charles White's Library," in Oehler and Adler, *Charles White*, 212 and 213.

13. Ilene Susan Fort, "Charles White's Art and Activism in Southern California," in Oehler and Adler, *Charles White*, 134.

14. Mark Pascale, "'Graphic Interpreter of the Black People': Charles White as Draftsman and Printmaker," in Oehler and Adler, *Charles White*, 46.

15. James, "Selected Inventory of Charles White's Library," 212 and 216.

16. Lerone Bennett Jr., *The Shaping of Black America* (Chicago: Johnson Publishing Company, Inc., 1975).

17. Bennett, *The Shaping of Black America*, 62.

18. Bennett, *The Shaping of Black America*, 146.

19. Bennett, *The Shaping of Black America*, 171.

20. Bennett, *The Shaping of Black America*, 208.

21. Charles W. White Papers, 1933–1987, bulk 1960s–1970s. Series 1: Biographical Material, ca. 1934–1987 (Box 1, Folder 9: Interview Transcripts, ca. 1965). https://ids.si.edu/ids/deliveryService/?id=AAA-AAA_whitchar_3199294&max=1300).

22. Bennett, *The Shaping of Black America*, 234.

23. Bennett, *The Shaping of Black America*, 340.

24. Charles W. White Papers, 1933–1987, bulk 1960s–1970s (Box 10, Folder 8). https://edan.si.edu/slideshow/viewer/?eadrefid=AAA.whitchar_ref500.

25. Barrett White, *Reaches of the Heart*, 172.

26. Barrett White, *Reaches of the Heart*, 172.

CONTRIBUTORS

Mora J. Beauchamp-Byrd is a teaching assistant professor of Africana Studies at Oklahoma State University. An art historian, arts administrator, and curator, her specialties include American art, with a focus on modern and contemporary African American art; art of the African Diaspora; British art and the Black Arts Movement in the UK; museum and curatorial studies; and representations of race, class, and gender in American comics. She has organized numerous exhibitions, which include *Transforming the Crown: African, Asian and Caribbean Artists in Britain, 1966–1996* (The Caribbean Cultural Center); *Picturing Creole New Orleans: The Photographs of Arthur P. Bedou* (Xavier University of New Orleans); *The Worldview of Katherine Dunham* (The Caribbean Cultural Center); and *Little Nemo's Progress: Animation and Contemporary Art* (Oklahoma State University Museum of Art). Beauchamp-Byrd has also taught at Duke University, Spelman College, The University of Tampa, and Xavier University of New Orleans. She is completing a manuscript on the portraiture of the New Orleans–born photographer Arthur P. Bedou. She is a member of the Board of Directors of the College Art Association. She received a B.A. in art history and an M.A. in visual arts administration from New York University, an M.A. in art history from Columbia University, and Ph.D. in art history from Duke University.

Nijah Cunningham is an assistant professor of English at Hunter College, CUNY. His teaching and research focus on African American and African diaspora literatures and culture. Through a transnational approach to Black literary studies and a critical archival approach, his current book project, *Quiet Dawn*, argues for a renewed consideration of Pan-Africanism as practice. His writing has appeared in platforms such as *Art Journal*, *Small Axe, The New Inquiry, Women and Performance, Current Anthropology, ASAP/J*, and *PMLA*. He is also the author of numerous catalogue essays on artists such as Oliver Jackson, Jennie C. Jones, Samuel Levi Jones, and Florine Démosthène. He is the curator of *Hold: A Meditation on Black Aesthetics* (Princeton University Art Museum, 2018) and co-curator with David Scott and Erica M. James of *Caribbean Queer Visualities* (The Small Axe Project, 2016) and *The Visual Life of Social Affliction* (The Small Axe Project, 2019–20). He received a B.A. from Boston College and a Ph.D. from Columbia University, and he was a Cotsen Fellow at the Princeton University Society of Fellows (2016–19).

Jill Deupi is the Beaux Arts Director and chief curator of the Lowe Art Museum at the University of Miami. Prior to assuming this position in 2014, Deupi was director and chief curator of University Museums at Fairfield University, where she was also an assistant professor of art history. Her professional experience includes work at the Royal Academy of Arts, the Art Institute of Chicago, the Snite Museum of Art, the National Gallery of Art, and the Wallace Collection. The recipient of a two-year Rome Prize, Deupi is a Fellow of the American Academy in Rome. She has served as a trustee of the Association of Art Museum Directors and a board member of the Academic Museums and Galleries, whose Task Force for the Protection of University Collections she co-chaired. Deupi holds a B.A. in French literature and political science from Mount Holyoke College; a J.D. from Washington College of Law, American University; an M.A. in the history of art from Birkbeck College, University of London; a Ph.D. in art history from the University of Virginia; and a graduate certificate in arts administration from New York University.

Will South is an independent curator, researcher, and artist whose career spans four decades, beginning with his 1981 survey show, *Utah Art: The Early Years*, and continuing through his 2020 blockbuster exhibition, *Van Gogh & His Inspirations*, for the Columbia Museum of Art. He has published widely in the field of American Impressionism, including *In Nature's Temple: The Life and Art of William Wendt* (Laguna Art Museum); *California Impressionism* (Abbeville Press); and *Guy Rose: American Impressionist* (Oakland Museum of California). Another area of major interest is African American art, with projects including *REMIX: Themes & Variations in African American Art* (Columbia Museum of Art), an exhibition and publication. He lectures regularly and is at work on a book about artist Henry Ossawa Tanner. He received a Ph.D. in art history from the Graduate Center of the City University of New York, specializing in early modern American art. His dissertation resulted in the traveling exhibition and publication *Color, Myth & Music: Stanton Macdonald-Wright and Synchromism* (North Carolina Museum of Art).

CREDITS

This volume accompanies the exhibition

CHARLES WHITE: A LITTLE HIGHER

Organized by and presented at:

Lowe Art Museum, University of Miami
November 10, 2022 to February 26, 2023

At the time of publication, the following further venues were scheduled:

Hickory Museum of Art
March 18, 2023 – July 30, 2023

Cincinnati Art Museum
November 10, 2023 – February 25, 2024

Charles White: A Little Higher was made possible by the Primas Family Collection. Additional funding was provided by the State of Florida, Department of State, Division of Arts and Culture, the Florida Council on Arts and Culture, and the National Endowment for the Arts; the Miami-Dade County Department of Cultural Affairs and the Cultural Affairs Council, the Miami-Dade County Mayor and Board of County Commissioners; the City of Coral Gables; the Funding Arts Network; Beaux Arts Miami; and Lowe members. Community partners include the University of Miami's Center for Global Black Studies; Miami MoCAAD; and Hampton Art Lovers/Historic Ward Rooming House.

Lowe Art Museum
University of Miami
Coral Gables, Florida, 33146

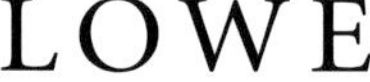

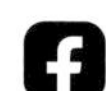   

@loweartmuseum
www.lowe.miami.edu

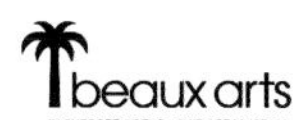

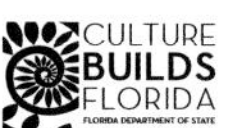

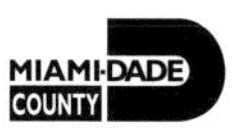

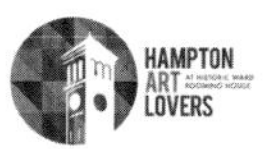

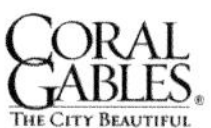

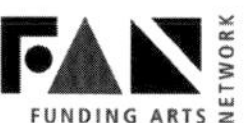

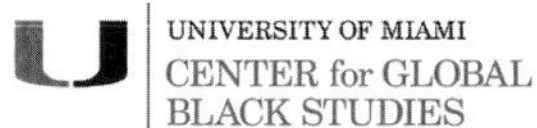

IMAGES

All artworks by Charles White in the figures and plates are copyright © The Charles White Archives unless otherwise noted. All artworks illustrated in the plates were drawn from the Primas Family Collection and were featured in *Charles White: A Little Higher*, except *Exodus II* (1966, plate 18), which was not exhibited at the Lowe Art Museum. Plates 29 to 40 were published in Lerone Bennett Jr.'s *The Shaping of Black America* (Johnson Publishing Company, 1975), while plates 6, 7, 8, 10, and 17 appeared in earlier books, periodicals, or other media. *Freeport Columbia* (1946, plate 6) was published in *Congress View* (March 1946). *Head of a Man* (1948, plate 7) and *Our War* (ca. 1948, plate 8) were included in the portfolio *Negro: U.S.A. A Graphic History of the Negro People in America Workshop Prints No. 2*. *Jazz Flute* (1955, plate 10) is associated with imagery White produced to illustrate album covers for the Sam Most Sextet (Vanguard). *Emancipation Proclamation* (1965–67, plate 17) was included in Philip Sterling and Rayford Logan's book *Four Took Freedom: The Lives of Harriet Tubman, Frederick Douglass, Robert Small and Blanche K. Bruce* (Zenith Books, Doubleday & Company, 1967).

Details of Works

All works are by Charles White. Cover: *Cat's Cradle* (1972, plate 24); back cover: *J'Accuse #2* (1965, plate 15); front endpapers and page 2: *Love Letter I* (1971, plate 22); back endpapers: *Prophet I* (1976, plate 43); pages 58–59: *Wanted Poster Series #14a* (1970, plate 22)

Photographs and Art

All efforts have been made to identify and credit photographers wherever possible.

Plates: Plate 27 photographed by Brad Flowers; all other plates photographed by Chad Redmon.

Front endpaper iii: Charles White in front of the left panel of *Struggle for Liberation*, n.d. Gordon Parks, photographer. Charles White Archives.

Page 4: Charles White working at his house on Kent St. in Altadena, California, n.d. Bob Moore, photographer. Charles White Archives.

FIGURES IN THE ESSAY "MEXICO WAS A MILESTONE—CHARLES WHITE'S *NEGRO: U.S.A.* PRINTS":

Fig. 4: Photo by John Wronn. Digital Image © The Museum of Modern Art / Licensed by SCALA / Art Resource, NY

Fig. 5: Digital image © Whitney Museum of American Art / Licensed by Scala / Art Resource, NY

Fig 8: The Art Institute of Chicago / Art Resource, NY

Fig. 9: Photo courtesy of the RISD Museum, Providence, RI

Fig. 10: Schalkwijk / Art Resource, NY

Fig. 11: Licensed by VAGA at Artists Rights Society (ARS), NY. Digital Image © The Museum of Modern Art / Licensed by SCALA / Art Resource, NY

Fig. 12: Licensed by VAGA at Artists Rights Society (ARS), NY

QUOTE

Page 160, Charles White quote: Charles W. White Papers, 1933–1987, bulk 1960s–1970s. Series 1: Biographical Material, circa 1934–1987 (Box 1, Folder 9: Interview Transcripts, circa 1965). Archives of American Art, Smithsonian Institution, https://ids.si.edu/ids/deliveryService/?id=AAA-AAA_whitchar_3199270&max=1300 and https://ids.si.edu/ids/deliveryService/?id=AAA-AAA_whitchar_3199271

Publisher & Creative Director
Ilona Oppenheim

Art Director
Jefferson Quintana

Graphic Designers
Eddymir Briceño
Jefferson Quintana

Managing Editor
Andrea Gollin

Proofreader
Ileana Oroza

Image Researcher
Amanda Belli

Printing
Printed and bound in Canada
by Friesens Corporation

First Edition

ISBN: 979-8-9856518-2-9

Library of Congress Control Number: 2022913924

Charles White: A Litte Higher is printed on Forest Stewardship Council certified paper from well-managed forests.

Tra Publishing is committed to sustainability in its materials and practices.

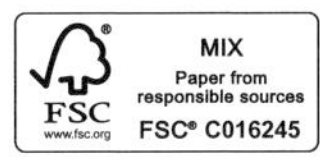

Tra Publishing
245 NE 37th Street
Miami, FL 33137
trapublishing.com

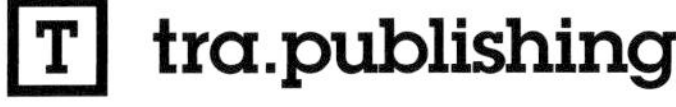

"I try to deal with the truth...Truth in a real spiritual sense...not spiritual meaning a religious spiritual... but the sense of inner man...I've tried to deal with beauty...the beauty in man, the beauty in life, the beauty that is the most precious possession that man has in life. And essentially, I feel that man is basically good... The other thing I try to deal with is...dignity."

—Charles White

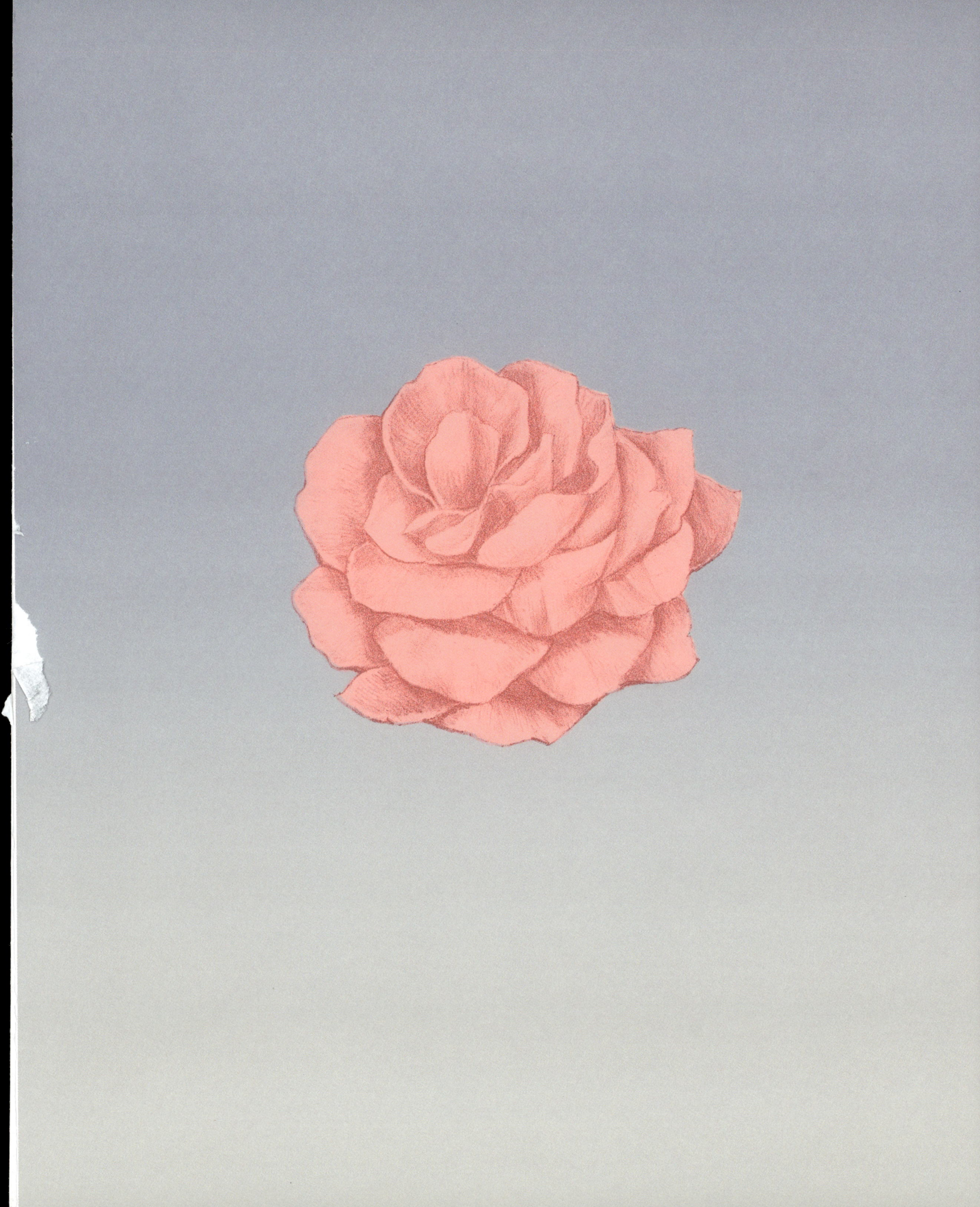